SEX
and Human Relationships

SEX
and Human Relationships

edited by

Cecil E. Johnson

*Associate Professor
of Sociobiology
Riverside City College
Riverside, California*

CHARLES E. MERRILL PUBLISHING CO.
A Bell & Howell Company
Columbus, Ohio

International Standard Book Number: 0-675-09392-9

Library of Congress Catalog Card Number: 78-101584

2 3 4 5 6—75 74 73 72 71

Printed in the United States of America

Contents

Introduction

In teaching undergraduate psychology and biology for the past sixteen years, I have come to realize, like Kinsey, Mead, and others, that we are dealing with sexual infants regardless of chronological age. I also realize, after lecturing and talking to hundreds of so-called sexually mature adults, that a great deal of ignorance and subsequent sexual incompatibility exists within the frame of modern American marriage. That ignorance and incompatibility result in a pyramiding divorce rate and considerable confusion within the family unit. The material of this book spotlights the American sexual scene in all its myriad ramifications. So much happiness and unhappiness orbits this core of our lives that it deserves major emphasis.

These essays do not concern themselves with a statistical approach to sex on its various energy levels. Americans are con-

stantly conditioned by numerous scientific "Pavlovs" to take their
sex, as they do their filter tips and breath sweeteners, on a statistical basis. Most average, middle-class, law-abiding citizens between the ages of 25 and 40, we are told, should have 2.7 orgasms
per week. Any deviation from this figure places the majority of
the people in the frigid or impotent camps, or tarred with saty-
riasis or nymphomania. Most marriage texts read like a manual-of-
arms for the young married couple, and often fail to recognize
the innumerable variations of the human population. In short,
most contemporary writers in the field seem obsessed by stereotyped sexual statistics. But those of us who have lived, loved, and
studied for many years know that the step-by-step outline of
what should or should not happen before the marriage, on the
honeymoon, and later in the marital bed, relegates what is beautiful and meaningful in our lives to a set of statistical sexual
calisthenics which are extremely unrealistic in view of individual
socio-psycho-biological differences.

The roles of men and women have undergone profound changes
since World War I, and the tempo has picked up since World War
II. We have more marriages between young people in their late
adolescence who are supposedly madly in love with one another
and have unrealistic visions of rose-covered dream cottages and
never-ending fun and games. Many young married couples also
have a materialistic, "I-want-everything-now" philosophy, which
poses often difficult problems for them. In middle-class circles, the
realities are usually quite the opposite: instead of a rose-covered
cottage, the young couple will probably end up in a rather drab
development, where battalions of look-alike tract homes march
across a treeless landscape. The home will be filled for the most
part with the same look-alike furniture of their think-alike neigh-
bors. Power mowers, deep freezers and other gadgets appear, and
the couple's dawning realization of these-things-cost-money-and-
how-do-we-pay-for-them syndrome hits home with soul-shaking
impact. Domestic battles suddenly erupt, and the "honeymoon
is over" period has arrived. If our hypothetical couple is sexually
compatible, they can hopefully iron out their financial and marital
difficulties. It will take years, however, because children will arrive
and new "essential" goods must be purchased for their continued
state of bliss. Dad has his nose to the grindstone and, to quote
from a satirical novel on middle class suburbia, he is "at home
only for spawning purposes and to hand over the check to his
wife." He has for the most part lost contact with the family and

is possibly even glad to hide within the warm confines of the work organization while "Mom" quarterbacks the team. Father, of necessity, has become, as D. H. Lawrence so beautifully points out, "a white-collar coolie waiting for his monthly hand-out of rice."

The distribution of roles between sexes and generations has undergone dramatic change with the spotlight on early marriages, new sexual freedoms and early parenthood.

Man has always solved his problems one way or another, and will probably continue to do so. Hopefully, I have not implied that I have a completely negativistic attitude toward sex, marriage, and the family. Like most of us, I have survived much of what has been mentioned and live a life which is more happy than unhappy. Too many people write in this field who are old maids or whose sex hormones have stopped flowing.

I believe that today's undergraduates are not too concerned with the "birds and the bees" approach which many texts espouse. Students' concern today moves with the new morality . . . The Pill . . . Role Changes . . . The Sex Drive—Demand and Expression . . . How to Gain New Respect for Home and Family and Mate Selection.

The selections in this book of readings represent a collaboration between myself and numerous other professors in psychology, sociology, and biology, who have graciously made suggestions to improve the impact and fabric of the project. Emphasis is placed on random grouping of selections, so that you, the student, will be hit with variations in content, as you move from one to the other.

Only one essay has been excerpted from a journal, while the others are drawn from whole chapters by authors whose literary styles place them among America's finest. All too often, books of readings for unfortunate college students are taken from boring, poorly-written journal articles whose main claim to fame is their sleep-conducive qualities. The one journal article, "Abortion—or Compulsory Pregnancy?" by Garrett Hardin, of the University of California at Santa Barbara, is the rare exception. Not only is the message vitally necessary in today's rapidly changing world, but his style is outstanding and real.

In the first essay, "Can Marriage Be for Life?" one of America's foremost anthropologists, Margaret Mead, brilliantly explores all aspects of modern American marriage and contrasts it with past patterns. The world-famous psychiatrist Albert Ellis, currently president of the Society for the Scientific Study of Sex, will mesmerize the reader with his contribution, "Romantic Love," which views the pattern of courtship in practically all of western civilized society as that of "the love tease." He methodically strips romantic love of its idealistic clothing and leaves a naked, honest reality.

The controversial researcher, sexologist Lawrence Lipton, in "Sexual Research on the Campus," will sometimes leave you breathless with the on-the-scene comments and case histories that dramatically point out what is really going on in the American college.

Following Lipton's essay is a series of real-life questions on contraception, followed in each instance by concise, scientifically accurate answers. Authors Fred Brown, Chief Psychiatrist at Mt. Sinai, and Rudolf Kempton, Professor of Zoology at Vassar, help to make it a classic of its kind.

The best selling *Human Sexual Response*, by William Masters and Virginia Johnson, ranks with the Kinsey Reports on the Male and Female. The excerpt from their book, titled "The Clitoris," is a masterpiece on the anatomy, physiology, and orgasmic qualities of that part of the human female body. The eminent psychiatrist Frank Caprio frankly discusses the physical and emotional causes of male impotence, how it can be cured, and how to achieve a happy and successful marital relationship.

For a change, both men and women students will be exposed to the brilliant, full-of-life prose of Marie Robinson, a prominent physician and psychiatrist. Male sexologists often attempt to feel and think like women, but this is impossible. Dr. Robinson possesses that rare combination of womanly scientist and author in one intelligent package. Her essay, "Sexual Surrender," is a beautiful contribution to American literature.

The world renowned psychiatrist, Milton Sapirstein, follows with a crushingly real essay titled "The Paradox of the Marriage Manual," dedicated to those newlyweds whose marriage is threatened by the unrealistic views espoused by their newly-purchased, by-the-numbers marriage manual. Professor James Leslie McCary of the University of Houston hits hard with an essay, "Sexual Attitudes and Sexual Behavior," one of the finest written in the English language. Completing this collection of essays is the eminent clinical psychologist and therapist, Allan Fromme, whose contribution, "Toward A Better Sexual Orientation," belongs with the truly greats of contemporary sexology.

I would hope that from reading and enjoying these selections, you will be able to live more happily, and that sexual love can be a joy, not a ball and chain rooted in outmoded puritanism.

Margaret Mead

Can Marriage Be for Life?

The American marriage ideal is one of the most conspicuous examples of our insistence on hitching our wagons to a star. It is one of the most difficult marriage forms that the human race has ever attempted, and the casualties are surprisingly few, considering the complexities of the task. But the ideal is so high, and the difficulties so many, that it is definitely an area of American life in which a very rigorous re-examination of the relationship between ideals and practice is called for.

In the American marriage ideal, choice by both partners is not only approved but demanded. Life is easier if parents approve, but

From: *Male and Female,* A Study of the Sexes in a Changing World, by Margaret Mead. Reprinted by permission of William Morrow and Company, Inc. Copyright © 1949 by Margaret Mead.

neither the law nor social expectation demands that they should. Young people who let their parents interfere with their marriages are regarded as either emotionally immature or trapped by bribes that parents with money and influence can pay. But the ideal girl and the ideal boy choose and marry each other in spite of all obstacles. They may have been school-mates all their lives. This is a familiar sentimental theme, "When you wrote on my slate, 'I love you, Joe,' when we were a couple of kids," or the opposite picture of male initiative, "I've loved you since you were a baby, since you used to crawl on the floor." They may have been members of the same high-school gang, dated together, and then finally realized that they were made for one another. They may have met on a train, on a boat, in an accident, at a fire, in a shipwreck, standing in line at the Grand Central Station, on a blind date, or by mail. "On Sunday, May 2, 1943, I got my first letter from her. I was in Albuquerque, New Mexico, and on Saturday, June 3, 1944, we were married in St. Louis, Missouri." Their acquaintance may have been launched into certainty by discovering that the brother of one and the uncle of the other had both played, at different times, on the football team of a small Middle Western college. But whether it is sitting side by side in the fourth grade while he dips her pigtails in the ink, or riding home on the same street-car line, or eyes that meet in a service club during a war, or the excitement that springs up between a man and the girl his roommate invited to the spring prom—all of this is the special lucky chance which brings the two together that each may choose the other. Same school, same town, same railroad wreck, have the same functional position in a romantic structure which disregards all of those realities of time and place, of common habits and common social background, on which marriage has usually been based. All the parents' compensatory efforts to keep their children in groups with their own kind of people, own religion, own class, own race, can be partly interpreted as precautions against this romantic ideal of choosing some one for themselves alone, reinforced, fortunately for the stability of American marriage, by the American fear of getting out of one's own class, or at least out of the class that one wants to belong to. Not only the parents, but the young people seeking a mate, do a good part of their seeking in approved quarters where the chance that brings true-lovers together can only operate on an approved invitation list. But counterpointed against this caution we find the recurrent theme in popular art of the boy or girl met under circumstances that make them seem unavailable, only to discover in the end that in addition to all the personal qualities that make them lovable, they are not really kitchen knaves or hat-check girls, but have been to the right schools and known the right people, or conversely, were poor boys or girls themselves who have just risen to success, and really understand. Very small primitive societies often phrase marriage as choice, but the choice is among some eight to ten girls, most of whom, usually all, the boy has known all his life, or if they are sought in the next village, all of whom at least come from a completely similar background. But in the United States, theoretically only the major racial divisions limit choice, so that several million boys and girls are potential mates if they meet and fall in love. This falling-in-love may happen anywhere, and for men at any time from the kindergarten to old age; for women it is regarded as dangerous, and leading to more trouble than happiness, to fall in love after their children reach adolescence and after they stop pretending that they are thirty-five.

Nor is this falling-in-love seen as patterned on the past and as reinstating an age-old way of life shared by their ancestors, one of whom died in the bed in which they were born. "I want a girl just like the girl who married dear old Dad," and the converse, "Oh, if Mother hadn't married Daddy, Daddy might have married me," are songs about parent-child relationships rather than any recognition that the future will repeat the past. The girl of a man's dream will neither dress like his mother nor look like his mother; she may speak with a very different accent, cook different food, manage her house differently in every respect, and she will be expected to disagree with both his mother and hers on most of the details of living. The choice of one's life, one's fate, comes out of the future, either unrelated to or definitely contradictory of the past. A first sign of assimilation of the foreign-born is the marriage out of the group, reinforced by the fact that it is easier for parents who see their children turning away from every Old World custom to blame a mixed marriage than to accept the defection of two young people of the same background. A recent popular novel, *White Fawn*, a paper edition, sums up the whole position. A girl of Boston blue blood meets under most unconventional circumstances—he runs over her dog—a promising young doctor of very simple Irish parentage. Both are presented as loving their families, and all the advisers in the case declare the marriage impossible, as both families live in Boston, and he has set his heart on success in spite of Boston's socially closed doors. Then comes the solution: not in Boston, never in Boston, but in some other city far away, in Seattle, they can "begin life over again." He has an education as good as hers, Seattle will be new to both of them, and any manners that he may have which fit another social level will quickly drop away under the tutelage of a wife who loves him enough to leave everything for him. Love wins, democracy wins; the honest pride of the Boston Irish, the faithfulness to the essentials of caste phrased in moral individualistic terms, are both vindicated, and a new growing American city gets a fine young doctor and a family on which it can depend. In this story there is a sub-theme of the girl's mother's flirtation with a younger man who is tied to a sick wife. The mother nobly "lets him go" as soon as his wife dies and he is free to marry. So while the absolute overriding importance of love as between the marriageable is insisted upon, love that cannot be expressed in marriage must be given up. The mother, although still young and charming and given to pretty négligées, is rewarded for her own self-denying life with a stern older husband by her joy in her daughter's solution. Thousands of marriages that, while not as dramatic, contain just as difficult background contrasts take place every year in America, and will take place even more frequently as young women become almost as foot-loose as young men.

Romantic love when the choice is among only ten possible girls, all of similar backgrounds and appropriate domestic skills, can safely follow the dictates of physical attraction. The nestling of a curl on the neck, a way of glancing from under the eyelids, a little trill of laughter in the girl, or in the boy a certain swing of the shoulders, a certain shyness or boldness of the eyes, can be used to distinguish one young farmer or one young fisherman from another. Such delicious qualities are not as safe guides when one is choosing a mate from a million otherwise unidentified people. Yet it remains the ideal for men, and only a little less the ideal for women. While the cautious may say, "I want to find out more about him before I fall for him," "I fell for him before I knew how to spell his name" remains the more romantic ideal and frequent enough practice. During the period when a marriage is regarded as successful and happy, it will be the incautious type of behaviour that will be dwelt on as proving that the marriage is based on real love. When her daughter repeats the same incautious gesture, the mother cannot repudiate the romantic story that has been told so often, unless she wishes at the same time to tell her daughter the ways in which her marriage has disappointed her in order to warn the daughter against the same lack of caution.

It has been pointed out that a frequent theme of modern movies is the "good-bad" girl, the girl who, met under compromising circumstances, turns out to be nevertheless a good, marriageable girl. Such an unconventional, anonymous meeting with a girl of suitable class and religion is the ideal solution of the American marriage dilemma, in which in order to prove love you must disregard every practical consideration in making a marital choice, but to have a happy marriage the mates should be as much alike as possible.

For here comes the other side of the romantic picture, the acceptance of women on a very close to equality status, and the hope of that companionship and understanding which comes from similar tastes, politics, athletic skills, choice of friends, and even, according to one style in predicting marriage success, the same amount of introversion or of self-confidence. There is less and less sense that the strong should marry the weak, that an intelligent man is better off with a frivolous wife (though he may prefer a non-intellectual one), that quantitative differences in education between husband and wife are a good thing. And since education is so similar for boys and girls, this means a premium on similarity. "Give-and-take in marriage" is one of our ideals. Simple contrasts, such as contrasts in height or colouring, may add piquancy; there is an insistence that the wife accept home-making as her status in order to settle at least one point of differentiation. But actual personality differentiation between the sexes is devalued. So the dilemma that is solved so neatly in film and novel is not solved so easily in real life. A man must find a girl who is the identical twin of himself in every aspect of background, religion, education, and experience, under circumstances which will convince both that each chose the other from among the millions of competitors for something intrinsic and independent of all these considerations. Young people exclaim over the pretty girl or the football hero who instead of venturing forth to new pastures marries the boy or the girl next door, and put them down as frightened and lacking in what it takes; they expect no good to come of it. Wiser heads shake over the chances for happiness when there are great differences in class and education, and expect no good to come of that.

As individual choice is expected to be the one criterion for planning a marriage, so also individual choice and the price of the marriage license and ceremony are all that is required, for any two unmarried people who are of age (subject to some racial bars in some states) to marry each other. A few states demand a doctor's examination; sometimes the couple is required to wait three days. But nothing else is required. There is no insistence that the man have a job or prove that he can make a living. There is no requirement that the girl have a single skill necessary for home-making. She may never have boiled an egg or held a baby in her arms, or even done her own hair or washed her own stockings. Not only is parental assent not required, but there is no invocation of any representatives of the past of either man or girl, who might introduce such considerations as the six months that one of the two has spent in sanitarium, mental institution, or prison. Alone, without a single record of the other's past, and without a single socially required guarantee of the future, the two are permitted to contract a state to which emotionally, as well as legally, they are theoretically bound for life. It is only during wars and in big cities that such marriages are very frequent, but the fact that they can occur high-lights the form of our marriage, the lack of protection that we give young people who attempt to act out completely the social expectation that they themselves are adequate to judge their own life-partners, and need neither help nor advice.

Nor are the newly married conceived of as needing material help. In fact the employer who pays a married man a better wage than an unmarried one is often thought of as having found a clever way of underpaying his unmarried employees. We also find con-demnation of the department-store that prefers unmarried girls who live cheaply at home with their parents and will accept low wages. Both are thought of as exploitive. A firm may prefer mar-ried employees because they are steadier, or refuse to employ married women because they have too many personal home prob-lems, but in that case the personnel policy is protecting the firm, not the married men and women. Unions, fighting for seniority privileges, override the needs of the married, even to putting women with young children on grave-yard shifts. The world in which the newly married couple have to fend for themselves does nothing about them, and if pregnancy is apparent, the young wife will find that house-hunting suddenly becomes much more dif-ficult, and that there are large blocks of apartments in which children are not wanted.

Nor are parents expected to do anything for them materially. A wedding is something that an indulgent father or a social-minded mother either "gives the daughter" or perhaps insists on against the young people's will. Friends may give showers, but here again this depends upon the exigencies of time and place. No dowry, no bride-price, no settlement on the wife, no wagon loaded with feather-beds and copper kettles, no cow whose calf will feed the new baby, no plot of ground, no newly built tent, no peasant cot in which the old people now take a back seat, no four-poster bed, no fine linen, are essential to the new marriage. This does not mean of course that many fathers do not give their daughters or their sons substantial gifts, even houses and cars, at marriage, but this is extra, it is not expected. Parents are not chided if they fail to provide for their children, and the children are a little apologetic about any such gifts—for young people ought to stand on their own feet. So strong is this feeling about independence that wealthy parents who plan to leave all their money to their children let the young people struggle along in poverty for years when their needs are greatest rather than give them help that would be bad for their characters. The fear of falling back upon father or father-in-law is always there to goad the young couple into renewed efforts, because maturity is never won finally in the United States, but is dependent upon the ability to support one-self.*

So without benefit of the careful sanctions and help with which many other societies have surrounded their new marriages, each young couple starts off life alone. They start to "make a life together." Ideally, they alone choose where they will live, what their style of life will be, whether their money will go for a car or a little place in the country, a living-room set or a bedroom set, a lamp or a radio. To the extent that their parents set the style in which they live, the parents are felt as interfering, which is one reason why it is so very difficult to be the children of upper-class parents in the United States, who have preserved a sense that they should be allowed to manage their children's way of life because it reflects on the family name. But the prevailing American ideal makes it more appropriate for children to remonstrate with their parents over their way of living than for parents to remonstrate with their children. This independence of parental interference is of course accompanied by the most meticulous attention either to the style of the clique to which they belong, or hope to belong, or to some image of such a clique derived from the maga-

---

* This same fear of loss of hard-won maturity can be found in American attitudes towards Great Britain, with the recurrent political appeal of preserving our freedom from British interference and political capital being made of the danger to Chicago, as in the thirties, of domination by King George.

zines and the department-store windows. The choice that is exer-
cised is often within very narrow limits, even when it seems to
have the enormous individuality of a modern Christmas-card
with a picture of your own dog or your own baby on it. But
whether to furnish a house in a style that is modern or period or
mixed, or whether to have a white or a mahogany radio, a Ford or
a Chevrolet, live in the city or become a commuter—these are
all felt as genuine choices, and choices that a married couple increasingly make together. It is no question of the bride's fitting
into the relentless domination of a mother-in-law, or the husband's
either imposing his own style of life or accepting that of his wife.
Although the consumption skills of the wife are more crucial to
the class position of a family, the ideal is that the husband be in
agreement with the choices; the details he leaves to her. Together
they plan when the first baby is to come—unless they belong to a
faith which feels these are matters which should be left to God;
they name it, and plan its future. Here again, all the details of
discipline and training are left to the wife, but the husband is
supposed to take an interest. It is no longer a question of a patriarchal bread-winner who asserts his right to rule his own home,
but rather of a wife who complains that a husband who doesn't
participate in that home is not living up to his rôle.

To the extent that their backgrounds are similar, they can
stylize their minor disagreements as part of the pattern of marriage and quarrel happily for twenty-five years over whether they
want to keep a dog or a cat, go to the seaside or the mountains,
go out or stay in, because the issues will all be minor ones within
an agreed-upon frame. But where class and region, nationality
and religious difference, are present, the small decision, expected
to be merely the next stitch in the firmly knitted new life, may
instead unravel the whole mesh. The smallest decision—whether
to eat a hastily assembled meal in the kitchen or to put the breakfast food on the table in one of the trade boxes that children have
learned from the radio to like; whether to turn out the light on
the wedding-night or send a telegram instead of writing a letter—
any one of these may suddenly make them see each other as
worlds apart, not because the personality for which each chose
the other is not there, but because the unrealized, unallowed-for
differences in background are deeper than either bargained for.

The sexual ideal with which young people come to marriage, always one to which men are expected to give only lip-service, is
that of chastity for both. The man who can say to a girl that she

is the first is still valued by American girls almost as much as the man values being his wife's first lover. Until the era of petting, all the husband's premarital experience had to be ignored, and if possible pushed out of the wife's consciousness. Now each is condemned to wondering how far the other has gone, with whom, under what circumstances. The various conventions of frankness that are growing up are an overlay on the old concealment based on a prevalent but repudiated double standard, but they are still an overlay. For the old requirement of real virginity in the bride and a decent reticence in the groom—which included a taboo on displaying any skill as a lover—there is being substituted a determination to start with a "clean slate." Starting with a clean slate often means making a clean breast of all one's past sex experience, but this is also a very effective way of making sure that it contributes nothing to the new marriage. Instead of offering each other the relaxation, the capacity to pause and listen a little to the beating of another heart because the sound of one's own quickened heart-beat has ceased to be so astonishing, the attempt is made to offer the new marriage, which is to be "for keeps," an *as if* position in which none of the past is relevant.

This ability to block out the past, to enter each new situation, be it job or love-affair, with the kind of innocence that it seems to Europeans could only be acquired by amnesia from a blow on the head is a peculiarly American characteristic, bred of the need to be both poised for flight and firmly rooted in the immediate landscape. Oriented outward, towards time and place and the actual concrete realities of life, we develop a capacity to respond quickly, learn and use first names, take the woes and joys of the man at the next desk or the woman across the aisle in a train as our own. Nostalgia for the past is out of place among a people who must always be moving, to a better job, a better house, a new way of life. To the immigrant from Poland to New Jersey or from Massachusetts to Iowa or from Illinois to California, nostalgia for the past way of life is an acute threat to good adjustment in the new environment. To the children of immigrants, there is a new danger, that they may absorb not the direct nostalgia for Poland or Massachusetts, but the parents' sense of unreality, of repudiated roots, of rootlessness. This too must be fended off, and it can be fended off by taking the present reality as the only reality and yet keeping one eye always on the future, which may be different. So Americans do not find it shocking to say to three different girls in a year, "You are the only girl I have ever loved," because the girl who came before is defined as unloved by the very fact that another is loved now. Past loves, past experiences, are named over to be by that very act eliminated. Each lover brings to marriage a conviction that this is the real thing, the only reality for either one. If it fails, then it is not the real thing, but the next experience may be. So each job, each home, each friend, and each lover can be eagerly accepted, optimistically, wholeheartedly, and no failure along the way finally disproves— for the health—the possibility of a later success.

Greater sex experimentation has not therefore contributed as much as it sometimes does to an easier sex relationship in marriage. Facility remains as a suspect reminder that the slate cannot be wiped clean after all, and past failures consciously repudiated are still there as a carking anxiety. The exaggerated overconcern with the other that is the American version of good interpersonal relations, in which each worries for fear the other will worry, puts an extraordinary strain on sex behaviour, and especially dampens spontaneity. The more women realize what sex satisfaction can mean to men, the more they worry for fear their husbands are not getting it, and the more men worry as to whether or not their wives are unsatisfied, the less able either one of a pair is to respond simply and immediately to the other. And American culture offers very little middle ground between continuous relatedness to other people's wishes, desires, hopes, thoughts, feelings, and a complete indifference to anything except one's own desires. This possibility that once an active concern for others is repudiated as too difficult, nothing will remain except a licensed self-indulgence runs through American sex behaviour, and makes marriage, all-exacting marriage, seem the only alternative to sheer rampant, meaningless exploitation of another's personality. Affairs that do not lead to marriage are seen as exploitive; sometimes both partners are exploiting each other, so the moral stigma of hurting another person is removed, but even so the general expectation is that anything but a final and difficult commitment is in the end unrewarding.

This hope for a complete commitment fits very well with our traditional marriage form, in which Church and State combine to insist that all marriages are for life, and that no marriage can be broken without branding the one who breaks it as a failure, if not a criminal and an enemy of society. All the poetry, the phraseology, the expectation of marriage that would last "until death us do part," has survived long after most states have adopted laws permitting cheap and quick divorces. The pressure for divorce is easy enough to understand on many counts. The emphasis on choice carried to its final limits means in marriage, as it does at every other point in American life, that no choice is irrevocable. All persons should be allowed to move if they don't like their present home, change jobs as often as they can get another, change schools, change friends, change political parties, change religious affiliations. With freedom to choose goes the right to change one's mind. If past mistakes are to be reparable in every other field of human relations, why should marriage be the one exception? If their choice of each other was what made a marriage a "real marriage," then once either makes another choice, its reality is gone. The spouse who clings to such a marriage is committing one of the worst acts in the American list of sins, limiting the freedom of another person, exploiting and taking advantage of some one else's past, dead impulse, freezing a past mistake into a present prison. The more modern psychology and modern literature emphasize the importance of impulse gratification, the tighter every spouse is caught in the obligation not to limit the impulse gratification of the other person. In every triangle, where two are married, three are trapped just because the man or woman who is desired by two others is free to choose between them. Because he and she can get a divorce if they really love the third person, not getting a divorce becomes a hostile act for the one who loves both, while failing to give a divorce on the part of the partially rejected spouse is limiting the freedom of two other people. Ethical dilemmas that do not arise in countries where Church and State not only advocate and teach, but enforce, marriage for life are recurrent, inexorably associated with the degree of freedom that exists in the United States.

So an ethics that is peculiarly American has arisen in the United States, to support a marriage-and-divorce code of great contradictoriness. Young people are still encouraged to marry as if they could count on marriage's being for life, and at the same time they are absorbing a knowledge of the great frequency of divorce and the ethics that may later enjoin divorce upon them. There has been much inveighing from the pulpit and the bench which assumes that all those who get divorces are selfish, self-indulgent creatures. But as long as divorce was limited to the selfish and the self-indulgent, there were very few divorces, and it was safe to encourage young people to think of divorce as something that could happen to other people, but not to them. Divorce has now been so absorbed into our ethics that husbands or wives lie sleepless and torn, wondering, "Ought I to get a divorce? Would she be happier with somebody else? Would he develop more with somebody else? Am I spoiling his life? Am I spoiling her life? Isn't it wrong to stay with some one out of mere loyalty? What will happen to the children if this goes on? Isn't it bad for the children to live in a home with this much friction?" Not only the possibility that any marriage except the marriage where *both* partners are deeply committed to some religious orthodoxy may end in divorce, but the phrasing of divorce as something that at least one of the partners in an imperfect marriage *ought* to get, is permeating the whole country, altering our expectations, making marriage many times more difficult.

It is difficult on two counts: because the expectation of permanency is still great enough to brand every impermanence as a failure, if not a sin, and also because to all the other insecurities of American life insecurity about marriage is added. In the United States, where all status is relative, where all jobs can be lost, where men are judged by how much they continue to advance, sometimes a little by how far they have advanced, but never simply by where they are—here marriage in former generations offered one refuge from this eternal uncertainty, this endless incitement to anxious effort. Whether a man succeeded or failed, his wife was there, and whether a woman was an invalid, a failure at housekeeping, an incompetent mother, or a paragon, her husband was there—in most cases, in enough cases to reassure every healthy person that here was one harbour in which his ship could ride at anchor where the winds of success and failure blew less harshly. It was safe to be romantic when there was no real danger that new romances could tempt you away.

> When I should be her lover forever and a day,
> And she my faithful sweetheart till the golden hair was gray;
> And we should be so happy that when either's lips were dumb
> They would not smile in Heaven till the other's kiss had come.

These were verses that could be appropriately written into a poem about one's wife entitled "That Old Sweetheart of Mine." The romance need not be scrutinized too carefully where there was no other choice; after the altar it was never again put to the test.

But to-day, with the growing recognition that divorce may come to any marriage, no matter how devoted, how conscientious, how much in love each spouse originally was, a marriage is something that has to be worked at each day. As the husband has to face the possibility of losing his job, so also the wife has to face the possibility of losing hers, of finding herself companionless, out of the job she chose, often with small children to care for alone. Both husband and wife face the need to re-choose each other, to reassert and re-establish the never permanent claim of one upon the other's choice. The wife in curl-papers is replaced by a wife who puts on lipstick before she wakes her husband, and the husband with a wandering eye finds that his eye wanders less happily because at any moment it may light on some one whom he will choose instead of his wife. As it is her obligation to make herself continuingly desirable, so it is his obligation not to put himself in positions where other women may become desirable to him. This means never going out in mixed company without his wife. It means that all casual flirtations take on a menacing quality that Europeans newly come to America find it very difficult to understand. Where there is freedom to divorce, there is less freedom for either casual relationships or passionate extra-marital love of any sort.

Yet the implied expectation of permanency, still based of course on statistics—for frequent as divorces are in some age-groups, most marriages are still permanent marriages—not only does not protect the new marriage, it actually compromises it. For American behaviour in marriage, the behaviour that young people have learned in their own homes, from their own and their friends' parents, is behaviour that depends on the finality of marriage. Quarrelling, sulking, neglectfulness, stubbornness, could be indulged very differently within a frame that could not be broken. But now over every quarrel hang the questions: "Do you want a divorce? Do I want a divorce? Does she want a divorce? Will that be the end of this? Is that where we are going?"

There is no reason why we cannot develop manners and customs appropriate to the greater fragility of marriage in the United States; they are very badly needed. For it seems unlikely that the other solution, tightening up on divorce laws, is likely to occur. Once freedom of divorce has become part of our ethics, as it has for many segments of the United States, simply going back becomes a genuinely retrogressive step. The very reasons that made divorce necessary, the enormous heterogeneity of our population and the great chances of maladjustment under our system of free marital choice, would remain. Rather the more likely development would seem to be forward to a new pattern of behaviour that fits the new conditions. And there are signs that such a new pattern of behaviour is developing.

In a pattern for marriage which accepts the fact that marriage *may* be for life, *can* be for life, but also may not be, it is possible to set to work to find ways of establishing that permanence which is most congruent with bringing up children, who are defined as immature until the early twenties. Although it is possible to argue and bring together much evidence that children are more damaged when they live in an unhappy home, resonant with the spoken and unspoken resentments of at least one parent, than when they live in a better relationship with just one parent, it is not possible at present to claim that children are better-off in a broken than in a whole home. One of the most important learnings for every human child is how to be a full member of its own sex and at the same time fully related to the opposite sex. This is not an easy learning, it requires the continuing presence of a father and a mother to give it reality. If the child is to know how to hold a baby in its arms, it must be held, and if it is to know how a member of the opposite sex holds a child, it must be held by both parents. It must watch both parents meet its springing impulse, watch both parents discipline and mould their own impulses so that the child is protected, and at adolescence be set free by both parents to go out into the world. Ideally, both parents will be there to bless and define the marriage, and to help their grown children assume the parental rôle by the way in which they take their grandparenthood. This is the way in which human lives have been given full stature, and as yet we know no better way.

We do know, however, that this continuity is of a different order in a changing society than it is in a stable one, and in a heterogeneous society than it is in a homogeneous one. In a changing society like ours the models can never be so perfect, and they must be far less detailed. Daughters do not learn to make the bread that mother used to make; at best they learn to enjoy feeding their families, with different food, differently prepared. The picture of how one will look and feel, act and think, at seventy cannot be filled in by concrete details of Grandmother's gold-rimmed spectacles and Grandfather's tapping cane. At best something of the vigour with which they set out on journeys at eighty, or the placidity with which they sit in the sun and remember the hymns they sang in childhood, may become part of the child's faith in the life that he will live. There is need of developing forms of education, forms that supplement the particularness of the single family, that will make it possible for the child to learn ways of feeling and acting which can be used in a world yet unborn, a world that the imagination of the elders is powerless to anticipate. The world will be the poorer if children learn patterns of behaviour so concrete and particular that twenty years later, as adults, they must wander homeless in nostalgia for a lost way of life. We now know a great deal about how to do this, how a nursery-school can translate and broaden the child's own home experience and make the experience of each child available to the others, how parental precepts can shift from the sureness of "Never eat on the street," "Never ring a door-bell more than three times," "Never accept a present from a man that you can't use up at once or return," to a different kind of teaching which includes the recognition that eating must always be disciplined to make it possible for people to enjoy eating in each other's company, that social fictions are useful and worth respecting, and that relations between the sexes need some kind of patterning to protect those who participate in them. But it is a complicated thing to learn how to transmit a pattern in such a way that the next generation may have its protection without making that protection a prison, may have its delicate discriminations without the inability to make new discriminations, may in fact neither simply repeat nor complete it, but develop a new pattern of their own. The casualties are bound to be greater than in those old traditional societies where five generations played hide-and-seek under the same apple-tree, were born and died in the same high bed.

One of the particular characteristics of a changing society is the possibility of deferred maturity, of later and later shifts in the lives of the most complex, the most flexible individuals. In very simple societies children have completed their acceptance of themselves and their rôles in life by the time they are six or seven, and then must simply wait for physical maturity to assume a complete rôle. But in most societies, adolescence is a period of re-examination, and possible reorientation of the self towards the expressed goals of society. In cultures like ours, there may be a second or a third adolescence, and the most complex, the most sensitive, may die still questing, still capable of change, starting like Franz Boas at seventy-seven to re-read the folk-lore of the world in the light of new theoretical developments. No one who values civilization and realizes how men have woven the fabric of their lives from their own imaginations as they played over the memory of the past, the experience of the present, and the hope of the future, can count this postponed maturity, this possibility of recurrent adolescent crises and change of life-plan, as anything but gain.

But a world in which people may reorient their whole lives at forty or fifty is a world in which marriage for life becomes much more difficult. Each spouse is given the right to and the means for growth. Either may discover a hidden talent and begin to develop it, or repudiate a paralyzing neurotic trend and begin anew. Ever since women have been educated, marriages have been endangered by the possible development or failure to develop of both husbands and wives. "He outgrew her," or less common but with increasing frequency, "She outgrew him." In a society where mobility is enjoined on every citizen and each man should die a long distance from the class he comes from—or devote his life to preventing downward movement, the only recourse left to the upper class— the danger that spouses will get out of step is very great. To all the other exorbitant requirements for a perfect mate, chosen from all the world yet in all things like the self, or complementary on a trivial basis, must be added "capacity to grow." Arapesh parents perform anxious little magical tricks to keep the girl who grows too fast smaller than her young husband, lest the marriage be ruined by the disparity. But American lovers have neither divinatory methods nor precautionary magic to ensure them that they will grow and change in step. Only the recognition of the problem itself can help to solve it, to make young people pause in their choices as they evaluate whether he or she will make a life companion, add to their other criteria "capacity to grow at something like the same rate." And they need to be able to treat failures to grow as tragedies, but not as personal betrayals. Some day a discovered and intractable discrepancy in rate of growth may seem a really legitimate reason for divorce, and one that both couples can accept as simply as do those people who accept childlessness as a reason for ending a marriage. Once there is recognition that change in rate of growth is simply a function of living in a complex modern world, then the marriage that is developing a dangerous discrepancy may be given professional help, just as the childless may seek the advice of the sterility clinic. And as in the sterility clinic, some of those who seek for help can and some cannot be helped. But the whole way of looking at life will be changed. For thousands of years men and women have blamed ghosts and demons, witches and elves and the sorcery of the next tribe, and most of all each other's inferiority or malice, for childlessness. But to-day it is possible to seek expert help from physiologist or psychiatrist, and the needless tragedies can be averted, and those which cannot be averted can be accepted gently by both. For just as there is no good marriage in which each does not wholly choose it, so there is no good divorce that is not chosen by both partners. Among the Negrito people of the Philippines, where vigorous little men and women obey their chief implicitly in a society that seems rather like the childhood of the world, when both partners agree on a divorce it is granted at once; there simply is no marriage. The acceptance of a religious faith that includes the ideal and the promise of indissoluble marriage carries with it dignity for man. But a civil marriage that marries any pair who choose each other and can show no legal impediment, and then will not permit them to choose to end that choice, is a travesty of all the values of human dignity. There are at best something like 71,000,000 church members in the United States, and many of these are no longer guaranteed by their faith that they will be able to stay married for life. For the other 61,000,000 a pattern must be found that will make it possible for them to treat divorce when it does occur with dignity and regret, and so make it possible for each married pair to work openly and to keep and keep on keeping their marriages safe.

There are signs that a vigorous younger generation are doing just that. They are learning to handle the unprecedented and contradictory premarital freedom that they have been accorded by society so that they know the rules and can keep them. They are learning to guard their expectancies of falling in love so that the chance-met girl in the railroad station who becomes one's fate will stay more in the movies, where she belongs, and less in real life, where she is more likely to be a disappointment. They are developing new patterns of learning to know each other, to replace the outmoded long engagement, with its stylizations that now seem artificial and lacking in sincerity. For the old theory that a girl would somehow become "awakened after marriage," and the later compensatory demand for trial marriages, new methods of getting acquainted and demonstrating confidence are being worked out. These include more stages of partial commitment, the slow involvement of more friends in the possible marriage, provision for more retreats with unimpaired dignity for each partner. They are making more realistic demands on the personality of the future partner, partly under a sobering recognition of how many mar-

riages in the war generation have gone to pieces under pressures
of absence, housing, and so on, revealing a lack of what it takes
to stay married in the United States to-day.* Meanwhile the society as a whole is becoming more conscious of the terrific strains
that have been placed on marriages, and of the need for a variety
of new measures, pre-marriage counselling, marriage counselling,
nursery-schools, house-keeping services, and so on, to reduce the
strain on each young couple asked to build single-handed a whole
way of life in a world in which neither they, nor any one else,
have ever lived. For the careful protective care that kinship groups
and tribal elders, family councils and parents, once gave young
people, wider social institutions that will serve the same function
in a new fashion are springing into being, slowly, and against great
resistance, but surely.

Meanwhile, young married people seem to be, if anything, more
anxious to have children than they have been in our immediate
past. Children are regarded neither as an inescapable part of life
nor as a penalty of marriage, but as a value that can be consciously sought and worked for, a value that makes life worth
living. The demand for symmetry between husband and wife is of
course being felt here, the demand that each share in the choice
made, in the planning for the children, and in the enjoyment and
care of the children. As working-hours are cut down and a free
Saturday becomes an American institution, many of the evils of
the household that lived in a suburb for the children's sake, and
so Father never got home in time to see the children, and was too
tired on Sunday, can be overcome. Two free days out of seven
provide enough leeway so that even very tired, overstrained men
can first relax, loosen their belts and kick off their shoes, and when
rested, be ready to start something sizable with the children. The
definition of children as joy rather than as duty is spreading
rapidly, though with all the hazards that a duty-ridden people
will then ask, "Am I enjoying my children enough?" and "Are my
children really enjoying me?"

But whatever the possibilities for anxiety, marriage that is a
responsible, chosen, and joyous way of life seems a more possible
goal for the descendants of Puritans than the mere unhappy reaction to a loss of orthodoxy in which duty to some unnamed

---

* Postwar divorces in 1945 were one for every three marriages, and will
probably, according to William F. Ogburn, drop to one for every five or six.

entity pathetically and inappropriately replaces a duty to God. To the extent that all marriage and all parenthood become more responsible, the religiously orthodox will also be safer, less threatened by the disintegrating standards of a society where so many live without even missing religion.

But if such responsible new patterns are to develop, then it is crucial that in theory, and in practice, the fact that divorce may come to any marriage—except where the religion of both partners forbids it—must be faced. The stigma of failure and of sin must be removed, the indignities of divorce laws that demand either accusation or collusion must be done away with. Social practices must be developed so that the end of a marriage is announced, soberly, responsibly, just as the beginning of a marriage is published to the world. This means a sort of coming-to-terms with sorrow that Americans have been finding difficult to practice in regard to death as well as divorce. We jubilate over birth and dance at weddings, but more and more hustle the dead off the scene without ceremony, without an opportunity for young and old to realize that death is as much a fact of life as is birth. A world in which one really says, "Let the dead bury the dead," is an ugly world in which corpses lie rotting on the streets and the living have to flee for their lives. A dead marriage is sad, a marriage that is broken by death is also infinitely sad (in 1947 of every 100 families, 12 were broken, 9 by widowhood, 1 by divorce and 2 by separation). Both are part of life. If we recognize that we live in a society where marriage is terminable, and in some cases should be terminable, we can then give every newly married pair, and every old married pair, a chance to recognize the hazards they face, and to make genuine efforts to survive them. Marriage was once a harbour from which some marriages set sail safely, some lay in it and rotted, some were simply wrecked on the shore. It is now a voyage in the open sea, with no harbour at any point, and each partner is committed to vigilance and deep concern if the ship is to sail at all. Each form of marriage can be dignified and rewarding if men choose to make it so.

As long as divorce is something disgraceful, for which however no one is punished, something to be hidden and yet something available to any one, we may expect an increasing number of irresponsible marriages in which one or both partners simply say, "Oh, well, if it doesn't work, we'll get a divorce." From such an attitude, many divorces are the expected crop. But if young people can say instead, "Knowing every hazard, we will work to keep our marriage," then the number of irresponsible marriages and irresponsible divorces may begin to fall. But society must recognize and honour those who try again, recognize the belief in marriage so well summed up in the movie title *This Time, for Keeps*.

Albert Ellis

Romantic Love

"We raise our daughters in convents," said Anatole France, "then marry them off to pirates." There is just about that degree of actual education for the lives they actually will lead, in the way Americans raise their children, particularly in their attitudes toward sex. What we teach is an unreality, and the failure to recognize reality is one of the first roots of neurosis and psychosis.

The pattern of courtship in American and in practically all of Western civilized society is, as we have just seen, that of the Sex Tease. In following this pattern, the modern woman, whether she consciously knows it or not, is forcibly striving to do two

From: Albert Ellis, *The American Sexual Tragedy* (2nd ed.), New York: Lyle Stuart, Inc., 1962. Reprinted by permission.

major things: First, to make herself appear infinitely sexually desirable—but finally approachable only in legal marriage. Second, to use sex as bait and therefore to set it up as something special. If she gives in too easily to sex pleasure, she loses her favorite man-conquering weapon. Hence she must retain sexuality on a special plane, and dole it out only under unusual conditions.

The idealized aspect of this philosophy of let-us-women-stick-together-and-only-employ-sex-for-special-baiting-purposes is what we usually call romantic love. For at the very core of modern romance is a tight rope tautly stretched between, and uneasily dividing as well as soldering, gratified and ungratified, over- and under-evaluated sexuality. Where non-romantic types of love prevail—as they do in numerous primitive, peasant, and Eastern cultures—sex is either enjoyed for its own sake or is hedged in by practical (socio-economic, status-giving, marital, or other) restrictions. Where romance is the rule, sex is virtually never enjoyed for itself. It is invariably hemmed in by idealistic, non-practical love restrictions. Romanticism, hand in hand with the sex tease game of American courtship, often plays up the verbal and plays down the active expression of human sexuality.

To understand modern romantic love, we should first know a little about its origins and history. Although the history of love may be traced to the beginnings of mankind, romantic love seems to have been born in Western Europe during the Middle Ages. It is, as Finck has pointed out, "A modern sentiment, less than a thousand years old."[1]

The so-called Dark Ages which preceded the twelfth century was an epoch of acute socio-economic, religious, philosophic, and esthetic rigidity. The individual of the day was born into a world which, to the largest possible extent, predetermined his work, his thoughts, and even his emotions. Against this church-bound and custom-ridden condition of living, romanticism was something of a reflexive, and certainly a healthy, rebellion.

Like most rebellious movements, however, romantic love at first tended to take to extremes its floutings of the established social order. Thus, where the amorous ideal had emphasized sexual fidelity, *courtoisie* love frequently glorified adultery. Where eighth century love was based on patriarchal traditions, tenth century troubadours extolled woman-centered, female-worshipping *amour*. Where the priests preached divine love, the courtiers deified human love. Where Christianized conjugality was truly coffined, cabined, and confined, romantic love emphasized freedom of choice—and of parting. As Denis de Rougement has observed: "The cultivation of passionate love began in Europe as a reaction to Christianity (and in particular to its doctrine of marriage) by people whose spirit, whether naturally or by inheritance, was still pagan."[2]

Just as an insurgent political group will often, both prior and subsequent to its victory, take over many of the trappings of the vested interests it is undermining, romantic love borrowed from the Christianized version of love that preceded it. It preempted many of the mystical, irrational, evangelical aspects of early Christianity. Fighting the restrictions imposed by a mighty religion, it eventually became almost a religion in its own right.

It should be noted that man achieves so-called free will almost in direct inverse ratio to his becoming a socialized human being. The mere fact that one has, and early in one's life is raised by, duly conditioned and biased parents reduces one's possible free will to meagre amount; the fact that one, additionally, is raised among hundreds of other human beings, and among humans who have a long history and an intrenched culture, further reduces one's potential free will to near-zero proportions. Romanticism, therefore, by very virtue of its being a philosophy with quite well-defined rules of the game of living, eventually leads to virtually as much restriction and human determination as do medieval or other non-romantic philosophies. To be human is to be, in one degree or another, predetermined in one's thoughts, feelings, actions. One mainly has a choice of what *kind* of determination one will live by. And even that choice is largely chimerical: since, as it for example happened, early Christianity and its heir-apparent, medievalism, actually determined most of the trappings of the romantic revolt that followed. Small wonder was it, then, that soon after its inception romantic love blanketed itself in religiosity and traditionalism.

Again, although romantic love was in part a reaction against the sexual repressiveness of early Christianity, it quickly took on so many characteristics of the Christianized love that it was trying to replace that, in its own right, it became antisexual. As Emil Lucka observed: "As time went on the barrier erected between true spiritual love and insidious sensuality became more and more clearly defined; the former pervaded the erotic emotion of the whole period. Parallel with chaste love, sensuality continued to exist as something contemptible, unworthy of a noble mind." The cycle, curiously enough, was then complete:

romantic love, which originated as a revolt against Christian antisexuality, soon was conquered by its victim: so that, at least in some of its extreme manifestations, it became itself a bulwark against pagan sensuality.

Three notable facts, however, kept the antisexual elements of medieval romantic love within the bounds of practicality and sanity. In the first place, it was not, when it first originated, a mass phenomenon. The troubadours and their ladies followed the romantic patterns, to be sure. But the peasants, footsoldiers, common tradesmen and artisans, and other members of the community tended to remain scrupulously orthodox. In the second place, while the troubadours and lords maintained romantic attachments to the ladies of the day, these were invariably adulterous, and not marital, attachments. Marriages, at this time, were socio-economically arranged, and had little or nothing to do with love either in their courtship or post-courtship stages. In the third place, although the troubadours and courtiers could fall romantically in love with their ladies, they also could, and invariably did, find plenty of girls from the peasant and other classes with whom they could roll in the hay. They could therefore well afford to use love as a special ritual for the unattainable lady while they used sex as a pleasant pastime and an essential ingredient of their relations with women of the lower classes.

Medieval romanticism was in several ways an exceptionally class-limited form of love; and it hardly interfered with sex activity, which the courtier could always have, practically for the asking, with a wife, prostitute, or girl of the lower classes for whom he had very frank sex desire and, usually, no romantic love whatever. Under such conditions, the courtier could easily build love into a mystical, religious, antisexual emotion—while he was gaily, and quite unromantically, fulfilling his sexual needs at the same time.

Up until the twentieth century, vestiges of this medieval pattern of romantic love have persisted. Although the nineteenth century male was supposed to show some degree of romantic love for his wife, several non-romantic aspects of sex and marriage also were so widespread in the 1800's as to be virtually socially sanctioned. Males of the upper class in Europe and America frequently had their regular mistresses; while lower class males often frequented brothels. Marriages, particularly among the gentry, were often arranged by parents, or at least had to be entered into with parental permission; and in a country like the United States, where the frontier still existed and where women tended to bear several children and to work just as hard as their husbands, there was relatively little opportunity for romantic love in marriage, even when some measure of it existed in courtship.

Only in our own day, for the first time in history, has romantic love become ubiquitous. Whereas our forefathers expected only relatively few gentlemen and gentlewomen to love romantically, we expect every male and female to do so. There are several reasons why romantic attitudes have become so democratized today. For one thing, romantic love is facilitated by small families, by weakened religiosity, by the freedom of women, and by social mobility, all of which are considerably more prevalent today than they were a century or more ago. For another thing, modern living arrangements and technological inventions (such as kitchenettes, automobiles, and birth control appliances) make it easy for households to be moved and for families to break up, and this in turn favors romantic views of love. Our present concepts of individual freedom, democracy, and personal adventurousness also encourage romanticism. Finally, we have literally taken up the cudgels for romantic love and actually preach its precepts in our schools, fiction, drama, movies, and television performances. "Romantic love is to a large extent a convention developed by society,"[3] and in our own society we have deliberately adopted this convention and promulgated it with a vengeance.

All love is not, of course, romantic love. Love itself consists of any kind of more or less intense emotional attraction to or involvement with another. It includes many different types and degrees of affection, such as conjugal love, parental love, familial love, religious love, love of humanity, love of animals, love of things, self-love, sexual love, obsessive-compulsive love, etc. Although *romantic* has become, in our day, virtually a synonym for *loving*, romantic love is actually a special type of love, and has several distinguishing features.

A summary description of the characteristics of romantic love —or more accurately of the romantic lover—will help clarify. The romantic lover is unrealistic: he over-evaluates and fictionalizes his beloved. He is verbal and esthetic about his love. As Tolstoy remarked of the lovers of his day, "Many people's love would be instantly annihilated if they could not speak of it in French."[4] He is aggressively individualistic: he insists, utterly, on his own romantic love choice, and on all but absolute lack of restraint in that choice. This aspect of romantic love was taken so seriously by the famous Comtesse de Champagne's twelfth century Court of Love that it held, in one of its decisions, that "love cannot extend its rights over two married persons. For indeed lovers grant each other all, mutually and freely, without being constrained by any motive of necessity, whereas husband and wife are holden, by their duty, to submit their wills to each other and to refuse each other nothing."[5]

The romantic lover, furthermore, frequently is in love with love rather than with his beloved; and he may well repeat, with Elizabeth Barrett Browning, "If thou must love me, let it be for naught except for love's sake only." He is monopolistic, in that he normally devotes himself to one paramount love object. As Folsom has noted, "Romantic love is intensely monogamous *at any one time*. Yet, essentially, its loyalty is to *love* rather than to a person."[6]

The romantic lover is demanding: he wishes to be loved, in his turn, by his beloved; to be loved madly, completely, monopolistically; and for himself, rather than for his position and accomplishments. He is perfectionistic: he strives for not merely a fine, good, lasting, happy relationship with his beloved, but for the finest, greatest, most lasting, most ecstatic amour.

The romantic lover is, as we previously noted, antisexual. He acknowledges the value of sexuality only when it is linked to love. He is sentimental and tends to overact and overstate the greatness of his love. He is passionate and intense: he is supposed to love madly and to be violently in love, rather than affectionately loving.

The romantic lover is changeable, and frequently goes from one violent passion to another. He is jealous, often intensely so, of his beloved. He tends to emphasize physical attractiveness above all else. Finally, in today's world, the romantic lover invariably stresses marrying only for love, and is likely to believe that one should never remain married when love dies. For him, too, the death of love from his marriage tends to become sufficient license for every sort of adultery. In the high name of romantic love, he is free to pursue his true passion at any cost.

The romantic lover believes, in sum, two basic propositions

which Ernest W. Burgess lists as follows: "1. That the highest personal happiness comes from marriage based upon romantic love. 2. That love and marriage are essentially personal and private and are, perhaps, even more than other aspects of life, to be controlled by the individual himself."[7]

This, in general, is what the romantic lover is; or, in other words, these may be said to be the *facts* of romantic love. Even more interesting, however, are some of the current American beliefs and attitudes—or folklore—concerning love. For several main tenets about romantic amour are constantly being drilled into the eyes and ears of the American public; and, apparently, some measure of belief in these tenets ultimately comes to be held by this public. Our mass media are full of assertions, implicit and explicit, about the nature of romantic love, some of which we shall now document.

1. *Romantic love is a feeling that takes you unawares, at first sight or a reasonable facsimile thereof, and quickly cooks your goose.*

(a) "Jordan knew he loved her the minute he saw her."—Story in *Man to Man Magazine*.

(b) "The first time I saw her, I knew that this was the woman for whom I would live or die."—Play broadcast over Columbia Broadcasting System.

(c) Some enchanted evening, if you see a stranger in a crowded room, and know she's your true love, you had better immediately *fly* to her side, and make her your own, unless you want to dream out the rest of your life alone.—Song, "Some Enchanted Evening," from *South Pacific*.

(d) "Putting Rajah to a gallop she covered the distance quickly, then frowned as she halted before a pair of surveyors and another man who seemed to be directing them. All three men looked up at her, but after a brief appraisal, Diana concentrated on the third man. As her eyes met his, she felt a strange impact, an uncanny sensation of suddenly and irrevocably meeting her destiny, as if she had lived all of her twenty-one years for this moment."—Story in *New Love Magazine*.

2. *When once you really and truly fall in love, your emotion is deathless, and not even complete rejection by your beloved will serve to make you fall out of love again.*

(a) "At last Jerry knew and understood the meaning of loving her, of knowing that nothing could ever wholly alter the need of her that had become a part of him."—Novel, *The Lonely*.

(b) "I made a declaration of my undying love. I would not, could not, ever love anyone else but her. It was impossible, unthinkable . . . Love like this was immortal."—Autobiography, *The Seven Storey Mountain*.

(c) "You're never going to lose me, dearest, I'm going to be right at your heels, tagging right along with you, as long as I live."—Story in *Gay Love Stories*.

(d) "You see, there's no escape from the truth of love. It exists and, no matter what you do or try to do to kill it, it will continue to exist . . . Now and forever he was hers!" Story in *Love Memories*.

3. *Romantic love is more than welcome at any age, and old-sters, as well as youngsters, should hasten to let themselves fall in love.*

(a) "Love has no age limit. The intelligent world is coming to realize that strong and fervent love, instead of blooming only during youth, often waits until maturity to reach its greatest ardor."—Article in *New Physical Culture*.

(b) It is only natural for a woman in her sixties to want a romantic love and marriage.—Comic strip in the *New York Post*.

4. *Romantic love, when it is reciprocated and fulfilled, leads to unalloyed, ecstatic happiness.*

(a) "Give me your love! And make life divine!"—Song, "Give Me Your Hand."

(b) "I looked at my love . . . and I knew that joy resounded in our hearts and I would find real happiness."—Story in *True Confessions*.

(c) When you find love, you'll "find your happy, happy time."—Film, *The Inspector General*.

(d) "Then I was in his arms, my eyes blinded by happy tears . . . But I didn't need my eyes—I could see him with my heart! . . . So it was that we came out of the darkness into the warmth of life and love!"—Story in *Honeymoon*.

(e) "Love leads to halcyon happiness."—Poem in *Voices*.

5. *When romantic love is unrequited, or when one's lover deserts, it is the most painful, agonizing feeling possible.*

(a) "Nothing ever had hurt so much in all her life [as her boyfriend being out with another girl], and yet she didn't want

to cry. She wanted just one thing: she wanted to be dead."—
Story in *McCall's*.

(b) "I lay on my bed, or sat in the armchair at the foot of the
bed. I clutched in my hands one of Mino's jackets which I had
found hanging up, and every now and again I kissed it passionately or bit it to calm my restlessness. Even when mother forced
me to eat something, I ate with one hand only and continued to
grip the jacket convulsively in the other hand. Mother wanted
to put me to bed on the second night and I let her undress me
passively. But when she tried to take the jacket from me, I gave
such a shrill scream that she was terrified."—Novel, *The Woman
of Rome*.

6. *Romantic love is a completely irrational, illogical feeling
that makes lovers do the maddest things.*

(a) "When people are in love, their minds cease to function
properly."—Novel, *The Woman of Rome*.

(b) "I even steal your handkerchiefs to have part of you with
me all the time."—Play, *I Know My Love*.

(c) " 'And you can't even kiss me!' wails the heroine as,
suffering from a deadly type of influenza, the hero proposes to
her. 'Bugs or no bugs,' said he firmly, 'that's just what I intend
to do.' "—Novel, *Dardanelles Derelict*.

7. *Romantic love is worth making any sacrifice for, and the
greater the sacrifice the greater, presumably, the love.*

(a) " 'You'll fail if you stick to me now,' Frankie warned
her. 'I'd rather fail with you than make it without you, Frankie.' "
—Novel, *The Man with the Golden Arm*.

(b) It is perfectly natural for a great ballet dancer to sacrifice
her career, and finally her life, for her husband.—Film, *The Red
Shoes*.

(c) A professional blackmailer, for the love of a woman who
is happily married and devoted to her family, sacrifices $2500
for her, falsely confesses to a murder in which she is involved,
and gets himself killed for her.—Film, *The Reckless Moment*.

(d) "If his life must be sold for the price of Lucia's, then it was
a price he was willing to pay."—Novel, *Divine Mistress*.

8. *True love is utterly monogamous, and once you fall in love—
honest and truly—you can never love another—even though your
beloved is worthless; unloving, or already married.*

(a) "If I ever love again, it will be you."—Song, "If I Ever
Love Again."

(b) "I'd wake up in the middle of the night with a dream of Tex, and cry silently so as not to waken Dane. And I'd pray, Oh, God, make him stop haunting me, make me forget him. I don't want to love him, but I can never love Dane as long as my heart goes on aching for Tex."—Story in *True Story*.

(c) "Love tends to produce a feeling of oneness, and genuine love is centered only on one person."—Article in *Your Marriage*.

9. *Romantic love is an all-important emotion, without which life is dull, pitiful, and meaningless.*

(a) "Suppose we could not love, dear; imagine ourselves as neither living nor dead."—Poem in *Wake*.

(b) "We both knew that our getting married was the whole point of our lives."—Story in *True Experiences*.

(c) "If ever I cease to love,
    If ever I cease to love,
    May the fish get legs and the cows lay eggs—
    If ever I cease to love!"—Mardi Gras song, quoted in the
    book, *Queen New Orleans*.

10. *Love has the power of life and death over men and women and can make them do, or not do, almost anything.*

(a) Even though a man has had several paralytic strokes and though neurologists have given him a short time to live, his wife's love can keep him alive and well indefinitely.—Article in *True Experiences*.

(b) Love can easily induce a King to give up his throne for a woman he loves.—Article in the *San Diego Union*.

(c) Love has the power to make a plain woman perfectly beautiful.—Article in *Woman's Day*.

(d) Love will redeem a man and change his entire character and existence; lack of love will literally drive a woman crazy.—Play, *The Madwoman of Chaillot*.

11. *Love transforms sexuality and makes it truly good. Sex without love is nasty and worthless.*

(a) A woman whose husband even hints that she can be physically attracted to a man whom she does not love should leave that husband immediately.—Novel, *The Long Love*.

(b) A normal, healthy man cannot possibly have sex relations with a girl without coming to love her.—Article in *Reader's Digest*.

(c) If any man ceases to love a girl, his kisses will suddenly become mechanical and passionless.—Story in *Private Detective.*

(d) Young people could never feel "white-hot burning thingamajigs" for each other unless they were violently in love.—Play broadcast over the National Broadcasting Company.

12. *A true lover gives in completely to his beloved, and becomes entirely subservient to her wishes and whims.*

(a) "She belonged to Jerry, everything she was—her thoughts, her person, her mind, her heart, the deep, swelling buds of womanhood that were bursting within her—awake, asleep, living, dying, breathing, walking, wherever she might be, to the ends of time, she belonged to him."—Novel, *The Lonely.*

(b) "If you crush the life out of me, I'll kiss you with my dying breath."—Film, *Samson and Delilah.*

(c) "All right, Jack, I'll go away with you—I'll do anything you want me to."—Film, *All the King's Men.*

13. *There may be many types of love, but there is only one* true *love, which is easily recognizable. When you really and truly love—*

you join your whole destiny to that of your beloved.—Story in *Cosmopolitan.*

you find your beloved beautiful even when you "see her with a shiny nose, blistered face, watery eyes, and a saffronish color."—Article in *Your Psychology.*

you are never cool to your loved one.—Story in *My Love Life.*

you want to be with your beloved *every* evening.—Article in *Your Marriage.*

you never doubt your love—Story in *Love Novels Magazine.*

you can never truly love anyone else.—Story in *Sweethearts.*

you will dream about your beloved constantly.—Story in *Ladies' Home Journal.*

It might be thought that, as the years go by and Americans presumably become more sophisticated in regard to sex-love matters, the super-romantic depictions that are common in our mass media would significantly decrease. If so, the decline in romanticism is not yet evident. A review of American love attitudes in the 1960's quickly turned up the following typical examples of extreme romanticism:

From the film, *The Miracle:* " 'Don't leave me!' she gasped. 'Don't leave me! I think I'll die if you leave me!' "

From the song, *I'll Always Love you*: "Day after day I'll always love you—live just to say I'll always love you."

From a story in *Personal Romances*: "I knew that if I lived a million years, I'd always love Ned Roberts."

From *Lois Lane Comic Book*: "All my love troubles are over at last! I've got the man I most adore!"

From the film, *The Gene Krupa Story*: "I'm no good for anybody but you, Gene. I never have been!"

From the song, *Why*: "We found a perfect love—Yes, a love that's yours and mine. I love you and you love me all the time."

From a play by William Inge in *Esquire*: "I get disgusted with myself sometimes, after he treats me bad, and promise myself I'm never going to have anything more to do with him, but . . . when he comes to me and puts his arms around me, I . . . can't help myself. I fall in love all over again. And that's the way it goes."

From a story in *Girl's Romances*: "Then I turned, and for the first time looked at the new boy . . . I felt as if—as if lightning struck my heart!"

From a poem in the *New York Journal American*: "Without you this life holds no meaning . . . not having you, stars cease to shine . . . and when you're away, little darling . . . my heart seems to endlessly pine."

From *Superman Comics*: "I will never forget our final, lingering, farewell kiss . . . 'Goodbye, Lori! I'll always love you!' "

From the song, *Guaranteed*: "Guaranteed is my love for a lifetime to your heart and your heart alone . . . I'll be there to fill ev'ry need; my devotion will grow, rain or shine, guaranteed."

From a story in *Alfred Hitchcock's Mystery Magazine*: "I told her I'd be an angel or anything else she wanted me to be. I was in love with Martha, faithfully, slavishly, completely, hopelessly."

Similar—in fact, almost identically similar—super-romantic sentiments were found (and may almost every month continue to be found) in such highly popular publications as *Life*, *McCall's*, *Family Circle*, *Look*, *Redbook*, *The Saturday Evening Post*, and the *Ladies' Home Journal*.

Although the best-selling novels of the 1960's are, as I pointed out in the recent revised edition of *The Folklore of Sex*, distinctly more sexually liberal and semi-pornographic than those of the 1950's, their apotheosizing of highly romantic love has, curiously enough, not been dimmed a whit by their increased sexualization. Thus, in Ruark's *Poor No More*, the ultra-sophisticated Susan Strong falls madly in love with the old roué, Craig Price, at first sight; and when he later treats her cruelly in almost every possible way she still insists on returning to him "because I love you because I can't help it, and I want to love you all my life, you miserable, stupid, arrogant, prideful, dishonest son of a bitch!"

In Nevil Shute's *On the Beach*, the hero, Dwight, refuses to get entangled with a most lovely girl, because he must remain true to his dead wife and children. In Costain's *Darkness and the Dawn*, Nicolan falls in love with Ildico when she is five years old and continues to love her "all my life." In Grace Metalious' *Peyton Place*, Michael Rossi, a most intelligent, sophisticated school principal, falls violently in love with a widow of 35 with a 15-year-old daughter; and he "admitted cheerfully . . . that he was hogtied and completely swozzled. He would wait for Connie MacKenzie if it took her 50 years to make up her mind." Similar ultra-romantic attachments are described in almost all the best-selling novels of the 1960's that were surveyed, including Jaffe's *The Best of Everything*, Uris's *Exodus*, Warren's *The Cave*, Drury's *Advise and Consent*, West's *The Devil's Advocate*, and Faulkner's *The Mansion*.

From the foregoing data, it may clearly be seen that romantic love, in today's America, is continually touted, over-evaluated, and deified. It is not merely a cardinal value of our culture; it almost *is* our culture. Amour is taken to such ultra-romantic extremes that we easily find examples, in our mass media, of the most exaggerated, distorted, and often downright silly manifestations of heterosexual affectability.

The impression could easily be given, from the material thus far presented in this chapter, that romanticism monopolizes our contemporary philosophies of love and marriage. This is not entirely true: since dissident, non-romantic voices are also heard from time to time. A *Modern Bride* writer, for example, tells us that "we are hampered by ideas of love that represent a combination of infantile and adolescent patterns, instead of those appropriate to a grown-up." In a tale in *Gay Love Stories* the heroine says: "I—don't want romance or glamour—I want—genuine affection, tenderness . . ." In an article in the magazine, *Wake*, we are informed that mature love is selfless and does not demand super-romantic requitement. An *American Sociological Review* article by William L. Kolb points out that our society puts considerable pressure on young people not to marry just for love, but for more logical, socio-economic reasons. Even some of our popular jokes contain unromantic implications, as this one from *Joke Parade*: "A young woman wrote in her diary, after the loss of her husband, 'My sorrow is more than I can bear.' Several months later, leafing through the diary she came to the entry, paused, and then added the word 'alone.' "

Despite these criticisms of romantic love, and for all the jokes current about it, the fact remains that our mass media overwhelmingly favor the belief that romantic amour is incredibly delightful, delicious, and delectable and that a life not rooted in romantic affection is detestable, deleterious, and damnably dull. While not even a dozen non-romantic or anti-romantic views were found in the course of surveying literally hundreds of mass media outlets, several hundred distinctly romantic attitudes were uncovered.

The ubiquity of ultra-romantic philosophies in our mass media, particularly when combined with the unromantic and often harsh realities of modern life, leads to serious (conscious and unconscious) conflicts and disturbances on the part of virtually all the members of our society. Some of the reasons for these conflicts and disturbances are as follows:

1. Romanticism is, almost by definition, passionately untrammeled and unrestricted. But our courtship customs, as we indicated in the previous chapter, are normally hemmed in by many practical and nonromantic considerations. Consequently, the swain who is romantically enamored of his girlfriend must almost necessarily encounter parental objections, financial difficulties, sexual tabus, and other limitations. It may therefore be predicted that, quite aside from his girlfriends' reacting negatively to him, most of his romantic attachments will never get the chance to bud or will be cruelly nipped before they have consequentially flowered. Although the sex tease of courtship which is prevalent in our society nicely dovetails with romanticism's antisexuality, our other courtship restrictions are mainly antithetical to romance: they, to some extent, encourage romantic dreams—but savagely combat the fulfillment of these dreams.

2. The kind of romantic love which is enthusiastically espoused by our mass media is based on many assumptions which, ordinarily, are not sustained by the realities of either living or loving. Thus, it is assumed that romantic love does not change; but, on the contrary, it most often does. It is assumed that romantic love survives the lover's aging processes and the beloved's loss of youth and beauty; but, most frequently, it does not. It is assumed that it

is easy to tell "true love" from "infatuation"; which, of course, it isn't. It is assumed that romantic love brings nothing but ecstatic joy; when, actually, it often brings worry, responsibility, loss of independence, and all kinds of anguish. It is assumed that having steady sex relations with one's beloved will make one romantically love her more; when, in point of fact, it frequently makes one love her less. It is assumed that if a pair of romantic lovers have children, their offspring will help increase their mutual ardor; when, in numerous instances, children seriously sabotage romantic ardor. Similarly, numerous other assumptions about romantic love are made in our popular publications and productions which, in reality, are distinctly false. Consequently, the utter, terrible disillusionment of many or most romantic lovers becomes eventually assured.

3. Romanticism, again almost by definition, implies a considerable degree of fiction, of facing away from instead of toward reality. The romantic lover exaggerates, overestimates, sees his beloved as she really is not. But life, particularly, in our technologically influenced world, is hardly fictional; and adjustment to life, as we psychologists have been stressing for many years, means full acceptance of reality. Neurosis, in the last analysis, invariably includes a considerable degree of failure to recognize reality. If, then, romantic love also includes a failure to recognize reality, we should expect it importantly to overlap with neurosis at several points. This means that we, on the one hand, are trying to raise our children to be realistic and, on the other hand, to be non-realistic—that is, romantic. Not only, then, are we directly raising them to be at least semi-neurotic, but we are heading them for a virtually irreconcilable conflict between their romantic and non-romantic aspirations: which conflict, in its turn, is only likely to intensify their neurosis.

4. Many romantic ideals, such as those concerned with purity, dedication, holy affection, and the deification of physical beauty, supply us with perfectionistic goals which will inevitably be unachievable by most of us, and will lead to grim disappointment and disillusionment. The result, particularly where sexuality is at issue, is likely to be neurotic and psychotic feelings of dirtiness, failure, guilt, inadequacy, profanation of what is considered to be holy, and so on. Human happiness, as has long been known, is a ratio between what people expect and what they get from life. When their expectations are ultra-romantic, and hence unrealistic,

failure to achieve their level of aspiration must inevitably ensue: with consequent unhappiness and a tendency toward emotional disturbance.

5. Romantic love, in our culture, is supposed to lead to engagement and marriage; but its tenets, actually, are largely opposed to the type of marriage which exists among us. Normal marriage has numerous socio-economic aspects which are antithetical to the maintenance of romantic (though not necessarily other types of) love. Thus, married couples must be concerned about purchases, repairs, sickness, insurance, child care, entertainment, business success, in-laws, relatives, friends, education, cooking, cleaning, shopping, mending, sleeping facilities, and hundreds of other practical aspects of modern living which are utterly nonromantic and which tend to restrict emotional outpourings of a romantic nature.

Romanticism, moreover, puts a premium on intense amative *feelings*: which are notoriously changeable and fleeting. Romantic courtship usually follows a highly erratic pattern, and includes considerable affectional promiscuity. Romantic marriage, quite logically, tends to follow this same pattern and to result in numerous separations and divorces—at which our society hardly looks with equanimity.

Marriage usually becomes a relatively calm, steady relationship that is not too demanding emotionally: since few married couples have available a great reserve of sustained, intense emotional energy. But romanticism, as Gross has pointed out, demands "constant and unequivocal demonstrations of affection."[8] An individual who is raised to crave romantic love is rarely content with anything but the sustained emotional intensity which is thoroughly non-indigenous to everyday marital domesticity. Hence the almost inevitable dissatisfaction of the arch romanticist who marries.

Romantic love, again, is partly based on the sexual teasing and blocking of modern courtship. Its very intensity, to a large extent, grows out of the generous promises combined with the niggardly actualities of sex fulfillment which exist during the courtship stages. When, after marriage, the sex blockings of the courtship days are necessarily removed, the intensity of romantic love which partly stemmed from these blockings may easily fade; and the result is a relatively (romantically) loveless marriage—which, by the very premises of romanticism, is considered to be worthless and must be broken up.

Romantic love, because it is an idealized, perfectionist emotion, particularly thrives on intermittent rather than steady association between two lovers. During courtship, fellows and girls see each other for relatively few hours per week, when they are well-rested, well-fed, and well-accoutered for having a good time. On such a basis, they are at their best and their handsomest or loveliest, and can reasonably well live up to perfectionist ideals. Marriage, however, invariably means domesticity: meaning, a constant, more or less monotonous, living together on an hour after hour, year after year basis. This type of domesticity, probably, is as well designed to sabotage romantic love as is any other mode of social living. Indeed, if romantic lovers wanted, with perfect logic, to induce their passions to endure for a maximum period of time, they might well ban, under almost any circumstances, marital domesticity. But, in our society, they do just the opposite: they, as it were, condemn themselves to living under the same roof, for perhaps forty or fifty years, with their beloveds. The result, in terms of their own romantic ideals, is almost invariably frightful.

6. Romantic love, in our culture, is essentially opposed to the other modes of love which we also, in one way or another, espouse. It is particularly opposed to conjugal or familial love which our religious institutions and (increasingly) our schools are continually upholding. Moreover, most of our married women, once they see that their early romantic love for their husbands does not last, tend to raise their sons and daughters, and particularly perhaps the former, in a Momistic, family-tied manner that brooks little romantic opposition. Mother-centered sons are not encouraged to fall madly in love with the girl next door; and many of them, in point of fact, are raised so that they cannot possibly romantically love anyone. When, because of the pressurizing and pulling influences of their culture (particularly, the novels, films, and television shows of this culture), they do become romantically attached to a woman, they are almost automatically propelled right into the center of a bitter struggle for their souls between their mother and their wife. Since romanticism, with its unrealistic idealizations and demands, can afford no such struggle, it usually gets the worst of the conflict, and the consequent wrestle with reality is often agonizing.

7. Of the several possible logical culminations of romantic love that theoretically may, and presumably should, occur, virtually none are consciously permitted to occur; so that its usual end is desultory, unplanned, and heartbreaking. Some of the possible logical culminations of romantic love are these:

(a) Romantic love may, under some circumstances, be sustained by severely limiting the period of its expression. Thus, Somerset Maugham has the heroine of his play, *The Constant Wife*, declare that she is going off to stay with her lover only for a period of six weeks: "Because I'm putting a limit to our love it may achieve the perfection of something that is beautiful and transitory."[9]

(b) Romantic love may flower indefinitely if lovers consciously become varietists and change their individual partners while continuing their romantic patterns of attachment.

(c) Romantic lovers may, quite logically, engage in plural love affairs and thus, by having two or more romantic partners simultaneously, avoid much of the monotony and domesticity which normally dooms romanticism.

(d) Romantic lovers may keep their love alive by consciously renouncing its fruition. Thus, Ibsen has his lovers in *Love's Comedy* break with each other just as they are about to marry, with the heroine ecstatically removing her engagement ring, casting it into the fjord, and exclaiming to her lover: "Now for this earthly life I have forgone thee,—But for the life eternal I have won thee!"[10] George Moore, in his *Memoirs of My Dead Life*, Andre Gide in *Strait is the Gate*, Walter Van Tilburg Clark in *The City of Trembling Leaves*, and Ben Hecht in *Erik Dorn* solve the problem of longevity of romantic love in precisely the way Ibsen solved it in *Love's Comedy*.[11] Theophile Gautier, in *Mlle. de Maupin*, gives one of the best summaries of this renunciation philosophy by having his heroine write a farewell letter to her lover in this wise: "You believe, perhaps, that I do not love you because I am leaving you. Later, you will recognize the truth of the contrary. Had I valued you less, I should have remained, and would have poured out to you the insipid beverage to the dregs. Your love would soon have died of weariness; after a time you would have quite forgotten me, and, as you read over my name on the list of your conquests, would have asked yourself: 'Now, who the deuce was she?' I have at least the satisfaction of thinking that you will remember me sooner than another. Your unsated desire will again spread its wings to fly to me; I shall ever be to you something desirable to which your fancy will love to return, and I hope that in the arms of the mistresses you may have, you will sometimes think of the unrivalled night you spent with me."[12]

(e) Romantic love, most logically perhaps, may be ended in the most drastic of all human acts: death. As Emil Lucka has pointed out: "One thing is certain: the great love cannot find its consummation on earth . . . The love-death is the last and inevitable conclusion of reciprocal love which knows no value but itself, and is resolved to face eternity, so that no alien influence shall reach it."[13] Denis de Rougemont concurs: "The mystic lovers in the Romance are compelled to pursue the *intensification* of passion, not its fortunate appeasement. The keener their passion, the more it can detach them from created things, the more readily do they feel that they are on the way to attaining the death in *endura* which they desire."[14]

Of these logical, or romantically self-consistent, ways of bringing romantic love to a climax, none are consciously espoused by any number of lovers in our culture: for the good reason that the general marital philosophy of our society is quite opposed to such acts as lovers limiting the period of their love, becoming varietists, engaging in plural affairs, consciously renouncing their loves, or arranging a suicide pact with their beloveds. Instead, we espouse what might be called the most illogical climax to romantic courtship and love: consummation. For sexual and marital consummation indubitably, in the vast majority of instances, maims, bloodies, and finally kills romanticism until it is deader than—well, yesterday's romance. Noting this, the famous troubadour Peiral maintained that "I cannot believe that a true lover can continue to love after he has received the last favor."[15]

The pernicious and widespread effects of our romantic ideologies may perhaps be illustrated by considering ten patients I have seen at the beginning of one of my regular work weeks. Patient No. 1, a 23 year old girl, keeps contending that she does not want to marry; actually, she has highly romantic ideals of marriage that aggravate her general feelings of inadequacy, so that she deems herself unworthy of ever acquiring the ideal type of partner she would like to marry; hence her stated lack of desire for the marital state. Patient No. 2, a 28 year old male, is living with a girl for whom he has considerable affection, but whom he will not consider marrying because, in some respects, she does not live up to his ideal of a tall, slim, beautiful, unearthly creature. Patient No. 3 has left his wife because, among other things, she has never lived up to his notion of romantic love during their twenty years of married life. Patient No. 4 has turned to homosexuality because, after twelve years of marriage, he still feels guilty about engaging in various non-coital sex activities with his wife (who is quite willing to engage in these activities) while he does not feel guilty, or as guilty, about engaging in these same activities with other males. Patient No. 5 feels that his wife does not love him because she is too close to her mother. Patient No. 6 cannot live comfortably with her husband, who she admits is a fine person and a good companion, because she is madly infatuated with another man who she says is quite inferior to him. Patient No. 7 has no special problems in relation to romantic love. Patient No. 8 cannot put his heart into sex relations with his wife, with whom he says he wants to keep living, because he feels that their marriage got off on the wrong foot when they married for practical, utterly non-romantic reasons. Patient No. 9 keeps falling intensely in love with males to whom she is absolutely afraid, because of fears that they may reject her, to show any indication of her feeling, and with whom she normally parts long before any chance for real intimacy arises between them. Patient No. 10, while saying that she would marry almost any normal male who loved her and wanted to marry her, actually goes with literally scores of boyfriends every year, most of whom she soon rejects because they do not live up to her impossibly romantic, perfectionist notions.

So it goes with most of my patients, particularly my female patients: although romantic aspirations and ideals are not necessarily their main source of difficulty and disturbance, romanticism is definitely one of the chief reasons for their being considerably more unhappy and maladjusted than they would be had they more realistic goals of love and marriage. Similarly, I am sure, if we had adequate statistics on the place of romanticism in the causation of modern neurosis, we would find literally millions of instances where romantic ideologies have caused or abetted emotional disturbance.

Psychologists, psychiatrists, social workers, and marriage counselors rarely, alas, keep the kind of statistics which would be most helpful in gauging just how much maladjustment results from the inculcation in our populace of super-romantic ideals. Many case histories and clinical observations, however, have been published in regard to this point. Alfred Adler, for example, shows how a person who invents a "romantic, ideal, or unattainable love . . . can thus luxuriate in [his] feelings without the necessity of approaching a partner in reality."[16] Karen Horney demonstrates how romantic, over-evaluated love may be made "a screen for satisfying wishes that have nothing to do with it . . . made an illusion by our expecting much more of it than it can possibly fulfil."[17] John Levy points out how an individual's romantically expecting too much from marriage inevitably leads to a "universal feeling of disillusionment about marriage."[18] W. Beran Wolfe contends that "romanticism is the sexual life of the adolescent. When practiced by mature men and women it reaps a narrow horizon, a high degree of subjectivity, a desire to be pampered, to be treated like a prince or a princess."[19] Sandor Ferenczi notes that a full appreciation of reality is lacking in persons who remain fixated at the romantic stage of love.[20] Freud stresses the fact that extreme romanticism may lead to masochistic submissiveness to the love partner and to actual sexual perversion.[21] Lorine Pruette discusses a number of the childish marital attitudes to which romantic ideologies may lead.[22] Theodor Reik and Edmund Bergler show how unrealistic love attitudes, sparked by literary productions, result in many sorts of neurotic phenomena.[23]

Sociologists and anthropologists, on the basis of their studies, have also consistently demonstrated the pernicious effects of ultra-romantic attitudes. Ray E. Baber has pointed out that "the fact that so frequently the response satisfactions in the early years of marriage do not come up to expectation is due to social misguidance. The literature of love has brought into being a cult of romance that dominates the thinking of both old and young, though not in exactly the same way. It is a wishful cult, ignoring the basic realities of life and building its castles in the clouds of fancy, where none but knights and ladies, princes and princesses exist."[24] J. B. Lichtenberger has noted that "we have here, in the perversion of the concept of the marriage of true affection and in the over-emphasis upon the romantic element, one of the obvious causes of the increases of divorces . . . Romantic love as the exclusive basis of marriage is hopelessly inadequate. Even connubial love can flourish only in a congenial atmosphere and often is killed by antagonisms which arise from other sources."[25] Sumner and Keller contended that it is romantic influences "which bring men and women up to matrimony with false and impossible notions and prepare them for speedy disillusionment, misery, divorce, a new attempt to reach the impossible, and so on."[26] Similar realistic observations on the effects of romanticisms have been made by many other outstanding sociological thinkers, including Folsom,[27] Green, Gross, Groves and Groves, Landis, MacIver, Mowrer, and Schmiedeler.[28]

This is not to gainsay romanticism's many valuable aspects: the democracy of choice, the freedom from restraint, the aspirations to high-level individualism, the frank avowal of hedonism, the glorious potentialities for human ecstasy, and the indubitable other benefits that it valiantly espouses. As Vernon Grant points out,[29] the amorous emotion has many lovely sensual and esthetic elements. Ortega y Gasset and Sorokin[30] have also emphasized its advantages. The conclusion is factually and clinically inevitable, however, that romantic love, in its present form, is a very mixed blessing. Unless it evolves (as, fortunately, it may) in a somewhat saner direction, and unless it becomes a more mature and more realistic path to marriage, serious trouble will continue to result.

References

1. Henry T. Finck, *Romantic Love and Personal Beauty*. New York: Macmillan, 1887, p. 1.
2. Denis de Rougemont, *Love in the Western World*. New York: Harcourt, Brace, 1940, p. 70; G. R. Taylor, *Sex in History*. New York: Vanguard, 1955.
3. Arthur Garfield Hays, in V. F. Calverton and Samuel D. Schmalhausen, *Sex in Civilization*. New York: Macaulay, 1929, p. 219.
4. Leo Tolstoy, in Frederick W. Morton, *Love in Epigram*, Chicago: McClurg, 1899.
5. Comtesse de Champagne, in De Stendhal, *On Love*. New York: Liveright, 1947; Alan Watts, *Nature, Man and Woman*. New York: Pantheon, 1958; R. H. Robbins, "Courts of Love." *Sexology*, 1962, 28, 392-396.
6. Joseph K. Folsom, *The Family*. New York: Harper, 1935, p. 74.
7. Ernest W. Burgess, "Sociological Aspects of Sex Life of the Unmarried Adult," in Ira S. Wile, *Sex Life of the Unmarried Adult*. New York: Vanguard, 1934, pp. 153-154.
8. Llewellyn Gross, "A Belief Pattern Scale for Measuring Attitudes Toward Romanticism." *American Sociological Review*, 1944, 9, 463-472.
9. Somerset Maugham, *The Constant Wife*. New York: Doubleday, 1932.
10. Henrik Ibsen, *Love's Comedy*. New York: Willey Book, 1911, pp. 470-71.
11. George Moore, *Memoirs of My Dead Life*. London: Heinemann, 1921, p. 72; Andre Gide, *Strait is the Gate*. New York: Knopf, 1936, pp. 187-89; Walter Van Tilburg Clark, *The City of Trembling Leaves*. New York: Random House, 1945, p. 395; Ben Hecht, *Erik Dorn*. New York: Modern Library, 1930, p. 130.
12. Theophile Gautier, *Mlle. de Maupin*. New York: Three Pay Sales Co., 1900, p. 223.
13. Emil Lucka, *Eros*. New York: Putnam, 1915.
14. Denis de Rougemont, *op. cit.*, pp. 123-24.
15. Peiral the Troubadour, quoted in Emil Lucka, *op. cit.*, p. 129.
16. Alfred Adler, *What Life Should Mean to You*. Boston: Little Brown, 1931, pp. 275-76.
17. Karen Horney, *The Neurotic Personality of Our Time*. New York: Norton, 1937, p. 387.

18. John Levy and Ruth Munroe, *The Happy Family*. New York: Knopf, 1938, p. 66.
19. W. Beran Wolfe, *How to Be Happy Though Human*. New York: Farrar and Rinehart, 1931, p. 261.
20. Sandor Ferenczi, *Further Contributions to the Theory and Technique of Psychoanalysis*. New York: Basic Books, 1952.
21. Sigmund Freud, *Group Psychology and the Analysis of the Ego*. London: International Psychoanalytic Press, 1922.
22. Lorine Pruette, *The Parent and the Happy Child*. New York: Holt, 1932, p. 9.
23. Theodore Reik, *A Psychologist Looks at Love*. New York: Rinehart, 1945, p. 67; Theodore Reik, *Love and Lust*. New York: Straus, 1958; Edmund Bergler, "Further Contributions to the Psychoanalysis of Writers," *Psychoanalytic Review*, 1948, 35, 33-50.
24. Ray E. Baber, *Marriage and the Family*. New York: McGraw-Hill, 1939, p. 203; Crane Brinton, *A History of Western Morals*. New York: Braziller, 1959.
25. J. B. Lichtenberg, *Divorce*. New York: Whittlesey House, 1931, p. 345.
26. William Graham Sumner and Albert G. Keller, *The Science of Society*. New Haven: Yale Univ. Press, 1927, p. 2049.
27. Joseph K. Folsom, *The Family and Democratic Society*. New York: Harpers, 1950.
28. Arnold W. Green, "Social Values and Psychotherapy," *Journal of Personality*, 1946, 14, 19-228; Llewellyn Gross, *op. cit.*, p. 469; Ernest Groves and Gladys Groves, "The Case for Monogamy," in W. F. Bigelow, *The Good Housekeeping Marriage Book*. New York: Prentice Hall, 1938, p. 157; Paul H. Landis, "Control of the Romantic Impulse Through Education," *School and Society*, 1936, 213; R. M. MacIver, *Society*. New York: Long and Smith, 1932, p. 145; Ernest R. Mowrer, *Family Disorganization*. Chicago: Univ. Chicago Press, 1927, p. 162; Edgar Schmiedeler, *An Introductory Study of the Family*. New York: Century, 1930, p. 169.
29. Vernon W. Grant, *The Psychology of Sexual Emotion*. New York: Longmans, Green, 1957.
30. José Ortega y Gasset, *On Love*. New York: Meridian Books, 1960; Pitirim A. Sorokin, *The Ways and Power of Love*. Boston: Beacon, 1954.

Lawrence Lipton

Sexual Research on the Campus

The notion is gaining ground among the young unmarrieds, on the campus as elsewhere, that unmarried sex is not at all identical with "premarital" sex; that sex is its own justification, without so much as a thought to marriage or any expectation of marriage.

Project Pan: An Interim Report

Although it is the most obdurately underfinanced experimental project on any campus, more students are devoted to Project Pan than to any of the other Life Sciences. This huge project is financed by its own researchers and technicians and carried on

From: Lawrence Lipton, *The Erotic Revolution*, New York: Pocket Books, 1965. Copyright © 1965 by Sherbourne Press, Los Angeles, California. Reprinted by permission.

without benefit of university or state funds, without Foundation
grants and, in most cases, without benefit of clergy. Guggenheim
Foundation grants and certain traveling fellowships have sometimes helped to finance such research, but the results do not
appear in the official reports.

Researching the researchers, I have found that in the high
schools the work is still carried on in an elementary trial and error
manner. What it lacks in scientific method, however, it more than
makes up in enthusiasm and single-pointed devotion. "I've been
going steady now for two years," one high school junior told me.
"The boy didn't want to go steady, at first, but he found out he
couldn't play around without missing out on a lot of Saturday
night dates." But don't you both miss out on variety of experience? After all, the idea is to experiment, isn't it? "Sure. But what
makes you think we don't experiment? We've tried out a *lot of*
things. There's a book some of us chipped in to buy and we've
been passing it around." (The book, I learned, was a dog-eared
paperback copy of the *Kama Sutra* published in Tokyo.)

A sophomore couple who had been going steady for a few
months had just broken up. "Going steady is for the birds," the
male member of this research team told me. "You lose out on a
lot of dates. If you don't connect for a Saturday date now and
then you can always make a quick pick-up at the Frostee-Freeze
drive-in where everybody hangs out on Saturday nights." Is going-
steady diminishing? "If a girl is a dog—some call 'em pigs—you
know, kinda not so good looking or something—she'll want to go
steady because she's afraid she can't make it on her own. It gets
to be a drag."

It is very rarely that professional sociologists make this important area of changing human relations a subject of study. This is
usually left to feature writers for the newspapers and magazines
and an occasional local reporter on the scent for a "hot" human
interest story with sexy, smirking undertones and pious editorial
overtones. From such sources one gets the impression that high
school sex is as code-bound and routinized as a fraternity initiation ritual. Nothing could be farther from the truth. It is a
free-wheeling affair, imaginative and improvised and constantly
changing. Going steady, for example, appears to have been SOP
about a decade ago, probably a high school imitation of the GI
Bill shack-ups which followed the Korean police action. Since then
it has tended to diminish and, at the present time, it is optional at
most. Those who opt for it, as most of my informants tell me, are

the less popular students, boy or girl, who feel insecure and are looking for a sure thing. The lack of good looks is evidently not the determining factor, as the informant I have quoted thought it was. Of more importance is the fear of being left without a marriageable partner "in case anything happens."

In high school circles contraceptives are on the same improvised basis as dating and sex relations. And more resourceful than they are (or need be?) on the college level. "We just don't do *anything*," one girl student told me. Further questioning brought out that "anything" meant sexual intercourse of the formal or primary sort. "There's more than one way of getting your kicks, you know," the girl told me, implying by her manner and tone of voice that I probably *didn't* know. It is one of the striking things about such interviews that youth at this age thinks it has *discovered* techniques and practices which are hoary with antiquity. Fear rather than deliberate caution seems to be at the bottom of the resourcefulness displayed by many high school students.

A favorite technique at this early stage of sex education is masturbation, sometimes solo, sometimes in duet. Another is oral coitus. "It's safe," more than one student asserted, "and it counts, the same as any other way." "Any way you make out, it's a score." What counts, socially, is to score; it's a matter of status, among the girls as well as among the boys. Oral intercourse, by the way, appears to be more common with the girl as the active agent than the boy. Cunnilingus is a refinement that comes only with practice and at a much later stage of sexual experience. Even at the college level it is still awkward—and lacks the status of an inside job. Anything else, at this age, seems to lack the masculinity which is so highly prized among boys, and among girls as well.

At the high school level contraceptives, when they are used, tend to be limited to the more easily obtainable devices. Condoms, safes, rubbers, as they are variously called, are obtainable in drugstores, legally in some states, extra-legally or illegally in others, but always behind the counter, especially for young customers. Druggists prefer a touch of the surreptitious, not for reasons of delicacy or prudishness; it is probably just a hangover from the early days. High school students do not resent the bootleg air that surrounds such purchases. It adds a touch of adventure to the transaction. Sixty cents for three is the going rate in most places, which brings this commodity within the most meager high school budget. The fancier sheep skins—the contraceptive, not the academic kind—go for as much as three for two dollars. The more economy-minded now make do with Saran-Wrap and the girls with 7-Up douches; cheap, and the bottles are returnable. And, for lack of any or all of these, the most ancient—and most precariously undependable —contraceptive of all, strategic withdrawal.

The more sophisticated contraceptives, Enovid pills and diaphragms, are still rare among high school students. It is almost impossible for them to get fitted with diaphragms or obtain medical prescriptions for the oral pills. The result is that the burden of preventing sperm infection falls upon the boys. Even the common condom has to be obtained under false pretenses; druggists (in California at least) are forbidden to sell them to boys under the age of eighteen. Even if they are married! Doctors who will fit an unmarried female with a diaphragm are hard to find. Those who do, try to invent some pious fiction which will serve for an excuse, "medical" reasons, or they limit such services to the daughters of friends, usually without the knowledge of the parents. At the request of one high school student I discussed the question of providing her with a diaphragm with her parents, with not unexpected but none the less amusing—or disgusting—results.

"If we do that," the girl's father told me, "what's to prevent her from going on a wild spree and having sex relations with every young snot-nose in the school?" It did not occur to him for one minute that the girl's problem was not a burning passion for promiscuity but the problem of finding boys of her age who were even slightly desirable. "But dad," she protested—mother, father and daughter were present at the interview—I would not have it any other way in this case— "But dad—you don't *know* how hard it is to find a boy I can *accept*—that way! Most of the boys I know at school are so messy I can hardly stand to dance with them, let alone—" Mother hastily interrupted at this point, to prevent any embarrassing disclosures. The question of daughter's virginity was being studiously, fearfully avoided. It hung in the air between them, like the question of the Immaculate Conception at an Anglican Church council. "We've never been the prying kind of parents," mother assured me emphatically. And, with heart-breaking humility, to her daughter: "We're only trying to do what's right." "What's good for me, you mean," daughter came back, with a touch of sarcasm. "No, what's right," mother insisted desperately, and father chimed in with: "Your mother and I were young once, too, don't forget. Maybe we weren't angels, but—" and left *that* one hanging in the air, lest he inadvertantly exceed "the customary limits of candor," as the California obscenity law phrases it.

Unfinished sentences, awkward pauses, hints and innuendoes—this was all that came of the "face to face dialogue between youths and adults" that Professor of Family Life Lester A. Kirkendall recommends so highly. One wonders, had he been present on this occasion, could he have missed the note of guilt and panic in the father's words: the unstated premise of his objection, that the only thing which could prevent his daughter from going hog wild in the carnal fleshpots was the hazard of seminal infection, venereal disease and, as the old limerick has it "the bother of having a child." One thing he said was a dead give-away: "I'll admit I was a bit of a heller when *I* was a youngster, but I'll be damned if I'll make it easier for my daughter to make the same mistakes I made." Which made mother wince and daughter so uneasy she was unable to look her parents in the eye again for the rest of the interview. As for mother, Dr. Kirkendall surely would not have failed to note her jealousy at the thought that her daughter was demanding the relatively safe enjoyment of pleasures which she had once denied *herself* or, what was just as likely, pleasures she had been unable to enjoy without morning-after-remorse, fear and guilt. Evident too in this interview was the father's latent incest wish and the guilt feelings which surround such fantasies. And the mother's secret, not always successfully concealed lust for her daughter's boy friends. Such undercurrents inhibit candor in these chummy little family discussions. The upshot: no diaphragm, or any other kind of contraceptive. Not even a better understanding between parent and child; if anything, a worsened relationship, filled now with suspicion as well as repression. One more recruit for the teenage Underground and the improvised sexways of the high school years. "It'll be different in college," daughter told me, "different and easier, I think—well, anyway, I hope."

Sex in the Parochial Schools

Going away to college which, for many (including the young woman I alluded to above) means going away from home, perhaps for the first time, not counting summer camp and such. Freedom from close surveillance by parents presents new problems of its own. What these new problems will be depends on whether the student lives in a dormitory on or near the campus, in a fraternity or sorority house, in a rented room, family style (room and board), in a private apartment or in a cooperative community house. If he or she is attending a college in the home town and continuing to live with the family, the problems will continue to be pretty much what they were in high school, only more so; at least during the freshman and sophomore years. Whether the student is able to support himself or remains dependent on his family in whole or in part will make a difference. And there is the overriding consideration: is it a state university, a privately endowed university, a denominational or an interdenominational school?

The gamut of sex supervision on the campus runs all the way from strict supervision and separation of the sexes to almost complete permissiveness in small coeducational schools where cohabitation in every sense of the word is permitted, or at least winked at, and the shack-up is common practice. By a kind of tacit understanding between school authorities and the press, the latter type of educational set-up is never alluded to in articles on the subject, making it one more well-kept secret of contemporary American sexways.

To begin with the most socially and sexually retarded institutions, the denominational colleges, what passes for moral regulations in such colleges is the nearest thing we have to a museum of moral anachronisms. As in the case of the parochial high and elementary schools below them on the educational escalator, sex is regarded as at best a necessary function of the human condition, somewhat less vital than urination and excretion, and the rules governing sex are accordingly drawn with a view to concealing, deodorizing and sanitizing—that is, in case the primary objective, deterrence, should fail. Deterrence, of course, is the consummation most devoutly to be wished, and enforced wherever possible, and nothing less than deterrence is officially envisaged, or provided for —as witness the fact that while there are rooms provided for urination and defecation (noncoeducational, of course), there is no room set aside for sexual intercourse, not even for non-coeducational masturbation. As might be expected, Project Pan is carried on in denominational schools only under the most adverse and unhealthy conditions. The results achieved in this branch of research are somewhat better, however, than one would expect considering the lack of plant and research facilities and the active policy of discouragement carried on by the administration and faculty.

Practice in the counter-measures devised by the students to outwit the official policy begins early in the parochial schools. At one Catholic high school for girls in Southern California two lines of research are currently carried on. One project, strictly lesbian, is carried on intramurally, and another, heterosexual, is carried on extramurally. The intramural experiments are confined to the dormitories in the after-lights-out hours of the night and embrace, so far as I have been able to determine from interviews with the researchers, all but the most advanced and arcane refinements of the lesbian arts. The extramural work is carried on by students who "go over the wall" to meet their male colleagues of the project in the abundant groves which surround the school, groves which, for all we know, were once pagan groves of erotic worship sacred to some early New World counterpart of the Great God Pan, who also favored wooded places.

The barracks-like togetherness of parochial school dormitories, which are designed to prevent auto-eroticism, are made to order for homosexuality, male and female. Heterosexuality can survive under such conditions only by stealth. Going over the hill is one way. Frequent leaves and holidays home are another way. At the Catholic school I have mentioned, the nuns do all they can to discourage such lapses from religious discipline. "If you ask for a week-end home," one of the students told me, "the nuns look at you as if you had just announced that you were running away to enter a whorehouse." Army red tape is nothing compared with what you have to go through to get sprung, if only for a weekend, from the holy precincts. "All right," one of the nuns said to me when I finally got permission, "all right, go ahead, *wallow* in the sin of the world, *roll* in the mud. When you get back it will be just that much harder for you to take up your cross again." When you returned after your weekend you were expected to tell the girls in your dorm all the sexy details, what you did on your holiday in town, how you did it and with whom. They *loved* it."

It is in this way that religious schools help to create in their students the "shameful or morbid interest in nudity, sex, or excretion" that the California obscenity law defines as obscene. The genitals, it is true, are not far from the anus, but they are never so near as they are in the minds of the religious purist and the legislative blue-nose.

Christian sacrifice and self-denial are only bootcamp training for the real test of faith: self-punishment. Didn't Jesus die for our sins? The least we can do for *Him* is suffer a little. In the Catholic parochial high school I have alluded to (and in all Catholic schools at this level) early, before-breakfast, mass is the rule. And self-punishment enough, to hear the girls tell it. It is said of the apostle Peter that the place on the Temple stones where he knelt in prayer was rubbed down to a high polish and his knees were like the knee-pads of the camel. "At ——," my informant told me, "nothing pleases the Sisters more than to see the girls faint during morning mass, the more the better. I faked it once, because I was hungry—I really did *feel* faint, you know, but I faked it. And, boy, did I get the treatment. I was carried off to bed, breakfast was brought to me on a tray. Sister ——, who usually hated my guts, brought in a vase of flowers. Even the girls, who've used this trick themselves, went through the motions of being concerned about me. The really devout girls, there *are* a few, offered up special prayers for me. You might say fainting at early mass is a kind of status thing. Anyway, it was a ball!" And, at a later interview: "You know what I've found out? The *real* fainters are the girls who go over the wall at night. In the morning they're dead on their feet for lack of sleep and just naturally keel over. But they get the full treatment, breakfast on a tray, flowers—and they get to sleep all morning."

Such are the honors which the Church heaps upon her martyr saints.

Christian Sex Education in Parochial Schools

There is nothing that even the most persistent advocate of sex education can complain of in the amount of time and attention given to it in the parochial schools. This is especially true of the Catholic parochial school system, at all levels of education, where it amounts to something like an obsession. Those whose knowledge of sex education in the Catholic parochial schools and in the confessional are limited to the views expressed publicly by Catholic churchmen and teachers in the newspapers and magazines and on television programs sponsored by the Church or by Catholic laymen, or the opinions voiced by spokesmen for the Church in panel discussions, may well come away with the impression that the Catholic Church and its schools are growing more liberal and progressive in such matters. This impression grows out of the fact that the only churchmen who are willing (or permitted) to make such public appearances are those of the more liberal wing of the Church; usually editors of Catholic publications, monsignors, teachers and Catholic authors—never members of the hierarchy. Between such public pronouncements and what is actually taught about sex in parochial schools, and what transpires in the confessional, there is a wide difference.

Listening to the sweet reasonableness and "modern viewpoint" of Catholic spokesmen on the television programs and panel shows you would never guess that among the "occasions of sin" which tend "to lead us into sin" are taverns, saloons, night clubs, theaters, office parties, parked cars on a lonely road, drive-in theaters, dance halls, "bad" pictures, movies, magazines, television programs, "books against faith or morals," steady dating or company-keeping between a young man and woman, petting and sitting up late at night after mother and father have gone to bed.

No man, the author tells us, can reasonably be expected to avoid the perils of mortal sin in such situations. If he exposes himself to the temptations that lurk in such occasions he is already guilty, he has already committed a mortal sin. He is guilty even if he does not *later* fall into the sin which the occasion exposed him to.

This according to M. A. Feit, C. SS. R., in one of the Liguorian Pamphlets issued by the Redemptorist Fathers at Ligouri, Missouri, carrying the *Imprimi Potest* of John N. McCormick, C. SS. R., Provincial, St. Louis Province and the *Imprimatur* of Joseph Cardinal Ritter, Archbishop of St. Louis (April 7, 1961).

The title of the pamphlet is *Whirlpools of Destruction, The Occasions of Sin.* It is distributed in parochial schools, chapels and churches as guidance and instruction for teenage students and teenagers in general. It by no means exhausts the occasions of sin which the Church regards as whirlpools of destruction; in actual practice, in the schoolroom and the confessional, the soul may be imperiled by home parties, dancing, parents, even Catholic parents who have themselves fallen into sin, non-Catholics, secular schools and schools of other Christian denominations, and the privacy of the bedroom and bathroom; even, on occasion, one might add, the choir loft and, as we have seen, the sacred precincts of the parochial school itself.

From *Sex—Sacred and Sinful,* by Rev. Gerald C. Treacy, S.J. and bearing the Imprimatur of Francis Cardinal Spellman, we learn that the Catholic school alone is qualified to impart sex education, because the Catholic school is instituted and staffed by the Church and the Church is the one Teacher that God has appointed and endowed with the proper qualifications to teach the moral law, and Sex, we are told, belongs to the moral law.

The student is also warned against *naturalism*, another grave danger to which students are exposed in the sex education which secular education approves, and that this secular sex education deals with that most delicate matter of purity in the spirit of naturalism, which the Catholic student is protected from in the Church and its schools. The Church does indeed advocate sex education, the author assures us, but from what follows we are given to understand that the Church is also the only qualified teacher and all others are propagandists of a "so-called" sex education only. Under the impression that they can forearm students against the dangers and perils which sex, and not only sex but sensuality in general, expose them to, such non-Catholic teachers provide a "foolhardy" kind of public instruction in sex and do so indiscriminately, even, we are told "in public." The author further warns that non-Catholic sex education exposes the students to such information at too early an age, thus leading them into occasions of sin in order to acquaint them with sexual situations on the theory that they are in this way prepared and hardened against the dangers of impurity and sin.

Such language, moreover, tells us more about Catholic sex education than it does about the "propagandists" it is directed against. Note the use of a phrase like "the dangers of sensuality" as if it was interchangeable with the word sex, and the use of the word "naturalism" as if it was synonymous with sin, an implication which is repeated in another part of the tract where it is equated with "paganism" and epicurianism, a philosophy which the author solemnly warns the reader—you can almost see him shudder at the thought—is a philosophy of night after night revels which drain body and mind to the point of exhaustion. How does one protect his soul against such debauchery and corruption? By attending Mass and receiving communion frequently. The Host, in the form of a wafer taken by mouth, like an Enovid pill but with more reverence and at least as much faith in its effectiveness, will lead to a life of purity. The essential ingredient in this spiritual medication is a genuine love of purity and the protective intercession of the Blessed Mother, Virgin Most Pure, Saint Joseph and the Guardian Angel.

Except for the theological dogma, every word of this tract might have been written by the Puritan Mathers, Increase Mather and his son Cotton, nearly three hundred years ago, a Puritanism that has held American lifeways and sexways, even literature and the arts, in a strait-jacket which it is only now shaking off. In some respects it goes even farther in the direction of anti-sexuality than Puritanism ever did. It extols complete life-long sexual abstinence even above sacred sex and Christian (i.e. Catholic) marriage, even above sexual "purity."

The author, quoting from a commentary by Father Walter Farrell on St. Thomas, offers the reassuring thought that the person who succeeds in fighting off temptation and remains a virgin is not giving up an illegal pleasure for the divine good of his or her soul; she (the emphasis is always on "she") is giving up a perfectly legitimate pleasure for some much more valuable: surrender to God. Matrimony, we are told, is sacred but virginity is its superior. Matrimony he describes as approaching the heroic, but when the human is put aside the reward is the divine, the soul has triumphed over the flesh. Christ, he reminds us, chose a Virgin Mother and made a virgin disciple his closest friend, Paul extolled virginity, but neither Christ nor Paul were enemies of love. It was just that they were aware of a truth everybody else had missed through the ages, that such rejection of human love, such complete devotion to the Divine, is a sacrifice which is demanded in order to express adequately the love of the faithful for the Virgin in one's own life. The love of the Virgin, we are given to understand, differs from the love of the wife in that the Virgin rushes immediately into the arms of God, while the love of the wife goes to God or Jesus only through the sacrament of marriage, which is holy, natural and beautiful, but is retarded on its journey to God through the slower, gradual steps of human love.

This is on a level of unreality, withdrawal from the facts of life which in any other context would be suspected of insanity, so far removed is it from contemporary thinking (and acting) about sex in present day moral behavior, a moral behavior which many religious thinkers, writers and clergymen (some of them Catholic) are already calling Post-Christian. What role does such Catholic anti-sexual sex education play in the parochial schools, among the students and the teachers who are expected to impart and enforce it?

The answers which parochial school students give to such questions may lack the subtle (i.e. evasive) and responsible (i.e. double-talk) character of a television panel show discussion, but they shed more light on the matter. Here are some examples:

"Some of the Sisters are good eggs, but—well—they're not very bright. I mean, they just don't know what's going on. When it comes to sex, just look at them, they're *past* caring—if they ever did. Maybe that's why they became Sisters in the first place. Except one, Sister ——. To her sex isn't just sin, it's a kind of poetry, *religious* poetry. But you can't talk straight with her about sex, either. Why does sex have to be something way up in Heaven or way down in hell? Why can't it be, well, just *human?*"

"Sure, I believe in God, what I understand about it. And I love Jesus. But when it comes to sex, I'm not God and I'm not Jesus. I'm not a saint. I'm flesh and blood. I'm a human being, so I act like a human being, and that includes sex. If that makes me a sinner, so, I'm a sinner. Isn't that what penance is for? And absolution? I think if I could explain it to God—well, maybe not to God but to Jesus—I think Jesus would understand."

Which calls to mind Voltaire's remark to the priest: "God will forgive me; that's his business."

From personal observation of student behavior I can report that religious practice is nothing for the Church to be jubilant about. Prayer is perfunctory, by rote, and rarely personal or related to student life or anything else in the life of the young. Except for the prescribed responses of the service and a few Hail Mary's by way of penance (which nobody is ever foolish enough to try and check on) prayer, when it is truly sincere, takes the form of such heartfelt exclamations as "God! I wish—," "I hope to Christ! that—," "God bless you!" and, of course, the universal and indispensable, "Go to hell!" or "Go to the devil!" The prayer of intercession is largely a formal affair, the student body praying for a sick Sister, a fellow student undergoing surgery (or, in the boys' schools, injured on the football field) or simply, praying for "the intentions of the Pope." One occasion does elicit devout prayer. "One of the girls was getting an abortion; the sisters didn't know a thing about it, of course, but we all prayed like hell!" The prayers, I learned, were addressed to the Virgin Mary, Mother of God. With one exception: "I prayed to St. Joseph," one of the girls confided to me. I thought he would understand *better*—and forgive—so I lighted a candle."

These, it will be noted, are *believing* students. Those who take it all with a large helping of salt dismiss all such questions with a shrug or a cynical grin. "I'm just here because my parents want me to. As soon as I can break away I intend to go to a *real* school and get a *decent* education," one student told me, and many others expressed themselves much to the same effect. It is good television manners to agree that religious schools uphold high standards of scholarship; it is the polite thing to say, even if you know that, with very few exceptions, it is *not* true. There is also a kind of gentlemen's agreement not to enquire, publicly, into the morality and the sex life of parochial school students. Every effort I made to obtain information on the number of students expelled for violating sex regulations was met by a conspiracy of silence. Except among the students, where it is a favorite topic of whispering gossip. One thing may be taken as certain: more students are expelled for flunking out in morals than in math.

The hush-hush policy on school morals makes it almost impossible to obtain any reliable figures, or even honest opinions, from faculty and administration. Since professional sociologists usually consider it unprofessional to question students of religious schools without permission of school authorities, such studies are left to the free-lance investigator and author. Studies are made of the sex life of prison inmates, even if they have to be smuggled out under the noses of the guards and wardens. Even mental hospitals have been the subject of such studies. But religious institutions still enjoy immunity in such matters, probably on the old and honorable American principle that no gentleman ever argues about religion. A principle, let it be noted here, which is now going rapidly into oblivion along with the whole Judeo-Christian anti-sexual moral code.

In the boys' schools discussion is freer, even where the faculty is concerned. A Father in one of the Dominican boys' schools told me that he has been able to discuss sexual matters with his students on a fairly high level of candor. "Not that it has done much good," he was quick to add. "In fact, the more candid a boy is the more likely he is to give you an argument—and a pretty good one too—in favor of freer sexual conduct than the Church permits. And these are often our brightest students. I'm afraid that in practice, if not in principle, I have tended to become—shall I say, more understanding, in such matters? After all, some of our most revered saints were hell-raisers in their young manhood. Only one thing gives me pause. I doubt, I strongly doubt, that any of our present-day problem boys will ever become Augustines or Loyolas."

Or even Kierkegaards, I might add. What they are more likely to become is pioneers of the New Morality.

I have dwelt at some length on the parochial schools because it is the most carefully concealed area of youthful sex behavior. In the Protestant parochial schools the problem is more openly recognized and dealt with. Here dogma plays a relatively smaller role than it does in the Catholic schools. The moral stance taken by Protestant clergymen in public discussions where, occasionally, a spokesman for Catholicism is present, is one of liberalism as opposed to the dogmatism of the Catholic position. What Protestant liberalism comes down to in such discussions is a social worker attitude with a light religious varnish over it. Lutheran Minister Martin Marty is quoted as saying that students "are piecing together lives which are at least as whole as their parents'," which sounds as if the Lutheran Church looks with sympathy on the youthful quest for a new morality. But such statements prove to be misleading when ministers are questioned further and students at denominational schools are questioned about what actually constitutes school policy in matters of student sex life.

According to one student, a psychology major at a West Coast denominational college, "Christianity is a hex on sex. There is still the stigma of evil and sinfulness that surrounds sexual relationships." Another denominational school student puts it this way: "There *is* something called sex education for students, but it always takes the form of what is called 'preparation for marriage.' It never even begins to touch the question of premarital sexual intercourse on campus. What we get is the physiology and anatomy of sex, and the medical aspects, always with marriage and children as the sole aim and purpose of sex; never sex as pleasure, or communion or mutual understanding. You can *talk* about such things with fellow students, but if you try to bring up anything like that in class, especially in mixed classes, there is either a dead silence, or snickers, giggles and coughing and, well, general all-around embarrassment for everybody concerned."

What student sexways are like in Protestant denominational colleges may be gleaned from a few typical answers volunteered at a private discussion of the subject:

"In the first place, you don't enroll in a denominational college if you want a free sex life. You go to a big university, preferably in a big city, a state university or some place like Dartmouth. Myself, I would have gone to UCLA if I could, but my grades weren't good enough, so here I am at——. The way *I* make out, I just don't pay any attention to the rules or ask advice from the counsellors and deans. The main thing is to make yourself invisible and anonymous, so far as sex is concerned. Anyway, I prefer the townies to most of the girls on the campus. The girls at a school like this come from religious homes. Their sex life is ruined for any kind of pleasure before they get here. As long as you don't get into any kind of scandal you're okay here. In fact, it's safer to be a fag on this campus than it is to be normal. Fags can shack up together —and they do—without anyone asking any questions, but try it with a girl and—well, you just don't, if you know what's good for you, unless you can find a place far from campus and both of you keep your mouth shut. If it gets to one of these religious creeps and they've got it in for you, you're in trouble with the dean. The place is full of stool pigeons, like some goddam military school."

"Scholastically, —— is one of the best schools in the state, but not in the arts and humanities. It's mostly in the arts and humanities that you have this sex problem—students, girls mostly, falling in love with some art teacher, or a music professor. Or a fellow Lit student who writes poetry. You know, the bohemian types. Well, you don't often find them at a school like this, so you haven't got *that* problem. But once you get mixed up in the arts you've got problems. Somebody thought it would be a good idea to start a theater group. The administration went along with it—it was set up in the Speech department. Well, before we'd gotten half through rehearsals on the first play half the cast was shacking up with someone in the cast, the thing was swarming with homos on the make for the male members of the cast. One of them got to the director and he had to resign, quietly, because the thing got to the dean—one of the girls who had a crush on the director blabbed about it. Like I say, it's in the arts that you have the trouble."

"What they're calling the Sexual Revolution, you've got it here like anywhere else, except that you don't call it that. I've gone to a state college and I haven't noticed that it's any different here, except, like I say, you don't talk about it. Or, if you do, you call it socializing, or dating, or something like that. Everybody knows what you mean, anyway. Those girls I was talking about, the ones who come from religious homes, I've dated a few of them and let me tell you, you don't need to show them any pictures in the doctor book. Only thing is you've got to take all the precautions yourself. They lay down and shut their eyes and that's it. I asked one: Why don't you get yourself fitted with a diaphragm, or take the pills? You know what she said? 'It's sinful,' she said."

"It's true, you find the same thing here as you do on any other campus—maybe not as much, but the same *kind* of things go on— only you don't come right out and *name* it. You don't call *anything* by its right name, not in class, not when you're talking with the deans, not when you're asking a girl for a date, not even when you're in bed with her. That's the *religion* part of it. It's a kind of make-believe."

The best place to hear the sort of double-talk this student was talking about is on any of the television discussions that pass for educational programs on any Sunday morning. Here is a sample from "Confrontation," a discussion of religion and sex with clergymen and students participating:

CLERGYMAN (Methodist): There seems to be an increasing interest in sex within our society here of late. Today we're going to talk about Christianity and sex.

STUDENT (male): I believe the Church today has evaded the responsibility of adequate and proper sexual instruction in education . . . I would suggest that the Church has not established concrete and definite sexual standards. Their standards are very nebulous. I would make this statement with one reservation; that when I speak of Christianity I speak of the Christianity that is practiced and not necessarily the teachings of Christ.

STUDENT (female): I think perhaps too that we would like to add that the Church does place a hex on regulation of premarital and extramarital relations, but it considers the sex act itself within the marriage as the highest form of communication between a man and wife, and it's a God-given thing that, if it's not abused, it's something beautiful, and I think it's the highest form of expression.

CLERGYMAN (Lutheran): I think it's always a dangerous thing to generalize. In recent years the main-stream denominations have done a great deal in the field of sex education and preparation for marriage. In fact, there have been more statements that have come from the major denominations on family life and premarital education than almost any other single problem or issue in our society. In addition, I think the major denominations are publishing a voluminous amount of material dealing with courtship and sex, dating, and these fundamental questions these young people today are asking. We require that getting married in our church they must have two to four hours at least of sessions, they must take the Johnson test, the Peterson premarital inventory, and we try to do a rather thorough job of counseling.

STUDENT (male): What is the attitude of Christianity or the Church on premarital sexual relations?

CLERGYMAN (Methodist): Well, I didn't say that Christianity in general has established standards, or that the information is necessarily adequate. What I'm saying is that I think we have made considerable progress in this direction in recent years.

STUDENT (male): The reason I am of the opinion that the Church has not is that, riding past churches or attending churches I have never seen a sermon topic with the title of sex in it. I have never been in a classroom that has discussed adequately or responsibly the topic of sex.

CLERGYMAN (Methodist): I think you're touching right on one of the problems now. That is that we generalize in terms of our particular experiences, and this becomes increasingly dangerous when we talk about religion and Christianity in general. In dealing with college students we try to come to terms with questions they have about sex. To be sure, the church has erred in the past and undoubtedly is erring in the present and will err in the future. But I always like to say, not as a defense but as a matter of fact, that the church, after all, is made up not of perfect people but of forgiven people. Consequently, very often what are taken to be the standards Christ set and the practice of the church today—and this kind of a charge, you know, which implies hypocrisy on the part of the church, and so forth, is the strange kind of tribute that vice pays to virtue. . . .

This sort of shadow boxing sham battle between hand-picked students and double-talking say-nothing clergymen is common in public discussions of love and sex among the younger generation. Note that the students in their prepared (and probably screened) statements are *asking* the church for standards of sex behavior and principles to guide them, reducing criticism by the students to zero. It is like nothing so much as Walt Disney's cute little two-dimensional animal world where none of the creatures are encumbered with genitals and even the rabbits are presumably born of an immaculate conception.

The Mosaic Code—after Freud

Except for religious seminaries where rabbis and religious scholars of all kinds are educated and graduated, there is no campus life in Jewish education. Schools like the Jewish Theological Seminary, Hebrew Union College and the University of Judaism draw their student body from a screened and selective group which is already committed to a moral system and little disposed to question it or experiment with revised or alternative moralities. Those who find themselves tempted to make such experiments know they will have to find other careers. Women students are few and those who do enroll are not likely colleagues for Project Pan. This is not to say that future rabbis do not have premarital sex problems. Such problems were once solved by early marriage, even symbolic child marriage, but modern economic and social conditions do not make early marriage any easier for future rabbis than for future lawyers or doctors. The rabbis with whom I have found it possible to discuss their student-day sex life leave me with the impression that their youthful sins were more like Onan's than Pan's. It is long since the Lord has slain anyone for onanism but the guilt feelings that surround masturbation—still called "self-pollution" among many gentlemen of the cloth—continue to plague the religious conscience. Uncompleted coitus is a small price to pay for technical purity. Levirate marriage no longer has the force of law in Israel and onanism is not a capital crime in the sight of God or man, but self-abuse—another one of those pious euphemisms— is still the most unmentionable transgression of the Jewish moral code, more agonizingly shameful and harder to own up to than fornication or adultery. Perhaps it is less flattering to the proud patriarchal male ego of the Jewish moral tradition than seduction, or even rape.

Trying to put together a plausible picture of the sex life of a *yeshiva bocher* (seminarian) from my interviews and discussions is like compiling a composite case history of a lecherous saint, a neurotic fantasist and a compulsive liar.

Having grown up as they did during their seminary years when Freudian theory and therapy was challenging traditional sexual mores, the rabbinical students had to come to terms with it somehow. To judge by my notes and interviews they seized on Freud's "sublimation" as the answer. What better way to sublimate the sexual instinct than putting it to the service of God through service to man? What it amounted to in practice, of course, was suppression and rejection of their own sexual instincts and serving God by teaching other men and women to suppress theirs by the same means. If the damning up of the orgastic energy resulted from such sublimation and if the sex life was crippled by fear and guilt, it was all part of man's upward rise from beastliness and paganism to purity and godliness. Granted that such a solution of the question might entail suffering, but it was a self-sacrifice demanded by God and enforced by society for its own preservation. By society they meant the existing culture, the Judeo-Christian ethos and its moral code. Liberate the sexual instinct by all means, then harness it to the glory of God and the demands of the existing culture.

Freud himself provided the arguments for this two-faced doctrine of "adjustment" to the culture and its mores when he rejected Reich's life-affirming support of the Sexual Revolution. Official Judaism, at least the more vocal Reform Judaism, accepted this interpretation of psychoanalysis and hailed Freud as a modern Moses. What it amounted to in practice we have seen in our account of the sex life of the Jewish seminarians who are now members of the rabbinate. How does it affect the sexways of the Jewish student today?

The Mosaic Code—after Fromm

What Freud was to the last generation, Erich Fromm is to the present generation of Jewish youth. To be sure, Fromm supports Freud's views in many respects but only in part where religion is concerned. Freud's views on religion were already out of date by the time they became available in English in *The Future of an Illusion* but Fromm's revisions of Freud have profoundly influenced student youth and especially Jewish students. Taking off from Freud's objection to religion, that it puts morality on very shaky grounds when it makes morality stand or fall on belief in God at a time when religious belief is on the wane, Fromm goes on to say:

> We do not have to rely on inferences from Freud's criticism of religion . . . If man gives up his illusion of a fatherly God, if he faces his aloneness and insignificance in the universe, he will be like a child that has left his father's house. But it is the very aim of human development to overcome infantile fixation. Man must educate himself to face reality. If he knows that he has nothing to rely on except his own powers, he will learn to use them properly.[1]

Fromm seems to be saying here that to be free from God is to be free from sex fear and sex guilt. Instinctual, inner-directed sex regulation is easier for those who have rid themselves of the Judeo-Christian God who slays onanists and makes such a big issue about a little tissue, but it still leaves them with the problem of main-

---

[1] Erich Fromm, *Psychoanalysis and Religion* (New Haven, 1950), p. 126.

taining their new-found freedom and finding a place to practice it, and sex partners to practice it with. Besides, there is no communal ritual in our society to give public sanction to it and protect it against the bluenose snoopers and policemen of the moral status quo.

For such a task the Jewish student seems, at first, to be better equipped than, say, the Catholic or the Lutheran. Once the Eighteenth Century Enlightenment had broken through the moribund religious orthodoxy of the European ghettos it swept away the myth of the Chosen People and much of the old morality of Genesis and Deuteronomy along with it. Mass immigration to America in the first decades of the Twentieth Century accelerated the process of enlightenment and liberation. Freudian psychology gave the Jewish enlightenment great impetus, providing it with an intellectual apparatus that rivaled the religious legalism of Leviticus in its impressive complexity. Only antisemitism, open and concealed, prevented widespread physical (sexual) assimilation in the U.S. during the first three decades of the century, so great was the drive, especially among the second generation Jews in America, to shake off the separatism to which they had been self-condemned for centuries by the Chosen People covenant with the God of Israel. In any case, if the alternative was the God of Paul and Luther and Calvin and John Wesley, there was little hope of liberation from the old Mosaic morality in conversion or assimilation. The Freudian psychology seemed to offer an alternative and the moral vanguard of the Jewish youth seized on it.

The Secession from Babbittry which marked the Twenties was also a secession from the Puritan morality which was the American version of the Judeo-Christian moral code. H. L. Mencken, who appointed himself the spokesman of the Secession and propagandized it (and aggrandized himself) through, first, *The Smart Set* and, later, *The American Mercury*, nursed a Germanophile distrust and dislike of the Jews, but the younger generation of Jews in the Twenties liked and trusted Menckenism. The two principle Bohemias of the time, Greenwich Village in New York and the Near North Side of Chicago, numbered many Jewish young men and women among their habitués and residents, far in excess of Jewish population ratios. These bohemian enclaves served a double purpose for Jewish nonconformist youth. They afforded a refuge from the repressive Judaic moral code and, at the same time, a refuge from an Old Testament American Puritanism reinforced by Pauline anti-sexual Christianity. Such literary spokesmen of the generation as George Jean Nathan, Alfred Kreymborg, James Oppenheim, Maxwell Bodenheim, Sara Teasdale, Louis Untermeyer, Ludwig Lewisohn and Ben Hecht provided the intellectual and moral underpinnings of what can now be seen as the Jewish contribution to, not only the literary renaissance of the Twenties but the Sexual Revolution which the press of the period sensationalized as Flaming Youth and The Jazz Age. Intermarriage—and, on a much larger scale, intersexuality—of Jewish and Christian youth flourished; it would be more accurate to call it post-Jewish and post-Christian youth, since both were in revolt against the Judeo-Christian anti-sexual morality.

In the Thirties another dimension was added to the secession, the Marxist alienation, in which the Jewish youth again participated in numbers far in excess of population ratios. Had not Marx, himself a Jew, been a product of the Enlightenment, German version? Socialism, in an uneasy alliance with the sexual revolution (later to be dissolved in the first years of the Russian soviet state) harbored such anarchist "free love" advocates as Emma Goldman and Alexander Berkman. Such influences on the youth of the Twenties had not altogether vanished in the Thirties; it had merely gone underground and become a blend of socialist, anarchist, sexual nonconformism. It was particularly marked among the Jewish students of the universities in the Thirties and became the credo of their community houses, a social phenomenon which I have dealt with elsewhere.[2] The literary contingent of this triple threat challenge to the social and moral status quo had a significant Jewish representation. Among those who were particularly influential with Jewish students (and off-campus Jewish youth as well) were Irwin Shaw, Clifford Odets, Albert Halper, Meyer Levin, Albert Maltz, Henry Roth, Waldo Frank, Michael Gold, Joseph Freeman, David Daiches and, on both sides of the Atlantic, Marc Blitzstein, Bertold Brecht, Stefan Zweig, Arnold Zweig and Stefan Heim. Today all these and many more are to be numbered among the precursors of a vast international movement of writers, artists, dramatists and film-makers of the Erotic Revolution, among whom Jewish talents are more numerous and influential than ever before in history. High on the list of these in his impact on the moral outlook of Jewish students (as well as other students) is Erich Fromm.

---

[2] Lawrence Lipton, *The Holy Barbarians,* New York, 1959.

To Fromm, religion is too important a matter to be left to the theologians, rabbis and priests; and he prefers to keep the word God and give it new and fresh meaning. Freud's main argument against religion, Fromm reminds us (in his *Psychoanalysis and Religion*) is that religion keeps man in bondage and dependence and prevents him from attaining "the paramount task of human existence, that of freedom and independence," and that the "kernel of neurosis" is the incestuous fixation, the Oedipus complex. But Fromm would go beyond "adjustment," which is the classical aim of psychoanalysis. Speaking of those "who have accepted the judgment of the majority so completely that they have been spared the sharp pain of conflict which the neurotic person goes through," Fromm tells us that "while they are healthy from the standpoint of 'adjustment,' they are more sick than the neurotic person from the standpoint of the realization of their aims as human beings," and goes on to say:

✓ It is the tragedy of all great religions that they violate and pervert the very principles of freedom as soon as they become mass organizations governed by a religious bureaucracy. The religious organization and the men who represent it take over to some extent the place of the family, tribe and state. They keep man in bondage instead of leaving him free. It is no longer God who is worshipped but the group that claims to speak in his name.

"This has happened," Fromm tells us, "in all religions," but he does not reject all religions on that account. Instead, he redefines religion, just as he redefines God. Fromm distinguishes between "authoritarian" religion and the religion which takes individual needs into account. But Fromm's nonauthoritarian religion does not leave much room for sexual experiment or envisage the total eclipse of the Judeo-Christian moral system. He does not go all the way and argue, as Wilhelm Reich does, for a restructuring of the individual sexual economy toward a self-governing character structure which is *self*-regulating: total orgasm as a good in itself rather than a service to the state, a duty to God or a debt to posterity. "In humanistic religion" (as distinguished from authoritarian) Fromm declares, "God is the image of man's higher self, a symbol of what man potentially is or ought to become." The key word in Fromm's thinking about religion and sex is love.

The command to 'Love thy neighbor as thyself' is, with only slight variations in its expression, the basic principle common to all humanistic religions. . . . *Analytic therapy is essentially an attempt to help the patient gain or regain his capacity for love.* (his emphasis)

The net effect of this emphasis on love in sex is to limit sexual experience and make experiment in new sexways—as well as new loveways—more difficult and confusing. If it is more humanistic to limit one's sexual experience to a *love* partner one is faced with an enigma: How can I *know* a love partner from a mere sex partner? We are back again with the whole bag of sex cliches: "I'm waiting for Mr. Right to come along." "When Mr. Right comes along I'll know it." How? Love at first sight, "across a crowded room," as the song lyric has it. We are back again with the whole Romantic Love mystique. Love, courtship, marriage, monogamy. And—the divorce courts.

The Jewish students in the colleges and universities accept ✓ Fromm as a safer guide to sex life than Wilhelm Reich. This is especially true of the female students. They can tell themselves that they have "liberated" their sexual instincts and will give free reign to them when Mr. Right comes along. The result is the "nice Jewish girl," a neurotic monstrosity which becomes Exhibit A of the diseases of sexual repressions when the case reaches the analytical couch—or the marriage bed. It is this sex-with-love syndrome which makes Herman Wouk's *Marjorie Morningstar* a horror tale. An earlier account of it may be found in Meyer Levin's novel of the Twenties, *The Old Bunch.*

My own investigations reveal that Jewish girl students who accept the sex-with-love theory only succeed in deceiving themselves with the notion that they are in love with every boy they have sexual intercourse with. They operate on the principle of the leprechaun in *Finian's Rainbow:*

> "When I'm not near the girl I love
> I'm in love with the girl I'm near."

Since it is based on a misconception and a self-deception, such sexual experiences do not constitute an experiment in the Erotic Revolution. Romantic make-believe love is precisely the kind of sex life on which authoritarian religion is based. It is the whole emotional content of most of the marriages that land in the divorce courts. It is the kind of serial courtship that ends in serial marriage. It is simply promiscuity under a fancy name, and a far cry from the kind of intelligent selectivity of sex partners, without any deception on either side, which is the aim of the Erotic Revolution in its present, exploratory stage. In the end, Fromm's revision of Freud proves to be only a revision in terminology. If any successful experiments are being made, looking toward a self-governing, inner-directed re-structuring of the human character and a sexually freer society, we must look for them not, I think, in the parochial and denominational schools but in the secular colleges and universities.

Some Successful Sex Experiments: A Progress Report

As befits the spirit of higher education, as distinguished from the cruder sexual experiments on the high school and junior college level, the university students proceed from hypothesis to empirical test, hoping for a definitive breakthrough. In the past it was the male researchers who made the first experiments, drawing on amateur female assistants of the town or the more professional but unscientific co-workers of the whorehouses. Today they are assisted by women students on campus in a genuinely co-educational, cooperative endeavor. The "houses of ill fame" which were once available for such experimental projects are now too few and too costly for student use. And the more modern "call girl" service is practically the monopoly of such post-graduate practitioners as business executives on tour of duty, buyers and salesmen, conventioneers and procurement officers of the armed services.

Lacking proper laboratory facilities, the students who volunteer for Project Pan are obliged to make do with improvised facilities which would tax the imagination and ingenuity of less enterprising, less dedicated experimenters. Some universities, as we shall see, have parietal rules[3] which give left-handed recognition to the social (read: sexual) needs of the students, but the right hand is always there in one way or another to know what the left hand doeth and enforce decorum and discretion if deterrence fails. On most U.S. campuses no aid or comfort is afforded the researchers of the Orgastic Revolution except by oversight or default. There are no double beds, for instance, in college dormitories; officially, beds are designed for sleep and single blessedness,

---

[3] Parietal: "within a college"; limited visiting hours during which students may entertain students of the other sex in their rooms.

or, at worst, for secret, solitary masturbation. Two students to a room is the rule, even in the most luxuriously appointed dormitories, with perhaps a few single rooms reserved for foreign royalty and the heirs and heiresses of wealthy donors. The motor car is put to uses never intended and probably never foreseen by Henry Ford, Sr., who was no friend of the Sexual Revolution. The old-fashioned detachable seat cushion, which is one reason why old jalopies are in great demand, has always been a favorite tool of research, *in situ* or removed to the seclusion of roadside bushes. The compact car of today may well be a plot on the part of Establishment to confine experimental sex research to midgets, who are, presumably, a smaller threat to the Old Morality.[4]

With motor car immorality becoming more and more of a contortionist's feat, the motel room becomes the principle off-campus facility for sexual co-education and experiment. A team of really determined researchers with the necessary funds can often con their way into a double bed without I.D. cards and, in emergency situations, even without luggage. Fraternity and sorority parties afford occasional opportunities for joint operations, and in some cases, for larger scale group analysis and mixed seminars.

But the really significant and successful breakthroughs are being made today in those relatively godless secular universities where sexual coeducation is at least tacitly recognized as a human, if extra-curricular, activity.

At Harvard the parietal rules permit students to entertain girls in their dormitory rooms from 4 to 7 p.m. weekdays, from noon to midnight on Saturdays, and from noon to 7 p.m. on Sundays. The word "entertain," widely used to describe such visitations, is not meant—not by the school administration at least—to describe sex, or optimum opportunities for sex, as "a fun thing." "Entertain" is used here only to denote the kind of thing that goes on when, their parents, for example, might receive guests in the home. At Harvard it might mean something quite different. Here is the way a 20-year-old Radcliffe girl describes it:

> If a Harvard man dates a Radcliffe girl consistently, their friends just naturally assume that they're being intimate. It's also assumed that they're going to bed during parietal hours. Most parents and

---

[4] In so-called "theatrical hotels" performing midgets are permitted to sleep three or four in a bed at special room rates, presumably on the pre-Freudian assumption that the "little people" are children and therefore sexually innocent.

deans believe sex is an after-dark activity that takes several hours. My generation knows that any time of day is a good time and that all you need is fifteen minutes.[5]

Increase Mather, Harvard, Class of 1656, must be spinning in his grave, counterclockwise.

A recent Harvard graduate described the workings of the parietal rules in this way: "If you've got a girl in the dormitory room with you, you're supposed to leave the door ajar. Occasionally the janitor or a campus cop will come by and say, 'Have you got a girl in the place?' and you say, 'Yes, but we're studying hard for exams and we'd rather you wouldn't come in.' If you're cool about it and don't make a scene you can usually get away with it, even if you don't exactly comply with the rules and you keep the door shut, or it's past the hour."

Not all the house janitors are so liberal and understanding. "There was this one janitor, he was a kind of a weird guy. He would spend a lot of his time reading those sexy girlie magazines. I guess he was jealous of the students having girls in their rooms. There were others like him but you could bribe them with a gallon of wine now and then. Not *this* guy. You couldn't sweet-talk him or give him presents. Most of the janitors were cooperative. It depends on who approaches them. Usually it was some student who was a smooth talker and knew how to shoot the breeze with the janitor and cool it with him, get him to accept a present or two. He might even say, It would be nice if you'd let me have the key to the swimming pool, and the janitor would say, You know that's against the rules. They didn't want us swimming at four o'clock in the morning, and some of the fellows liked an occasional swimming party, especially at the Adams House. It had a gargoyle at one end and a fireplace. Cozy, you know. But if the right guy approached him the janitor would give him the key to the place. No mixed swimming in the nude, of course. There was always the chance a campus cop might walk in."

One could search in vain through the newspaper and newsmagazine accounts of sexways at Harvard without finding a single reference to the actual workings of the parietal rules, or suspecting that it is ever necessary for the students to flatter, cajole or bribe the dormitory janitor in order to receive the full benefits of the rules so far as sex is concerned. In other words, the official assump-

---

[5] *Newsweek* (Vol. LXIII No. 14, April 6, 1964), p. 52.

tion behind the parietal rules at Harvard is that men and women visiting together in the dorms will conduct themselves in the same sexless ways which are presumed to prevail in the drawing room of a well-bred Christian or Jewish household when guests are being entertained. Or say, at a formal student-faculty social affair. The four to seven o'clock weekday visiting rule is really a tea time arrangement, or, at worst, a cocktail hours affair, at which nothing sexier than a polite flirtation is envisaged by the rule and the university authorities who made the rule. The noon to seven o'clock Sunday rule, too, is carefully kept within afternoon limits on the assumption that sex, as the Radcliffe girl observed, is exclusively an after-dark activity. The only exception is the Saturday rule, noon to midnight. Here the assumption is that midnight is well within the limits well-bred Christian-Jewish parents would set for a Saturday night visit between young people, in their homes or in the homes of their friends.

There is something profane, unholy and potentially pagan and depraved about anything that might happen in a mixed company of unmarried young people after the witching hour of midnight. Even saloons, cocktail lounges and night clubs are, in many of the smaller cities in the U.S., still required to close at midnight and few even in the bigger cities, are permitted to remain open after 2 A.M. or all night. The later the hour, after the critical hour of midnight, the more potent become the powers of Satan over the natural (and therefore sinful) instincts of men and women, and especially young unmarried men and women after the age of puberty. In the case of the commercial establishments which cater to the entertainment needs of the public, bribery of policemen and other law enforcement officials is the course commonly resorted to by saloon keepers and night club owners. It should come as no surprise, therefore, that college students resort to flattering, cajoling and, if necessary, bribing dormitory janitors in order to outwit the university authorities who wrote the parietal rules.

Of course it would be naïve to believe that the university authorities at Harvard or any other university really expect all of their students to observe Cotton Mather or Mrs. Grundy rules and Nice Nelly manners in the dormitories during parietal hours, to say nothing of forbidden after-hours behavior. But neither, it should be added, would it be realistic to assume that the city fathers expect all proprietors and patrons of saloons and night clubs to observe the rules of good behavior and the closing hours.

Infractions, they know—and no doubt the university authorities also know—must, in practice, be winked at or sparingly enforced, unless things get out of hand and lead to a public scandal. Bribery is another matter. The possibility is acknowledged, of course, and penalties are provided for it, but the official attitude toward it is something like the social rule against breaking wind in the parlor, that is, something that can be overlooked and even condoned up to a point—as long as it is kept reasonably quiet and doesn't raise too much of a stink.

There is no reason to suppose that the Overseers of Harvard are unaware of the effects, good and bad, of the parietal rules, even if we are willing to accept the opinion of one Harvard grad that "they are pretty much straight, square Anglo-sexual types" (an echo of comedian Woody Allen). Along with the Deans and other administrative officials, they probably subscribe to the traditional academic clichés that boys will be boys, that they must be expected to sow a few wild oats (as long as they don't sprout, at least not during the school year), and that the "modern thing to do" is give youth its head "up to a certain point." What that point is, is not difficult to define: it is the point at which pious and/or Puritanical parents begin to give the institution a suspicious going-over, pressure groups like the religious *cum* patriotic organizations come sniffing around, and the commercial smut-mongering press starts raising embarrassing questions. The fact that students, faculty and administration must always be prepared to face is that, to the official and self-appointed guardians of public morals, college students who stray from the straight and narrow into moral experiments, however successful these may prove to be in terms of human health and well-being, are just so many cases for moral and religious rehabilitation, fallen sons and daughters, especially the latter, who need to be helped back into the Anglo-sexual (or anti-sexual) straitjacket. In any case, the parietal rules at Harvard, Princeton or any other university where they have been tried, are finally only as effective, for good or ill, as the people who are depended on to enforce them at the scene of the crime. This is as true on campus as it is on the playing fields of Zuma Beach, Fort Lauderdale, Balboa or Sloppy Joe's in Nassau or in the Bermudas. "Teenage riots" on the public beaches, Spring vacation rites in the beachside motels, love in the afternoon of a Harvard fawn, or hi-jinks in the after-dark after-hours wind-up of a frat house or dormitory party, it is the sheriff, the motorcycle cop, the campus policeman, the janitor and the house mother who finally determine what the laws, rules and regulations *are* and what "up to a certain point" means in terms of what is permissible and what is not. In sexual politics the art of the possible is what you can get away with and still avoid arrest, or expulsion.

The sort of sexual toilet training which passes for sex education in the schools is mercifully absent at Harvard. "At least that much was spared us," to quote one Harvard student. "There are no lectures on sex. The students wouldn't stand for it. The only thing that came anywhere near it that I can remember was a lecture at the Catholic Newman Club. He was a Catholic physician and he gave us one of those man to man, buddies kind of sex talk. Things like, 'Contraceptives really don't work. You've got to be careful, that bag might not hold out.' It was the lewdest thing I ever heard in all the time I was at Harvard. Lewd and vulgar. It just about killed all the Catholicism I had left in me. Up to that time I still took Catholicism half-way seriously. I had a Catholic upbringing. I never went back to the Newman Club again."

What the dormitories lack in true privacy is almost made up for in the community houses. Community, or cooperative houses as they are usually called on the East Coast, are organized by a group of girls who share the rent and take turns shopping and cooking. The parietal rules for cooperative houses are more liberal than those for the dorms and fraternity houses. There is less surveillance and what there is is friendlier. "At Harvard it is usually the Radcliffe girls who start cooperative houses," my informant told me. "The coop girls are less inhibited. I knew male students who lived in a girls' co-op house for weeks, even for months, because they didn't have enough money to live alone. The girls kept mum about it; they protect each other that way. I lived in a dorm because my family was well off at the time, but some of the boys who couldn't afford the dorms started cooperative houses of their own. They paid about two-thirds of what it costs to rent a room in the dorm." There are other ways to stretch out the parietal hours. "The Radcliffe girls have to be back at their dorms by one o'clock on Saturday nights. That means our parties had to be over by midnight, as required by the Harvard parietal rules. Radcliffe is half a mile away, fifteen minutes' walk. But, if the girl didn't sign out when she left the dorm, she could stay out till any hour of the morning. To stay with you all night all she had to do was leave the house without signing out and quietly slip in next morning. She could depend on the other girls to give her an alibi in case anything leaked out. She'd do as much for them and they knew it."

Much of the research connected with Project Pan on the campus is concerned with the invention and perfection of such M.O.'s and operating procedures to get around the rules and avoid detection. This would seem at first blush, if you are given to blushing at such things, to argue a lack of gratitude on the part of college students towards school authorities who are trying so hard to be liberal about sex. Yet, seen from the students' standpoint, the parietal rules are designed more for curbing rather than condoning, to say nothing of encouraging, sexual experience and experiment. So evasions and countermeasures flourish. At Yale a necktie hung out on the doorknob denotes MAN (and WOMAN) AT WORK, but the signal is only as safe as the traffic will allow. One is always at the mercy of snoopers, official and self-appointed. Besides, it is often pointed out by students that *any* rule designed to control or regulate sexual relations has an inhibiting effect. The feeling is that Big Brother is always watching. Whether the closing hour is seven P.M. or midnight, the restriction is an inhibiting one for, as any successful experimentor will tell you, in sex nothing succeeds like excess.

In colleges where the open-door policy is in effect your privacy is measured not only in time but in inches. Where the rule is "the width of a book" you might get away with the cynical use of a book of matches. But, again, only as long as you have loyal dormitory mates and careless, or indulgent, janitors, house mothers and campus cops. At Brandeis University several hundred students staged a two-day demonstration when the administration announced a new open-door policy. The new regulation "makes impossible any meaningful relationship between boy and girl," the editors of the student newspaper protested, a protest in which one may hear the voice of youthful experience—and experiment— but also the echo of Lester A. Kirkendall. No wonder his book, *Premarital Intercourse and Interpersonal Relationships* is kept out of the hands of undergraduates in many school libraries by being kept on restricted shelves or only in the medical library. Book desegregation may yet become an issue on the campus and the civil right of sexual privacy may yet become as acute an issue as racial integration, with mass lay-in demonstrations being staged behind closed dormitory doors.

Despite all the restrictions and risks, Project Pan has had its experimental successes on the college campus. Anything which breaks down barriers between the sexes may be chalked up as a success. The Right of the First Night, which was anciently the right of the god-priest of the hierogamy and later the *droit du seigneur* of the lord of the castle is now a right that the college undergraduate may exercise, if some high school student hasn't already beaten him to it. Undergraduates at the University of Georgia call such girls "first-nighters" and use the term with an increasing measure of respect; their fathers used to call them "push-overs."

Any time is the right time and any place is the best place for sex, if I understand the views of my informants. "When fraternity boys at Michigan State talk excitedly about 'grassers' (a blanket, some beer, a coed, and a grassy spot along Red Cedar River), all they are describing is an elaborate version of the old-fashioned blanket party," says *Newsweek*, but it may just as accurately, and more sympathetically, be described as "a book of verses underneath a bough, a jug of wine, a loaf of bread, and thou . . ." What begins with a night before exams cramming session and ends up in bed together is certainly a step ahead, in health and beauty, to the old-fashioned catch-as-catch-can, under-the-blanket wrestling match. "So, sure, some girls roll in the hay a little, but they get rid of their anxieties and frustrations that way," a girl columnist of *The Daily Californian* is quoted as saying, and a Vassar girl says, "It's a load off my mind, losing my virginity." For one thing, the boys and girls talk with one another more than they used to. More than one psychologist has observed that sexual foreplay is more common among young people than it once was under the old hit-and-run conditions. And so is good conversation. As one University of California coed described it to me: "I never knew conversation was so important, before and after. Before it's exciting and after it's—I don't know *what* it is, exactly, maybe reassuring. Anyway it makes you feel loved." What do they talk about? "Anything, really. Anything interesting, but when you get to know each other it's mostly about ourselves and each other. The things we like, the books we read, the movies we see and what we think about them, the teachers, the class work. We study together a lot, help each other with writing assignments and looking up things in the library. Best of all, though, is finding out things about each other, about ourselves. It leads to intimacy and understanding and that leads to better sex, more sex enjoyment. But for that you've got to have a place where you aren't going to be spied on. That's why I live ten miles from campus. Most of the boys I date do, too. There's only one old car in our whole crowd so we make up a car pool and take turns driving and chip in for gas. Two other girls and I are talking about getting an apartment together next semester and starting a community house, like the ones I've seen in Venice." (That is, Venice by the sea, a slum suburb of Los Angeles.[6]

I have seen and recorded a number of such "covenants of intimacy," to use the term applied to such relationships by Wally Toevs, Presbyterian pastor of the University of Colorado. It is not the "little marriage" which is supposed to be in preparation for the "great marriage" which is to last. It is a series of passionate friendships which are usually regarded as having performed their purpose if they succeed in helping the participants to overcome the "pleasure fear" to which early miseducation in sex condemns most of the youth in our culture. "After the age of 16 or 17," the adolescents in our culture, reach a point in their miseducation where "the striving for pleasure has been replaced by a fear of pleasure," according to Wilhelm Reich.[7] "They have acquired *pleasure anxiety*. This pleasure anxiety, or fear of pleasurable excitation, is something basically different from the fear of punishment for sexual activities which, if intense, usually is fear of castration. The increasingly defensive attitude toward sexuality is anchored in this pleasure anxiety . . . (resulting in) painful genital excitation." Self-repression of sexual excitation and erection, which is society's most highly recommended remedy, "becomes anchored in this pleasure anxiety. In this way, the adolescent very often becomes himself the advocate of sexual prohibitions."

This sort of rationalized self-frustration is illustrated by the case of the Radcliffe girl who said: "I used to think it perfect nonsense to lie down with a boy, get undressed, or let him undress you—and then say let's stop. It's probably bosh, but I have built up this idealistic thing about the final act itself."

No sexual experiment can be considered a failure if it enables the student to diseducate himself out of pleasure fear and self-frustration. Even at the risk of pregnancy and abortion? "Yes," was the answer I got from one coed. "It was worth it. I held out all through high school, and believe me, it wasn't easy. I was a nervous wreck by the time I got to college—nearly jumped out of

---

[6] Lawrence Lipton, *The Holy Barbarians*, New York, 1962.
[7] Reich, *The Sexual Revolution*, p. 104.

my skin if a boy so much as made a pass at me. In high school I used to date boys like mad, never the same one twice, of course, because I never finished anything I started. Got a reputation for being the worst prick-teaser in our crowd. Everybody thought I was being promiscuous in the *worst* way—and all I ever got out of it was frustration and those morning-after jitters. The abortion . . . that was in my freshman year, before I knew what to do. It was my own fault. But it was worth it. Now I don't date so many boys anymore. I'm cool about it. I can pick and choose, and take my time about it, because I've overcome my fear of it. I'm comfortable with boys. I enjoy it. For the first time in my life I really enjoy it. I even have favorite records I put on—music to screw by."

There is little that Theodor Reik, the esthetic expert "on the psychoanalysis of romantic and sexual emotions" could teach this young woman. She is a graduate student of Project Pan.

Reaction and Counter-Reformation

University and college administrators have not been entirely silent about the sexual revolution on the campus. Some have taken a firm stand against it; some have attempted something like a counter-reformation from within; a few have gone all the way and left the students free to make their own sex arrangements in their own way—and at their own risk.

"Wild sex parties at Harvard University, the nation's oldest and richest college, disclosed Thursday by Harvard officials," was the lead paragraph of a UPI news dispatch on Nov. 1, 1963. "Dean John U. Monro said visits by coed and other women to Harvard dormitories have 'come to be a license to use the college rooms for wild parties and sex.' . . . Monro's disclosure of the parties of 'a few' of the university's 13,700 students were made in the *Crimson*, Harvard's undergraduate daily newspaper. . . . Monro said he and Dean of Students Robert Watson 'have been badly shaken up recently by some severe violations of our rules and recent standards of behavior and the feeling that the college itself seemed to be contributing to an atmosphere of "don't care" ' . . . A series of meetings between students and officials was held recently but failed to resolve a disagreement over changes in house rules." Complaining that there was danger of "outright scandal,"

Monro warned students after college opened in September against "orgiastic parties" and told them that intimacies "between unmarried individuals" could not be tolerated. "Many thoughtful students feel that the university has the responsibility to provide facilities for sexual adventures," he was later reported to have said (*Time*, Apr. 6, 1964). "Looking back on the incident, the likable, crew-cut dean regrets the sensationalized headlines about 'Wild Parties at Harvard' but insists: "I now think I'm dealing with a larger number of people than I believed last October."

I have it from Harvard students who have been present at "orgiastic parties" that what actually takes place on such occasions is a more sophisticated version of the juvenile gang-shag. Liquor is the solvent employed to flush away the built-in inhibitions against self-abandonment to sexual pleasure. Not all those who are present participate in the orgy; it attracts chiefly those boys and girls who have had the most difficulty overcoming their inhibitions and achieving orgasm in one-to-one sex partnerships. The near-hysteria of the "wild party" excites them and enables them to throw off the fears and guilt feelings which usually prevent them from enjoying sexual intercourse as fully as they have heard it can be enjoyed. Naturally, when the party takes this turn it also attracts the young nymphomaniacs and satyriasists in whom repression has taken the extreme reactive form of uncontrollable sexual gluttony. In the resulting permissive atmosphere a temporary *consensus gentium* is set up which draws in other, more normally sexed individuals, and you have a wild party, or, what a Harvard dean who is presumably learned in the Greek classics, would call "an orgiastic party."

A little more reflection by Deans Monro and Watson might have made them hesitate before applying to a wild party the term "orgiastic." They might had consulted any one of a number of academically authoritative works of classical scholarship, say, *The Greeks and the Irrational* by E. R. Dodds, and reminded themselves that the orgy, far from being an irresponsible outburst of sexual vulgarity, is the name originally given to what was once a highly respected kind of mental therapy. Speaking of "the old Dionysiac cure," Dodds observes that it was essentially similar to the later corybantic cure, and that "both claimed to operate a catharsis by means of an infectious 'orgiastic' dance accompanied by the same kind of 'orgiastic' music—tunes in the Phrygian mode played on the flute and the kettledrum."

The malady which the Corybantes professed to cure is said by Plato to consist in "phobias or anxiety-feelings arising from some morbid mental condition.[8]

"A casual phrase of Plato's," Dodds goes on to tell us, "appears to imply that Socrates had personally taken part in the Corybantic rites; it certainly shows, as Linforth has pointed out, that intelligent young men of good family might take part in them. Whether Plato himself accepted all the religious implications of such ritual is an open question . . . but both he and Aristotle evidently regard it as at least a useful organ of social hygiene— they believe that it *works*, and works for the good of the participants."

I do not think it would be altogether too farfetched to assume that there may be students at Harvard's occasional wild parties who are well aware of the connection between classical, prehistoric and contemporary tribal rites and a dormitory or frat house orgy. I would be surprised if this were *not* so. I have myself been present at similar orgies in less scholarly surroundings and found young men and women who knew perfectly well that they were trying, in their own way, to reenact Dionysiac, Corybantic and primitive tribal rites. The books on prehistory, classical culture, primitive rite and modern psychology (which often deal with such matters) are available in cheap paperback editions not only to Harvard students but to young and old everywhere, at least in the larger city bookstores. So it is conceivable that there are "intelligent young men of good family," and young women too, at Harvard, who might have had such ideas and comparisons in mind, even if Deans Monro and Watson failed to take note of them in their public pronouncements.

At the same time, it would be misleading to leave the reader with the impression that I regard a wild party in a Harvard dormitory as a Corybantic dance, a Dionysiac "cure" or a tribal fertility rite. It is there, of course, sometimes more sometimes less conscious in the minds of the students who participate in a dormitory gang-shag, but it is felt more like an atavism than the divine madness of the ancient Bacchanalia, approved by men and blessed by the gods. If it brings with it no catharsis and no cure for the armored rigidity of the sexually crippled, it is because the larger

---

[8] Dodds, p. 77.

consensus of society is not there to approve and support it, with the result that it remains a clandestine affair, legally criminal, socially unspeakable and religiously sinful. Under such conditions it is almost bound to leave a feeling of remorse behind it in those who are not altogether free from social and religious guilt feelings, and a feeling of over-compensatory bravado and infantile exhibitionism in those who are not yet orgastically liberated but only neurotically rebellious against their still unmastered guilt and fear. True and lasting liberation from what Reich defined as "fear of pleasure" is not so easily won; you cannot achieve it in a few gang-shags by just letting yourself go, as they say.

The "responsible" school authorities do not care to look behind the wild party, or any other student sex activity, for that matter, for historical analogies and explanations, or raise the question: is it beneficial or detrimental to the sexual health, the orgastic economy of the participants? They are *against* letting oneself go no matter what the cause or the effect. Their aim is to restrain, regulate, control and deter. Even the most liberal among them.

No better example of the liberal professor is to be found anywhere than Lester A. Kirkendall. He has himself been the frequent target of bluenose clergymen, professional smut-hounds and school administrators bent on "holding the line." Writing in *The Nation* (Feb. 17, 1964) about "Sex on the Campus," Professor Kirkendall still accepts the assumption that it is up to the adult generation and the college deans to guide and counsel the poor perplexed students "who are grappling with the 'sexual revolution.'"

> I am a teacher and have dealt with young people for years. I have coped with the sex problems of two generations: young people with whose parents I worked are now coming to me for help. Thus I know that through all these years, youth in its teens has seriously sought help with sexual perplexities, and has consistently had its pleas ignored by the adult generation which should have helped it.

> Morally speaking, today's youth is no better, and no worse than its parents or grandparents. But because of the confusions and contradictions with which they are faced, young people today are certainly a mixed-up generation.

This might have passed for friendly and helpful support with the pre-war generation of college students Professor Kirkendall worked with, but if he will ask around among students of the present teenage and young twenties generation at Oregon State, and do so with a mind open to the sexual revolution—without the quotation marks he still wraps the phrase in—he will hear things like:

"*Who's* problem is it? It's the school administration that has the *problem*. We're finding the answers." And if he enquires further: "What are some of your answers?" he will be told: "Well, one of our answers is, Talk less and *do* more. Consult less and *screw* more." In other words, one learns not by talking but by doing, especially in such a personal, empirical field of learning and research as sexual health and happiness.

He will find that today's students would rather have help with contraceptives and private, snooper-proof accommodations than advice on how to live a liberated, life-enhancing sex life on campus and still live by the moral code prescribed, openly or by implication, by school, church and state. For the student knows, long before he comes to college, that everything his instincts and his sense of life tell him is good for him is regarded by his pastor, his teacher and the policeman in the prowl car as evil, wicked, dirty, sinful, antisocial and illegal.

Professor Kirkendall may even be looked straight in the eye and asked: *Who's* mixed up? The student who is trying to break out of the sex-crippling strait-jacket, or the deans and counselors who are trying to stuff him back into it again. Yes, even the sympathetic, understanding, liberal-minded Professor of Family Life, because it isn't family life we are most concerned about during the student years but how to avoid and prevent the forced, premature marriage and the unwanted, unplanned parenthood which lack of contraceptives and dangerous illegal abortions too often force upon us. We'll trade any amount of "talking things over" and marriage counselling for one good birth control clinic, preferably on or near campus, where we can get contraceptive advice and devices and safe, legal, socially-approved abortions when we need them.

All this may sound like ingratitude to the good counsellor, but gratitude is more than anyone can reasonably expect from young men and women who are today part of the most determined— and most intelligently informed—sexual revolution in history, in the face of public misrepresentation, parental hostility, churchly condemnation, legal threats and police harassment. Professor Kirkendall's mission is not so much to the student any more as it is to the school authorities, churchmen, judges, lawyers and self-appointed censors and snoopers. There he has done and is doing a good job as the Devil's Advocate. He would do an even better job if he dropped the role of *advocatus diaboli*—who was never anything more, historically, than the church-appointed, church-directed "defense" attorney putting on a well rehearsed show—and step out, instead, as the objective analyst of the sexual revolution if not its partisan advocate. It is too late for criticism of the college curriculum or to hope for a "college instructional program" closer to the facts of general present-day sex life. It is no longer as true as it once was that what "the students need (and want) is some very down-to-earth discussion," nor is it any longer true that "in our culture sex is seldom a topic of serious discussion among adults, and even less so between youth and adults." On the contrary, it is *more* so, not less so, among adults as well as among students. It may still be so in the public pronouncements of university officials, but it is not true of their private discussions, among themselves, and it is certainly not true of the students, privately *or* publicly. It is not more discussion projects of the sort which Professor Kirkendall praises, but more experimental sex projects, free from academic supervision, regulation or even "open discussion," which students need today.

Far from relaxing or, God forbid! abolishing the parietal rules (and from all accounts God is on the side of *all* restrictive rules), Harvard officialdom has no intention of abandoning its policy of supervising student morality. Dr. Graham Blaine, Jr. is on record as scoffing at students' claims that restrictive parietal rules increase guilt feeling. "Admittedly," says psychiatrist Blaine, "a percentage of all these people who are having love relationships benefit from them, but they are a decided minority. It's a question of balancing the small amount of increased pleasure for the few against great potential harm to the many. Strict enforcement of parietal rules bolsters the girls who aren't sure if they want to have an affair." The picture evoked by this touching statistical concern for the moral balance of the student community is: Behind every tempted but undecided demivirgin who falls under the spell of a Harvard man stands a Harvard dean, psychiatrist, overseer, house mother, janitor or campus cop, to help keep her shoulder straps from slipping and hold up her panties.

Among the King Canutes who have come forward to command the orgastic juices to stop flowing is the president of Notre Dame, the Rev. Theodore M. Hesburgh, who has issued the warning that "if anyone seriously believes that he cannot become well-educated

here without . . . girls in his room (he should) get free of Notre
Dame." Among other Canutes are president Sarah Blanding of
Vassar, who has publicly denounced premarital sexual experiments, and Vassar's Dr. Florence C. Wislocki who opines that,
"We don't know if there's more or less sex among students, but at
least Miss Blanding made some of the girls stop and think. Before
then, many felt we condoned sexual experimentation."

"What ever made them think we had any such illusion about
school policy?" was the question many Vassar girls were asking
each other at the time and, according to my own information, the
prevailing attitude, even among girls who were still holding out
for Mr. Right (on the No-Sex-Without-Love principle), or saving
it for the bridal bed, was: "What business is it of Sarah B's *what*
we do or don't do about sex?"

All over America, universities and colleges, large and small, are
imposing curfews or curtailing or rescinding dormitory visiting
privileges; others are settling for sex lectures and discussion seminars, like Oberlin's "Sex in Human Relations" seminar; and still
others are rallying to the breach and prescribing cold showers and
character-building athletics. And the parochial denominational
schools continue to stand pat on God and prayer.

Meanwhile, behind a wall of silence and jealously guarded privacy, a few of the smaller, privately supported schools are managing to survive and maintain high standards of scholarship and
financial solvency without imposing restrictive regulation on the
sex life of their students.

Curfew Shall Not Ring Tonight: Project Pan, Unlimited

The defenders of the Old Morality on campus always come
around sooner or later to posing what seems to them the question
to end all questions: What would happen if *all* restrictions were
removed and sex was left completely unregulated? The implied
answer is, of course, sexual anarchy; not a state of innocence but
a state of unbridled licentiousness and sin of the sort implied in
the biblical verse: "In those days there was no king in Israel:
every man did that which was right in his own eyes."

What is right in the eyes of students who live and work in a
permissive moral climate?

At Bennington, where there are no set limits to dormitory
visiting hours, no one has had to call in clergymen or psychiatrists

to bolster the virtuous or policemen to break up midnight revels. Scholarship and the arts flourish right along with sexual experimentation and there seems to be ample time for both, and both, if we are to believe the fond reminiscences of graduates, are conducted on a very high level of planning and performance. If any coed is agonizing about her virginity at Bennington, as the *Newsweek* report[9] has it, she is not likely to go unravished long, at least not for any lack of opportunity. "If a girl reaches 20 and she's still a virgin, she begins to wonder whether there is anything wrong with her as a woman," a Bennington junior is quoted as saying. From all accounts the answer to that one must be Yes. If the school administration ever starts looking around for sex problems at Bennington this would be a good place to begin. Cases of ingrowing virginity are not easy to cure after atrophy sets in.

Reed College, in Portland, Oregon, has had dormitory visiting hours for two decades and is a pioneer in enlightened permissiveness. Here, too, academic achievement runs high. High marks and high IQ's are no guaranty of high orgastic potency but they help to lend variety and imagination to sexual experimentation and hold down the incidence of seminal infection. Reed is presently undergoing considerable expansion. It remains to be seen whether the size of the student body is as much of a factor in campus morality as some claim it is.

Hunter College, in New York, has three times the number of students Reed has (as many as Harvard and Radcliffe put together) and no one has found it necessary to conduct moral revival meetings on campus or call in the minions of law and order to protect the innocent and virtuous.

Not only the size of the student body but the size of the city in which the school is located determines whether the student feels he or she is experimenting in a gold fish bowl, where every date is a dormitory case history to be "staffed" before and after; or a private affair, one of a multitude of such affairs, and providing for this reason a measure of anonymity that only an exhibitionist would find unpleasant.

At Oberlin, which long ago became known as "God's College" (because it trained Congregationalist missionaries), God is honored today in pre-Judeo-Christian ways that are closer to Baal than they are to Jehovah. In other words, it is an outpost of *post*-Judeo-Christian morality. This despite the fact that Oberlin is not

---

9 *Newsweek* (Vol. LXIII, No. 14, April 6, 1964), p. 52.

distinguished for administrative permissiveness. No cars are permitted students and the dormitories are ruled by restrictive visiting hours and afford a minimum of privacy. Which only goes to show how much can be accomplished by really determined and ingenious researchers of Project Pan. Why college administrators should think they can stifle profane love with rules and regulations when popes and priesthoods using the whole armor of God have so often failed is one of the mysteries of the Puritanical mind. "Love laughs at locksmiths" is a folk saying which may help to explain why antiquarians have found more chastity belts than keys. A voluminous manual could be compiled of the ways which high school and college students have devised to outwit restrictions and prohibitions in religious as well as secular schools. A similar concentration of human effort, channeled into a year's crash program, could conceivably find a cure for the common cold.

The principle on which most of the stratagems are based seems to be "Let them beat us in the trifles; we shall conquer them in the broad consequences," a piece of sage counsel which I vaguely remember as coming from a profound and highly respected source which I have long ago forgotten.

At another Ohio college, Antioch, fewer stratagems are needed than at Oberlin. "What I learned at home," one interviewee (female) told me, "was *not* that sex is dirty—nothing as vulgar and stupid as that—but only that sexual intercourse was *so* important and so *beautiful* a thing that it shouldn't be indulged in except with the most carefully chosen partners. And what I found out was that, in the eyes of my parents, there was practically *no* young man who met the requirements. All through high school I sublimated instead, which meant that I masturbated like mad, mostly with some fantasied Mr. Right who looked—I realize now —a hell of a lot like dad: after all, what high school kid could compete with *him!* who could it be more important and beautiful with? It wasn't till I went away to college that I found out that sex could be fun, and it didn't have to be so damn important or so damn beautiful in order to be deep-down satisfying. That it could be Mr. Wrong, and you could learn a hell of a lot from a lot of Mr. Wrongs, till Mr. Right came along. Do you know, it wasn't till I was in my junior year that I finally shook off my father fantasy and all his sublimation and Mr. Beautiful and Important bullshit and learned to fuck for the fun of it."

What had undoubtedly started out as a well-intentioned and intelligently inculcated home education in sex turned out to be as severe a case of rigid moral armoring as any Sister Superior of the most cloistered parochial high school could wish for her charges.

"Sublimation" also proved to be the undoing—or should I say the *over*doing?—of another college student (male) who told me that his psychoanalyzed and sexually "progressive" parents, aided by "progressive" grade school teachers, filled him with such a "hifalutin" and "medical" picture of the sexual act that, to quote his own words, "I literally *talked* myself out of it every time; it took me that long to set the stage for it, and by that time I'd lost my erection and the girl couldn't care less anymore." In the case of this young man it took a whole series of unsublimated whores to diseducate and re-educate him and bring him back to the instinctual genital level. Of one of these prostitutes he said, "She never heard of Freud or Jung or anybody, but she taught me more about fucking as an art and a pleasure than my educated parents, all my teachers and all the books I read. She was even *cleaner* than many of the nice girls I dated, but she never made me feel medical about it. In fact, the only dose of clap I ever got I got from a nice girl who didn't even know what clap *was*, she was that nice."

At Oberlin, Antioch or Hunter our young man would have found nice girls who know what clap is and how to look before leaping into bed with a suspiciously leaky cock. At Bard College he would have been able to conduct his remedial re-education without going off campus and at a good deal less cost. And if he had been lucky enough to be going to school within dating distance of Sarah Lawrence College he might have graduated from his early "progressive" mis-education without running the risk of a cat house police raid.

But even at best there are risks. Officially, *no* school, public or private, goes out of its way to make it easy for premarital sex. Officially they are all committed to the Judeo-Christian moral code, respectful of the mores of the tribe, and obedient to law and order. If it comes to a showdown, say, a public "scandal," they must pay lip service, at the very least, to the moral *status quo* on pain of losing their private bequests, public funds, Foundation grants, or the loyalty of the alumni. Administrators, deans and faculty, if they are inclined to be soft on sex, to adapt a phrase from the politicians, are compelled to appear tough on sex, publicly, no matter how they think or feel about it privately. Students know this and expect the deans and administrators to act as a buffer between themselves and "the outside world," as quite a few of them phrased it in their conversations with me. "I don't blame her (the head of a womens' college) for lying to the reporters," a knowledgeable junior reasoned. "After all, we lie to *her* and do everything *we* can to get around the rules." In the most enlightened and best regulated schools there is a sort of tacit pact between students and administration: the student tries to be as discreet about it as he/she can and, in case of trouble, "keep the school out of it," and the administrators are expected to make only a token show of enforcing the rules, if any, and, if anyone comes snooping around, to deny everything with righteous indignation. If things get really tough and the witch-hunters are out for blood, the students will accept a few temporary restrictions and a public scolding, all for the sake of the alma mater, but this is about the limit of their school loyalty. More than this and the pact is broken; there is open rebellion on the campus. The arrangement is not unlike that of the whorehouse madame and the police: if the pressure of the Good Citizens or the "Reform element" gets too hot to be ignored, the madame is willing to "take a pinch" and, if necessary, pay a reasonable fine as long as it doesn't disrupt business too much.

Still, so advanced is the state of the Erotic Revolution in some quarters, that even this sort of mild regulation is unacceptable to the student. In that case he or she seeks out a school where no restrictions at all are put on sexual behavior, or they cooperate with teachers to found such a school. There have been a number of such attempts. Notable among these is—or was—Black Mountain College.

Neo-Pagan Groves of Academe

It did not start primarily as a sexual revolution against repressive moral regulation. The founders of Black Mountain College took seven-hundred and fifty acres at Black Mountain, North Carolina and turned it into an experiment in education and student-faculty community living. The plant consisted of an old country inn overlooking a lake, and a few two-storey frame buildings. The dining room of the inn became the common dining room and the kitchen was presided over by two Negro cooks, who were "part of the Black Mountain family, wonderful, lovely people," the way one student remembers it. After World War II the school acquired four extra one-storey wooden buildings, army surplus barracks, and an added enrollment consisting of ex-GI's who were taking advantage of the GI Bill of Rights. The school, even with the added accommodations, was hard-pressed to provide proper housing for the more than one hundred students and faculty. By this time the student body was about equally divided between boys and girls and each had their own dormitories, but visiting was unrestricted as to days and hours.

This is not to say that the faculty members did not have their own private opinions about morality. Some of them were quite conventional in their opinions and practices. "The farther back you go in history of Black Mountain College the more formal it was, sexually. John Rice, the original founder, was no sexual revolutionary. Neither was Joseph Albers, the architect, who followed Rice. Albers was a fairly stiff-necked old guy, German type. One time he let it be known that he disapproved of students putting sleeping pads in the cubicles. He said they were intended for study only. But nobody paid much attention to that. If anybody wanted a sleeping pad in the study cubicle he had one, and that's all there was to it."

With two or three students to a room on the lower floors of the dormitories and five or six to a room on the upper floors, there couldn't have been much privacy for sex. As to that, my informant remarked, "What the hell, there were 750 acres of grounds." Which is, of course, the most honored of all traditions in the arts of love and sex: fucking *al fresco*, a practice immortalized by an Illinois grad in a poetic salute to those "who fuck *al fresco* in the park / Their bed the Sunday comic page."

Were there any unplanned consequences? "Pregnancies? Sure, now and then. But there wasn't any policy about that sort of thing. It was your own business if you wanted to have a child or an abortion. Either way you were welcome to stay or go as you pleased. If the students wanted to help they could take up a collection." It is interesting to note this fact, for it is precisely at this point that faculty and/or administration usually step in with: "You see, it *is* necessary to have rules or this sort of thing can happen. It can be dangerous to health, even to life, and it's the sort of thing it is hard to conceal for long or keep from becoming a public scandal. Besides—" and this is always considered the retort magnificent, "it interferes with class attendance and tends to depress scholarship standards and grades." What was Black Mountain's experience in this respect? "There were no tests, no grades. The student was expected to look to himself if he wanted such measurements."

Historian Arnold J. Toynbee has expressed the view that if the trend toward sexual freedom continues our universities will no longer be institutions of higher learning but social clubs for sexual mating. Black Mountain College was, until it folded in the late Fifties, about as free in this respect as any educational institution can be. It's educational principles and techniques never elicited any praise from academician Toynbee, if indeed he ever took the trouble to find out about them or even knew there was such a place, but many of its teachers and students have made world-wide reputations in their chosen fields. It must be admitted that Black Mountain failed to turn out its quota of atomic scientists and college-educated police chiefs, but in the arts it looms large. Among the poets anthologized by Donald M. Allen in *The New American Poetry*, Charles Olson, Robert Duncan and Robert Creeley were on the staff of Black Mountain College in the early Fifties, and Edward Dorn, Joel Oppenheimer and Jonathan Williams studied there. The literary magazine of the school, *Black Mountain Review*, published some of the first work of Paul Blackburn, Paul Carroll, Larry Eigner and Denise Levertov, as did *Origin* magazine which was closely tied to *Black Mountain Review* by virtue of a kind of interlocking directorate. The poet John Weiners studied at Black Mountain College and founded *Measure*, another influential avant-garde literary magazine of the Fifties. From 1955 to 1957 *Black Mountain Review*, under the editorship of Robert Creeley, published some of the best and now most widely known work of William Carlos Williams, Jack Kerouac, Allen Ginsberg, Michael McClure, Philip Whalen, Irving Layton, Louis Zukofsky, Gary Snyder, James Purdy, Paul Goodman, Gael Turnbull, Michael Rumaker and some of the first excerpts from the work of "William Lee," later revealed as *Naked Lunch*, by William Burroughs. Painters Ben Shahn and Robert Motherwell taught summer courses at Black Mountain.

It is worthy of note, I think, that the writers and artists whose names are connected with Black Mountain College fall into the category of avant-garde. Does this mean that a permissive moral climate "produces" trail-blazers, movers and shakers? I am inclined to answer that question in the affirmative, with one qualification: it also *attracts* them. The point is that an atmosphere which does not stifle free enquiry and encourages experiment is more likely than not to attract and nurture original minds and talents. At Black Mountain, those teachers who after a longer or shorter residency could not bring themselves to go along with new concepts and practices in their field had to leave voluntarily or found themselves deserted by the students.

Sexual freedom at Black Mountain was not a matter of approved or disapproved behavior. It was simply taken for granted and there wasn't any need to make an issue of it one way or the other. In all my conversations with Black Mountain students and teachers I cannot recall a single case where anyone brought up the subject of sexual freedom, it was so much taken for granted. From Rice to Albers to Olson opinions and attitudes of the leadership changed, as the climate of sexual attitudes changed everywhere in America over the twenty-five years of Black Mountain, but freedom to experiment was never an issue so far as the students were concerned; philosophical, esthetic and educational questions far outweighed moral questions and made or broke teaching careers and student loyalties at Black Mountain College. It folded up in the Fifties, but did it end because it failed? By the middle Fifties there were springing up all over the country small enclaves of sexual permissiveness of the Beat variety in which many Black Mountain students were able to find something like the community feeling they had grown used to at the college. Besides, some of the smaller colleges of long standing were offering a climate of sexual permissiveness that almost equalled that of Black Mountain. Some of Black Mountain's teachers were finding academic hospitality and freedom in these smaller colleges, and their students followed them there. When *Black Mountain Review* ceased publication it had already spawned five or six other publications where its editors and contributors could publish their work. Both school and publication had served their pioneering purpose. In this respect they could be said to have died of success.

Unmarried Sex: A Summary and Trial Balance

Surveying the sexual behavior of the unmarried, on and off campus, the first conclusion must be that "premarital sex" is a misnomer. Premarital sex is a term which implies that sexual experience before marriage is *a preparation for marriage*. Social workers, preachers and popular magazine writers use it because it makes public discussion of the subject easier and presumably more defensible if you wish to give the impression that you are defending it, without running the risk of appearing to justify it. Thus it becomes, at worst, "the little marriage before the big marriage which is to last." Stated in this way it is almost indistinguishable from Victorian "wild oats," except that it appears to extend to girls the indulgence once allowed only to boys to "sow a few wild oats before settling down." "Settling down" is, of course, a kind of fallen-cake, old shoe down-at-the-heels, stick-in-the mud, shrug-it-off expression for wedded bliss.

There are enough pressures from every source to restrain, inhibit and punish sex without the school adding to them. If we are ever to be delivered from the straitjacket of the Judeo-Christian antisexual moral code it will have to *begin* in the schools. That the Erotic Revolution has already made as much progress as it has is in large measure due to the increasingly affirmative response of an enlightened minority of school officials and faculty to student pressure. In assessing the value of school policy in such matters it must be borne in mind that the students' choice of schools is determined by it in the first place. This must be further examined in the light of student sex in European colleges where, except for religious schools, restrictions on dormitory visiting are the exception rather than the rule; where traveling vacations across the borders into neighboring countries in pairs and groups —on hiking trips, over mountain trails, in sports cars and on motor scooters—is the accepted practice. Compared with Denmark and Sweden, for example, sex life on the American campus brings up the rear of the Erotic Revolution. From all accounts even the family-dominated youth of Japan may now be in advance of American youth.

While Americans were ogling Alfred Kinsey's statistics and charts of "kissing, lip" and "kissing, deep," his frequency studies of "animal contacts," "homosexual contacts" and "nocturnal emissions," Europeans were reading D. H. Lawrence's *Lady Chatterley's Lover*, Henry Miller's *Tropic of Cancer*, both verboten in the U.S., and Wilhelm Reich's *The Function of the Orgasm*, actually burned by court order in the U.S.

Censorship, legal, illegal and extra-legal, must be assigned some of the blame for the relatively unprepared condition of Americans, young and old, to understand and cope with the Erotic Revolution which is sweeping the Judeo-Christian world. Ignorance in such matters is not the same as innocence, but whether one knows little or nothing about sex or knows everything wrong, the results are strikingly similar. Among these results is the armoring of the musculature of the body, the rigidity which marks the "square," as he is so fittingly called today. The damage does not end there. Many case histories attest to the crippling effects of such conflicts between sexual instincts and social pressures.

Many of the interviewees quoted by Gael Greene in *Sex and the College Girl*, in the chapter titled "To Each Her Own Morality," are cases of instinctual-moral conflict and more or less severe disturbance of genital potency. It is true that in a transitional period of changing moral values each person is obliged to make his decisions, but such decisions do not constitute a private morality. "To each her own" can only mean an acceptance of the prevailing moral code or a decision to experiment with new sexways and lifeways, the details of which are usually discussed with others and shared with others and do not isolate the person so completely as Gael Greene implies. It is not a simple "decision for God," as Billy Graham keeps repeating in his sermons to the teenager; it is usually not a choice or a decision at all. It is an acceptance of sexual repression and premarital abstinence *on faith:* that is to say, faith in the Judeo-Christian moral code as defined by Billy Graham.

The "love-smitten San Diego State sophomore or junior" who said, "I don't think God cares about *that,*" and the "devoutly Catholic coed at DePauw University" who said, "My church says even French kissing is wrong," and therefore refrains from it, are both appealing to the same authoritarian moral code. So is the girl who said, "I felt so guilty, we almost broke up," when a boy French-kissed her. The fact that she called it "terribly intimate petting" is a clue to her sense of guilt, even though she later rationalized it with: "The Church's rules apply only to the non-thinking masses." I have known members of the nonthinking masses (by which she undoubtedly meant the non-collegiate rabble) who were farther along the road to moral and sexual liberation than French-kissing, and healthier in their sexual life and moral outlook.

Fear is a deterrent, of course, but it is not often the kind of deterrent the fearsome think it is.

Religion is almost universally recognized by researchers in the field of sexual behavior as a deterrent.

Some persons have expressed a fear that a long-time sex study of the sort in which we are currently engaged will fall into error if it averages histories obtained early in the study with histories obtained ten or twenty years later. There are persons who have regretted the fact that it was not possible to complete this study before World War II. They indicate that it is not correct to compare data obtained before the war and data obtained since, for patterns change so much in times of war and during post-war adjustments that we probably should begin the study anew. Not only do the press, propaganda agencies, and moral and law enforcement groups encourage this notion, but scientists have been inclined to accept it. There are persons who have suggested that we should rule out all histories of men who have been in the armed forces, inasmuch as their patterns of behavior have, inevitably, been so changed that they are no longer representative of a peace-time population. There are persons who have thought that the publication of the present volume might so affect the pattern of behavior for whole segments of the population that we could no longer find histories that would be representative of the conditions that existed before these data were made available. There are more persons who have thought that it would be important for us to get re-takes on histories of subjects who had previously given histories—not for the sake of testing the validity of memory and the extent of the cover-up (as we have in actuality used such re-takes), but for the sake of recording the presumably great changes in behavior that must follow such discussions of sexual matters as are involved in the contribution of one's history.

These persons do not seem to have realized the ancient origins of our current patterns and their deep foundations in the basic thinking of each cultural group. We have repeatedly pointed out that many of our present-day attitudes on sex are matters which were settled in the religious philosophy of the authors of the Old Testament and even among more ancient peoples, and there is no evidence that scientific analyses will quickly modify such deep-rooted behavior.[10]

Churchmen may have taken comfort from that last sentence but, if Kinsey's statisticians had gotten away from their adding machines, charts and questionnaires long enough to get a close-up look at what people were *doing* about sex and not so exclusively what they were *saying* about it, they might have concluded that the current patterns of sexual behavior were no longer so deeply-rooted as they thought. They might even have discovered that

---

[10] Kinsey, Pomeroy, Martin & Gebhard, *Sexual Behavior in the Human Male* (Philadelphia, 1948) pp. 414–415.

people were not waiting for "scientific analysis" to help them modify their sex behavior. Even as they were compiling and printing their charts and figures, in 1948, the Sexual Revolution was already on the march, having recently been given a tremendous forward push by the experience gained by millions of American men and women in the far-flung "theaters of war."

Kinsey had reported three times as much premarital intercourse among inactive Catholics as there is among those who strictly follow church teachings and that active and inactive Protestants were not so very different. Ten years later, 1958, Kanin and Howard reported in a study of premarital sex that regular churchgoers among married couples they studied showed 28% premarital coitus, couples with one regular and one non-regular churchgoer, 48%, and non-attenders, 61%. A Kinsey Report, on the *Sexual Behavior of the American Female*, 1953, showed an average of Catholics, Protestants and Jews who reported premarital intercourse as: devout, 16%, moderate, 29.2% and inactive, 35.5%. (P. 415, Kinsey.)

There is no way of correlating such percentages or even comparing them, although they do indeed show an increasing incidence of premarital intercourse among women as well as men, but in any case, like most social statistics, they merely document the obvious. Obvious, that is, to anyone who has gone through the last two or three decades with his eyes open. Education, Kinsey concluded, was a bigger factor in increased premarital sexual activity than religion, but this can only mean that as the educational level rises, churchgoing and religious allegiances fall, so that the one index is just about as useful as the other, and probably follows it closely. Churchmen are in some cases inclined to "reevaluate" their position, as where Dr. Roger Shinn of Union Theological Seminary writes:

> A good deal of the old repressiveness is gone—what we generally associate with the word Puritanism. Arising out of Biblical scholarship of the last twenty years is the recognition that the Bible's attitude toward sex is affirmative and that the repressive attitude is really a heresy. Sex is God-given, and man realizes himself through it.[11]

---

[11] "The Second Sexual Revolution," *Time* Magazine, Vol. LXXXIII, No. 4 (January 24, 1964), pp. 42–43.

It would surely come as a surprise, and a somewhat confusing one, I suspect, to such luminaries of the Higher Criticism as Archibald Henry Sayce, Julius Wellhausen and Henry Preserved Smith, all of whom have now gone to whatever reward the Author of the Word of God has in store for his critics, to learn that they are being credited with the decline of Puritanism and the restorers of sex to its God-given function. They might even be expected to take issue with Dr. Shinn's premise, that the new permissiveness "arose" out of biblical scholarship, or that the Bible's attitude toward sex is affirmative. Nothing in my own interviews or any that I have read in the work of others indicates that the scholarship of the Bible critics in this century or the last had any such effect on anybody, except perhaps on other Bible scholars.

Puritanism has become the whipping boy of the Counter-Reformation, but it is only an exercise in lip-service to moral reform. So far as institutional rules, censorship laws and religious teachings and sermons are concerned, they are still under the dead hand of Cotton Mather. If sex is God-given it is also God-regulated, and in practice that means subject to the moral code of the Judeo-Christian ethos. Denominations differ in the details of its application but none has come out in favor of premarital sex. The few clergymen who have let slip so much as a guarded hint of it have been set upon by their fellow clergymen and superiors. Even the liberal clergy has never accepted the evidence that sexual repression of *any* kind is dangerous to health. Sex may be God-given in the eyes of a few "forward-looking" clergymen, but marriage is still the God-ordained condition of the gift.

Meanwhile the outstanding fact of sex life in our time is the increase of unmarried sex, not as a preparation for marriage but as an end in itself. In effect it does, of course, prepare boys and girls for a more successful sex life in marriage, but only if they succeed before marriage in wriggling out of the straitjacket of guilt, fear and psycho-physical armoring. Permissiveness is no guarantee of sexual freedom on the genital level. Complete freedom of action on the social level is no guarantee of freedom on the sexual level. It is not the frequency of the orgasm but the quality of the orgasm that matters. Reich is explicit on this point. Orgasm anxiety may continue even in the most permissive situation and regardless of how active the individual may be.

As distinguished from the pyschoneurotic stasis of the orgasm, the healthy natural orgasm is marked by tension, charge, discharge, relaxation, with involuntary, unforced pelvic action and a pleasurable backflow of biosexual energy.

Does this mean that natural, uninhibited orgasm can be achieved only by resorting to a longer or shorter period of analytical therapy? Not at all. Despite the social and religious booby-traps there are young men and women who have matured naturally into normal self-regulated sexuality. How did they do it? As often as not it was simply a case of being let alone during infancy and puberty to explore, experiment and discover for oneself what the organism needs. Instinct is a good teacher if one is left free to follow it. But sex is an art as well as an instinct. If one has been left to develop instinctually during the pre-pubertal years, one stands a good chance of finding a proper teacher of the arts of love and sex when he or she is ready for such instruction. At the college level it is sometimes—more often than the formal "studies" of the subject would lead one to believe—a teacher. Or a post-graduate student who doubles in the arts of love and sex. I introduce the word love here because at the college level, or, in off-campus life, the feeling of love begins to have a mature meaning for the orgastically healthy young man or woman.

Arnold Toynbee, who views with alarm the Erotic Revolution of our time because he sees it as the spread of non-Western sexual mores that Western society condemned with good reason, wants to return to the Victorian ethic and advocates the postponement of sexual awakening and sexual experience beyond the age of puberty. In the trend toward early sexual experience he sees only a return to the biological limitations which man inherited from his prehuman animal ancestors, and speaks of sex as "a still more awkward feature of our biological inheritance than death." Later we shall have occasion to examine sex among our prehuman ancestors, in the light of what we know now about the bio-sexual function of the orgasm, but for the present it will be enough to suggest to Mr. Toynbee that he look into the scholarship and achievement records of those colleges and universities where the climate is most permissive and the students still manage to make sex a major subject of study even though it is elective and not required by the curriculum. Otherwise he may yet find himself, unwittingly, on the same public platform with another celebrated historian and viewer-with-alarm, Billy Graham, who has given it as his informed opinion that Rome fell because of broken homes.

Or, if he prefers to keep his reading on at least the college level, he may turn to E. R. Dodds' *The Greeks and the Irrational* and let his eye rove over those observations on a major source of Project Pan, the rituals and therapeutics of Dionysos, "a god of joy . . . accessible to all, including even slaves, as well as those freemen who were shut out from the old gentile cults." Scholarly Mr. Toynbee may prefer Apollo, but "Apollo," Dodds tells us, "moved only in the best society, from the days when he was Hector's patron to the days when he canonized aristocratic athletes; but Dionysos was at all periods a god of the people. The joys of Dionysos had an extremely wide range, from the simple pleasures of the country bumpkin, dancing a jig on the greased wineskins, to the ecstatic bachanal. At both levels, and at all levels in between, he is Lusios, 'the Liberator'—the god who by very simple means, or by other means not so simple, enables you for a short time to *stop being yourself*, and thereby sets you free."

It is this freedom that is the goal of the Erotic Revolution on campus, off campus, before marriage and, as we have seen, *in* marriage as well.

Fred Brown
Rudolf T. Kempton

Problems of Contraception

One of the great problems in modern society is the control of pregnancy. The extent of one phase of the problem is shown by the fact that of 8,524,148 marriages between 1910 and 1930 in the United States, 1,704,830 have not yielded children. This represents about twenty per cent of the marriages. While in some cases the marriages were childless by choice, these figures probably mean that well over a million couples married during that twenty-year period were unable to have children even though they wanted them. On the other hand many couples have had children more

From: *Sex Questions and Answers* by Fred Brown & Rudolf T. Kempton. Copyright 1960 by McGraw-Hill, Inc. Used by permission of McGraw-Hill Book Company.

frequently than is best for the health and well-being of both the mother and the offspring. The general problem of control of pregnancy, therefore, has two broad aspects. First is the problem of overcoming the inability to have children. The second phase, to be considered . . . is the problem of spacing birth of children for the betterment of the entire family.

Why is the spacing of children important?

Spacing is important because modern medicine and psychology have shown that if children are born at proper intervals it is better for the physical and mental health of both the children and the parents. As a general rule it is much better to have a given number of children spaced two years apart than the same number at yearly intervals. Economic factors also enter. The cost of having and rearing children is so high, especially in the cities, that if there are many in a family there cannot be proper care for all of them. In country districts, where the children may be a help around a farm, and where the expense of housing and feeding them is not so great, there is less pressure toward small families. The seriousness of economic pressures is indicated by the fact that it is estimated that there are probably close to three hundred thousand illegal abortions each year. A large proportion of these are performed on married women. The medical dangers of this procedure are great and prevention of these pregnancies seems a much more reasonable step than this dangerous and illegal ending of pregnancies which have already taken place.

Is this a problem only in the United States?

In one way or another the problem of controlling pregnancy is world-wide. Millions of people, well distributed over the entire world, attempt to control pregnancy. It is not a new situation, for there are records of contraceptive methods two thousand years ago. Birth rates which are too high or too low cause very serious national and international problems, some of which have led directly to war.

How does pregnancy normally take place?

Normally pregnancy occurs following sexual intercourse which has taken place within a day or two of ovulation. Sperm cells deposited in the upper end of the vagina find their way into the uterus and up the Fallopian tubes. When the egg leaves the ovary, it is then quickly fertilized and slowly passes along the tube to the uterus, where development takes place.

Can pregnancy take place without sexual intercourse?

Normally sexual intercourse is necessary for pregnancy to occur. In artificial insemination, the sperm cells are introduced by instruments used by a physician and no intercourse is involved. This question arises more frequently, however, in regard to semen which has come in contact with the external genitalia of the female; or in some cases there is worry lest sperm cells be introduced into the vagina on the fingers. It is unlikely that either situation will lead to pregnancy. Study of sterility has shown that large numbers of sperm cells must be introduced near the upper end of the vagina in order to ensure pregnancy. In these cases the smaller numbers entering the vagina and their position near the entrance tend to rule out the likelihood of fertilization of the egg. In addition, if a thin film of semen is spread on the fingers, evaporation is very rapid. This would cause death of the sperm cells even before the semen was fully dry.

Does the fluid which collects at the tip of the penis during sexual excitement contain sperm cells? What is its function?

This fluid does not usually contain sperm cells but sometimes it may contain a few. There is little likelihood of pregnancy from this source because of the small number of sperm cells.

The fluid which appears during an erection is produced by small glands. They are in the wall of that part of the urethra which passes along the penis. The urethra carries both urine and sperm cells at different times. The function of these secretions is to neutralize any traces of urine which may be in the urethra, so that its presence cannot damage sperm cells when ejaculation takes place.

Why not control pregnancy simply by not having sexual intercourse?

Total abstinence from sexual intercourse certainly would prevent pregnancy but its effect on the married couple psychologically and physiologically would be very serious. Lack of sexual intercourse in the unmarried causes no serious damage but in marriage, with constant sexual stimulus, refraining from having sexual intercourse would be certain to have harmful effects. This is not a desirable or practicable way of controlling pregnancy. The fact that in most states a lack of intercourse is considered a cause for annulment of a marriage indicates the viewpoint of society toward such an abnormal situation.

Are there any natural methods of controlling pregnancy?

If by "natural" methods are understood those in which no artificial appliances are used, we can consider that there are three widely used methods of this kind. They are: having sexual intercourse in such a way that the male never reaches a climax and does not have an ejaculation (coitus reservatus); the sudden withdrawal of the penis just before ejaculation, so that the semen is emitted outside the vagina (coitus interruptus); and engaging in sexual intercourse only at the time in the menstrual cycle when pregnancy is presumably not possible (rhythm method or "safe period").

The first of the three is to be condemned. There is a very strong feeling among physicians that this practice of not reaching a climax leads to serious difficulties with the prostate and other glands. The withdrawal method is not highly recommended. It requires good judgment as to when the ejaculation is about to occur, a considerable amount of will power to withdraw at that moment, and the psychological effects of the sudden interruption of intercourse are considered undesirable. This is true especially if the woman has not undergone an orgasm.

The rhythm method has many advocates. Where women have regular menstrual cycles and where suitable precautions have been taken in estimating the "safe period," it seems to be satisfactory. It has the advantage of placing the contraception in the hands of the woman; it requires no appliances; and it permits entirely normal sexual intercourse with no disturbing factors before, during, or afterward.

What is the basis for the rhythm method of contraception?

This method is based on the fact that there is only a short period each month during which a woman can become pregnant. Probably conception can take place only for about forty-eight hours before and forty-eight hours after ovulation. In women who menstruate with perfect regularity ovulation may be expected fourteen days before the first day of the next menstrual period. Theoretically conception could take place only two days before and two days after this time. To be safer one can allow four days each side of ovulation. This is because there is some variation in the time of ovulation and four days will take in most of the cases.

However, very few women are perfectly regular. As a whole they are more irregular during adolescence and as menopause approaches; between these two periods the irregularities are less. Yet among those women who think of themselves as being regular there may be much variation. Four-fifths of all women may vary as much as five days or more in the length of cycle, and some as much as eight or nine days.

With this irregularity how is it possible to predict the day of ovulation and to use the rhythm method of control?

With a moderate amount of irregularity the rhythm method can still be used by making two estimates each month, one based on the earliest day menstruation might be expected to start, the other based on the latest day. In both cases subtract fourteen days to get the probable time of ovulation, then assume that there should be no intercourse during the four days on each side of this date. If one is not particularly concerned with safety, the four days may be cut to three, or even to two. To obtain maximum protection, however, one should allow the full four days. This double estimation allows for variation in the length of cycle; four days allows for variation in the time of ovulation.

1	2	3	4	5	6	7
8	9	10	11	12	13	14
15	16	17	18	19	20	21
22	23	24	25	26	27	28
29	30	31				

For example, if a woman has a variation from 25 days to 30 days, and if she started to menstruate on the first day of the month, then the earliest time for prediction of the start of the next period would be the 26th, the latest the 31st. Using the shorter time, and counting on the calendar given above, fourteen days before the 26th would be the 12th. Counting back from the 31st would give the 17th as the latest day for ovulation. Counting four days on each side of the 12th and 17th would give a period from the 8th to the 21st, inclusive, as the time when conception might take place. If safety were sacrificed somewhat, this might be cut to three days, from the 9th to the 20th. Therefore the dates which are *not underlined on the chart* should be safe for sexual intercourse without danger of pregnancy.

This method shortens the "safe period" but it takes into account not only the individual variations in the day of ovulation but also the complete range in variation of the individual's menstrual cycle. Methods which do not take both of these variables into consideration are liable to fail.

Before starting the use of this method it is desirable that a record be kept of the exact time of menstruation extending over a period of at least a year. The record should be kept month by month while the method is used. If a shorter or longer cycle should appear, this should be used in future calculations.

When it is desired to have a child, it is well to use a few months in experimenting to see if three, or even two, days before and after ovulation are enough to allow.

It is the possibility of sudden and unpredictable changes in the cycle which gives the method its degree of uncertainty even when practiced as outlined here.

Are plugs for the uterus advisable?

There are a large number of such appliances and the whole group can be eliminated immediately. Plugs are appliances which are inserted into the opening of the uterus from the vagina. Many of them are designed to be left in place over long periods, even a year or more at a time. They are based on the theory that they will prevent semen from entering the uterus. Their use is dangerous because they may cause serious injury to the uterus, may lead to abortions, and can contribute to the formation of cancer.

What are condoms and how are they used?

The condom is a thin sheath worn over the penis. It may be made of rubber or thin animal tissue ("fish skin"). The former should be discarded after being used once, but the latter may be rinsed, dried, and used repeatedly. The rubber type is probably preferable. The "fish-skin" condom has to be moistened before use. Not only does this cause a disagreeable interruption but the moisture is often unpleasant to the woman. In addition, because it is not elastic it fits loosely, and in the sexual movements it may slip off the penis. It is often advisable to use a non-greasy lubricating material on the outside of the condom; and if the condom chafes the glans of the penis, a small amount should also be applied to this part before the condom is put on.

Certain precautions should be observed in using condoms. They should be tested before using and after use. The rubber condom can be blown up like a balloon before being used and can be examined for small holes by holding it in front of a light. By filling it with water, the fish-skin condom can be tested for leaks. This method of testing can also be used for the rubber condom after use. In case a leak is found after use, it is well for the woman to use an antiseptic douche. Unless the condom is really torn, there is probably not a great deal of danger of pregnancy. If torn badly, however, the danger is as great as it would have been without the condom. How much the douche will help in this case is not certain but it is about all that can be done.

As a whole, the condom is one of the safest of the contraceptive methods. It has the added advantage that this is the only form of contraception which provides the male with protection against infection. This is not of concern merely in venereal disease, but, as has been mentioned before, is of value if sexual intercourse is carried on during the menstrual period.

What are vaginal diaphragms?

Diaphragms are appliances which are worn by the woman and which form a cover over the opening into the uterus from the vagina, thus keeping out sperm cells. Because a close seal around the edges cannot be made, the diaphragm is covered before insertion with a special jelly or crème containing substances which kill sperm cells. The appliance may be inserted hours before use, and must be allowed to remain in position long enough for the jelly to kill the sperm (6-8 hours). It is recommended that a douche be taken when the diaphragm is removed, but this is for hygienic purposes rather than as a contraceptive measure.

One of the advantages of this method is that the appliance may be placed in position hours before use and therefore its insertion is not a disturbing factor in the period of sexual excitement. Secondly, when it is fitted by a qualified physician and *used with intelligent care*, it has a very high record of reliability.

Intelligent use involves several factors. The correct size must be selected to give a proper fit. It should therefore always be fitted by a physician experienced in contraceptive methods. It should never be simply purchased from a drugstore where one can only guess at the proper size and can get no instructions in proper methods of use. Such teaching is given, however, in Planned Parenthood Clinics, which are found in most counties. In the event that the location of the nearest clinic is not known, a letter to the Planned Parenthood Federation of America, Inc., 501 Madison Avenue, New York 22, New York, will give the writer this information. Reexamination every six months is another intelligent precaution encouraged by Planned Parenthood Clinics. This examination is very valuable in detecting abnormalities of the uterus and other organs in early stages when treatment is most simple and also most effective, besides ensuring proper fit and condition of the diaphragm.

How are sponges used in contraception?

The use of a sponge is sometimes suggested when diaphragms cannot be fitted. They are made of either natural or artificial material and are inserted in the vagina, usually with a thread attached to aid in their later removal. Before insertion the sponge is saturated with one of a large number of substances which are designed to destroy sperm cells. These come in the form of powders, jellies, and foams. This method is frequently unsatisfactory.

Are douches a satisfactory method of birth control?

As a method of birth control douches have one great fallacy. In the douche, warm water containing a substance which supposedly can kill sperm cells on contact with them is introduced into the vagina. Since some time necessarily must elapse between the ejaculation and the douche, sperm cells may have already entered the uterus. Furthermore, unless the douche is properly taken with precautions to distend the vagina, millions of living sperm cells may lodge in the folds of the vagina. Later they may enter the uterus.

Another objection to douches as a contraceptive method is that they interfere with the complete relaxation which is considered desirable following sexual intercourse.

If douches are used, the precaution should be taken to distend the vagina. This can be done by using the type of douching appliance which permits the fluid to flow into the vagina but retards its outflow. Lacking this, the same effect can be obtained with some difficulty by holding together the lips of the external genitalia for a short time while the fluid is running into the vagina. The low pressure distends the vagina enough to ensure the penetration of the fluid to all parts.

Douches are considered more effective if taken while lying down. However, with most people, this seems to be impracticable when taken for contraceptive purposes.

Are there any methods of applying chemical substances other than by douches?

There are many methods. Sponges have already been mentioned. Jellies, substances which form a foam in the vagina, and suppositories are all used. They are designed to produce, before intercourse, a film over the surface of the vagina and cervix. In addition, foam is designed to form a mechanical barrier to the movement of sperm cells. The difficulty common to all substances of this group is that they may not cover all the parts adequately and so fail to give complete protection. Some jellies are slow to spread; some foams last only a very short period before the bubbles disappear; and some suppositories have too high a melting point and resist melting for a period of hours.

What other methods of contraception are there?

It is difficult to make a complete listing. X rays have been used in an attempt to produce temporary sterility. While in some cases this appears to be successful, there is danger of permanent sterility when this method is used. Also there is a theoretical possibility that an egg cell might not be killed, but only so changed by the X rays that an abnormal child might be produced. Attempts have been made to produce a temporary immunity to sperm cells by inoculating the woman with sperm cells or an extract made from them. This is like inoculating against diseases. The process is intended to induce the female body to produce substances which kill sperm cells introduced into the vagina. These attempts so far cannot be called successful.

Is it possible to sterilize a person in such a way that the sexual characteristics are not lost?

This can be done very easily in the male and with somewhat more difficulty in the female. The procedure has no effect on the sexual mechanism other than producing sterility. But this sterility is permanent. In the male all that is necessary is to make a small incision in the scrotum and to tie the vas deferens and cut it. This is done on both sides. It is done under a local anesthetic, takes only a few minutes, and does not incapacitate the patient in any degree. In the female it is more difficult. Formerly it was necessary to open the abdomen and tie the Fallopian tubes. Now it is possible to dilate the cervix of the uterus, pass instruments into the uterus, and cauterize (burn) the opening of each tube. The scar tissue that forms is an effective barrier to the passage of sperm cells into the Fallopian tubes and therefore conception cannot take place. These operations do not produce any changes in sexual desire or the ability to carry on sexual intercourse.

Is it better psychologically for the woman or the man to have control of contraception?

Authorities are in agreement that it is better, other things being equal, for contraception to be in the hands of the woman. This is because she bears the main brunt of failure of the method. If the male has been practicing the contraception, and there is an undesired pregnancy, there is a tendency for the woman to blame him, with resulting strained relationships.

What is the effectiveness of the various contraceptive methods?

The effectiveness of any method (except complete sterilization) depends upon the people using it; without care the best method may yield poor results, and with the greatest care the poorer methods may give better results than indicated below.

Some recent figures give an idea of the relative value of the different methods:

Condom: average of reports gives a value of 95 per cent effective, with some reports as low as 70 per cent. The manufacture is now under government supervision and there are fewer failures due to tearing and to defects.

Diaphragm and jelly: average reports 90 per cent effective with a range from 85 to 95 percent in different clinics. In one report on private patients the effectiveness ran higher, with only one failure reported in 1,600 uses.

Jelly or crème alone (without a diaphragm): there are insufficient data to give a reliable estimate.

Foam powders on sponges: estimated as 55 to 95 per cent effective. As further study of the method is made the estimates are falling rather than rising.

Withdrawal: reports from 35 to 80 per cent effective. To an even higher degree than with the other methods, the results are dependent largely upon the user. This, as pointed out before, is one of the disadvantages of the method.

Douche: 16 to 70 per cent effective. In other words this is the least reliable of the methods for which there are good data.

Suppositories: no reliable information applying to the United States. English reports indicate the results are "good." However, part of this may be due to the fact that in England suppositories of a lower melting point can be used than in the United States, where the higher air temperatures cause the English type of suppository to melt on the druggist's shelf.

Garrett Hardin

Abortion—or Compulsory Pregnancy?

The problem of abortion is usually seen as one of justifying a particular surgical operation on the assumption that great social loss is incurred by it. This approach leads to intractable administrative problems: rape is in principle impossible to prove, the paternity of a child is always in doubt, the probability of defective embryos is generally low, and the socioeconomic predicament of the supplicant has little power to move the men who sit in judgment. These difficulties vanish when one substitutes for the problem of permissive abortion the inverse problem of compulsory pregnancy. The latter is a special case of compulsory servitude, which the

From: Garrett Hardin, "Abortion—or Compulsory Pregnancy?" *Journal of Marriage and the Family*, 30:2 (May, 1968), pp. 246-251. Reprinted by permission.

Western world has agreed, in principle, has no valid justification.
Unfortunately, state legislatures are now in a process of setting up
systems for the management of compulsory pregnancy. The ex-
perience of Scandinavia indicates that women do not accept bu-
reaucratic management of their unwanted pregnancies; therefore
we can confidently predict that the reform bills now going through
our legislatures will have little effect on the practice of illegal
abortion. Only the abolition of compulsory pregnancy will solve
the erroneously conceived "abortion problem."

The year 1967 produced the first fissures in the dam that had prevented all change in the abortion-prohibition laws of the United States for three-quarters of a century. Two states adopted laws that allowed abortion in the "hardship cases" of rape, incest, and probability of a deformed child. A third approved the first two "indications," but not the last. All three took some note of the mental health of the pregnant woman, in varying language; how this language will be translated into practice remains to be seen. In almost two dozen other states, attempts to modify the laws were made but foundered at various stages in the legislative process. It is quite evident that the issue will continue to be a live one for many years to come.

The legislative turmoil was preceded and accompanied by a fast-growing popular literature. The word "abortion" has ceased to be a dirty word—which is a cultural advance. However, the *word* was so long under taboo that the ability to think about the *fact* seems to have suffered a sort of logical atrophy from disuse. Popular articles, regardless of their conclusions, tend to be over-emotional and to take a moralistic rather than an operational view of the matter. Nits are picked, hairs split. It is quite clear that many of the authors are not at all clear what question they are attacking.

It is axiomatic in science that progress hinges on asking the right question. Surprisingly, once the right question is asked the answer seems almost to tumble forth. That is a retrospective view; in prospect, it takes genuine (and mysterious) insight to see correctly into the brambles created by previous, ill-chosen verbalizations.

The abortion problem is, I think, a particularly neat example of a problem in which most of the difficulties are actually created by asking the wrong question. I submit further that once the right question is asked the whole untidy mess miraculously dissolves, leaving in its place a very simple public policy recommendation.

Rape as a Justification

The wrong question, the one almost invariably asked, is this: "How can we justify an abortion?" This assumes that there are weighty public reasons for encouraging pregnancies, or that abortions, per se, somehow threaten public peace. A direct examination of the legitimacy of these assumptions will be made later. For the present, let us pursue the question as asked and see what a morass it leads to.

Almost all the present legislative attempts take as their model a bill proposed by the American Law Institute which emphasizes three justifications for legal abortion: rape, incest, and the probability of a defective child. Whatever else may be said about this bill, it is clear that it affects only the periphery of the social problem. The Arden House Conference Committee[1] estimated the number of illegal abortions in the United States to be between 200,000 and 1,200,000 per year. A California legislator, Anthony C. Beilenson,[2] has estimated that the American Law Institute bill (which he favors) would legalize not more than four percent of the presently illegal abortions. Obviously, the "problem" of illegal abortion will be scarcely affected by the passage of the laws so far proposed in the United States.

I have calculated[3] that the number of rape-induced pregnancies in the United States is about 800 per year. The number is not large, but for the woman raped the total number is irrelevant. What matters to her is that she be relieved of her unwanted burden. But a law which puts the burden of proof on her compels her to risk a second harrowing experience. How can she *prove* to the district attorney that she was raped? He could really know whether or not she gave consent only if he could get inside her mind; this he cannot do. Here is the philosopher's "egocentric predicament" that none of us can escape. In an effort to help the district attorney sustain the illusion that he can escape this predicament, a talented woman may put on a dramatic performance, with copious tears and other signs of anguish. But what if the raped woman is not an actress? What if her temperament is stoic?

---

[1] Mary Steichen Calderone (ed.), *Abortion in the United States,* New York: Hoeber-Harper, 1958, p. 178.

[2] Anthony C. Beilenson, "Abortion and Common Sense," *Per/Se,* 1 (1966), p. 24.

[3] Garrett Hardin, "Semantic Aspects of Abortion," *ETC.,* 24 (1967), p. 263.

In its operation, the law will act against the interests of calm, undramatic women. Is that what we want? It is safe to say also that district attorneys will hear less favorably the pleas of poor women, the general assumption of middle-class agents being that the poor are less responsible in sex anyway.[4] Is it to the interest of society that the poor bear more children, whether rape-engendered or not?

A wryly amusing difficulty has been raised with respect to rape. Suppose the woman is married and having regular intercourse with her husband. Suppose that following a rape by an unknown intruder she finds herself pregnant. Is she legally entitled to an abortion? How does she know whose child she is carrying anyway? If it is her husband's child, abortion is illegal. If she carries it to term, and if blood tests then exclude the husband as the father, as they would in a fraction of the cases, is the woman then entitled to a *delayed* abortion? But this is ridiculous: this is infanticide, which no one is proposing. Such is the bramble bush into which we are led by a *reluctant* consent for abortion in cases of rape.

How Probable Must Deformity Be?

The majority of the public support abortion in cases of a suspected deformity of the child[5] just as they do in cases of rape. Again, however, if the burden of proof rests on the one who requests the operation, we encounter difficulties in administration. Between 80,000 and 160,000 defective children are born every year in the United States. The number stated depends on two important issues: (a) how severe a defect must be before it is counted as such and (b) whether or not one counts as birth defects those defects that are not *detected* until later. (Deafness and various other defects produced by fetal rubella may not be detected until a year or so after birth.) However many defective infants there may be, what is the prospect of detecting them before birth?

The sad answer is: the prospects are poor. A small percentage can be picked up by microscopic examination of tissues of the fetus. But "amniocentesis"—the form of biopsy required to procure such

---

[4] Lee Rainwater, *And the Poor Get Children*, Chicago: Quadrangle Books, 1960, p. *ix* and chap. 1.
[5] Alice S. Rossi, "Abortion Laws and Their Victims," *Trans-action*, 3 (September-October, 1966), p. 7.

tissues—is itself somewhat dangerous to both mother and fetus; most abnormalities will not be detectable by a microscopic examination of the fetal cells; and 96 to 98 percent of all fetuses are normal anyway. All these considerations are a contra-indication of routine amniocentesis.

When experience indicates that the probability of a deformed fetus is above the "back-ground level" of 2 to 4 percent, is abortion justified? At what level? 10 percent? 50? 80? Or only at 100 percent? Suppose a particular medical history indicates a probability of 20 percent that the baby will be defective. If we routinely abort such cases, it is undeniable that four normal fetuses will be destroyed for every one abnormal. Those who assume that a fetus is an object of high value are appalled at this "wastage." Not uncommonly they ask, "Why not wait until the baby is born and then suffocate those that are deformed?" Such a question is unquestionably rhetoric and sardonic; if serious, it implies that infanticide has no more emotional meaning to a woman than abortion, an assumption that is surely contrary to fact.

Should the Father Have Rights?

Men who are willing to see abortion-prohibition laws relaxed somewhat, but not completely, frequently raise a question about the "rights" of the father. Should we allow a woman to make a unilateral decision for an abortion? Should not her husband have a say in the matter? (After all, he contributed just as many chromosomes to the fetus as she.)

I do not know what weight to give this objection. I have encountered it repeatedly in the discussion section following a public meeting. It is clear that some men are disturbed at finding themselves powerless in such a situation and want the law to give them some power of decision.

Yet powerless men are—and it is nature that has made them so. If we give the father a right of veto in abortion decisions, the wife has a very simple reply to her husband: "I'm sorry, dear, I wasn't going to tell you this, but you've forced my hand. This is not your child." With such a statement she could always deny her husband's right to decide.

Why husbands should demand power in such matters is a fit subject for depth analysis. In the absence of such, perhaps the best thing we can say to men who are "hung up" on this issue is this: "Do you really want to live for another eight months with a woman whom you are compelling to be pregnant against her will?"

Or, in terms of public policy, do we want to pass laws which give men the right to compel their wives to be pregnant? Psychologically, such compulsion is akin to rape. Is it in the public interest to encourage rape?

"Socio-Economic"—An Anemic Phrase

The question "How can we justify an abortion?" proves least efficient in solving the real problems of this world when we try to evaluate what are usually called "socio-economic indications." The hardship cases—rape, incest, probability of a deformed child—have been amply publicized, and as a result the majority of the public accepts them as valid indicators; but hardship cases constitute only a few percent of the need. By contrast, if a woman has more children than she feels she can handle, or if her children are coming too close together, there is little public sympathy for her plight. A poll conducted by the National Opinion Research Center in December, 1965, showed that only 15 percent of the respondents replied "Yes" to this question: "Please tell me whether or not you think it should be possible for a pregnant woman to obtain a legal abortion if she is married and does not want any more children." Yet this indication, which received the lowest rate of approval, accounts for the vast majority of instances in which women want— and illegally get—relief from unwanted pregnancy.

There is a marked discrepancy between the magnitude of the need and the degree of public sympathy. Part of the reason for this discrepancy is attributable to the emotional impact of the words used to describe the need. "Rape," "incest," "deformed child"— these words are rich in emotional connotations. "Socio-economic indications" is a pale bit of jargon, suggesting at best that the abortion is wanted because the woman lives by culpably materialistic standards. "Socio-economic indications" tugs at no one's heartstrings; the hyphenated abomination hides the human reality to which it obliquely refers. To show the sort of human problem to which this label may be attached, let me quote a letter I received from one woman. (The story is unique, but it is one of a large class of similar true stories.)

> I had an illegal abortion 2½ years ago. I left my church because of the guilt I felt. I had six children when my husband left me to live with another woman. We weren't divorced and I went to

work to help support them. When he would come to visit the children he would sometimes stay after they were asleep. I became pregnant. When I told my husband, and asked him to please come back, he informed me that the woman he was living with was five months pregnant and ill, and that he couldn't leave her—not at that time anyway.

I got the name of a doctor in San Francisco from a Dr. friend who was visiting here from there. This Dr. (Ob. and Gyn.) had a good legitimate practice in the main part of the city and was a kindly, compassionate man who believes as you do, that it is better for everyone not to bring an unwanted child into the world.

It was over before I knew it. I thought I was just having an examination at the time. He even tried to make me not feel guilty by telling me that the long automobile trip had already started a spontaneous abortion. He charged me $25. That was on Fri. and on Mon. I was back at work. I never suffered any ill from it.

The other woman's child died shortly after birth and six months later my husband asked if he could come back. We don't have a perfect marriage but my children have a father. My being able to work has helped us out of a deep financial debt. I shall always remember the sympathy I received from that Dr. and wish there were more like him with the courage to do what they believe is right.

Her operation was illegal, and would be illegal under most of the "reform" legislation now being proposed, if interpreted strictly. Fortunately some physicians are willing to indulge in more liberal interpretations, but they make these interpretations not on medical grounds, in the strict sense, but on social and economic grounds. Understandably, many physicians are unwilling to venture so far from the secure base of pure physical medicine. As one Catholic physician put it:

Can the patient afford to have another child? Will the older children have sufficient educational opportunities if their parents have another child? Aren't two, three or four children enough? I am afraid such statements are frequently made in the discussion of a proposed therapeutic abortion. [But] we should be doctors of medicine, not socio-economic prophets.[6]

To this a non-Catholic physician added: "I sometimes wish I were an obstetrician in a Catholic hospital so that I would not have to make any of these decisions. The only position to take in which I would have no misgivings is to do no interruptions at all."[7]

---

[6] Calderone (ed.), *op. cit.*, p. 103.
[7] *Ibid.*, p. 123.

Who Wants Compulsory Pregnancy?

The question "How can we justify an abortion?" plainly leads to great difficulties. It is operationally unmanageable: it leads to inconsistencies in practice and inequities by any moral standard. All these can be completely avoided if we ask the right question, namely: *"How can we justify compulsory pregnancy?"*

By casting the problem in this form, we call attention to its relationship to the slavery issue. Somewhat more than a century ago men in the Western world asked the question: "How can we justify compulsory servitude?" and came up with the answer: *"By no means whatever."* Is the answer any different to the related question: "How can we justify compulsory pregnancy?" Certainly pregnancy is a form of servitude; if continued to term it results in parenthood, which is also a kind of servitude, to be continued for the best years of a woman's life. It is difficult to see how it can be argued that this kind of servitude will be more productive of social good if it is compulsory rather than voluntary. A study[8] made of Swedish children born when their mothers were refused the abortions they had requested showed that unwanted children, as compared with their controls, as they grew up were more often picked up for drunkenness, or antisocial or criminal behavior; they received less education; they received more psychiatric care; and they were more often exempted from military service by reason of defect. Moreover, the females in the group married earlier and had children earlier, thus no doubt tending to create a vicious circle of poorly tended children who in their turn would produce more poorly tended children. How then does society gain by increasing the number of unwanted children? No one has volunteered an answer to this question.

Alternatives: True and False

Of course if there were a shortage of children, then society might say that it needs all the children it can get—unwanted or not. But I am unaware of any recent rumors of a shortage of children.

---

[8] Hans Forssman and Inga Thuwe, "One Hundred and Twenty Children Born after Application for Therapeutic Abortion Refused," *Acta Psychiatrica Scandinavica*, 42 (1966), p. 71.

The end result of an abortion—the elimination of an unwanted fetus—is surely good. But is the act itself somehow damaging? For several generations it was widely believed that abortion was intrinsically dangerous, either physically or psychologically. It is now very clear that the widespread belief is quite unjustified. The evidence for this statement is found in a bulky literature which has been summarized in Lawrence Lader's *Abortion*[9] and the collection of essays brought together by Alan Guttmacher.[10]

In tackling questions of this sort, it is imperative that we identify correctly the alternatives facing us. (All moral and practical problems involve a comparison of alternative actions.) Many of the arguments of the prohibitionists implicitly assume that the alternatives facing the woman are these:

abortion——*no abortion*

This is false. A person can never do nothing. The pregnant woman is going to do something, whether she wishes to or not. (She cannot roll time backward and live her life over.)

People often ask: "Isn't contraception better than abortion?" Implied by this question are these alternatives:

abortion——*contraception*

But these are not the alternatives that face the woman who asks to be aborted. She *is* pregnant. She cannot roll time backward and use contraception more successfully than she did before. Contraceptives are never foolproof anyway. It is commonly accepted that the failure rate of our best contraceptive, the "pill," is around one percent, i.e., one failure per hundred woman-years of use. I have earlier shown[11] that this failure rate produces about a quarter of a million unwanted pregnancies a year in the United States. Abortion is not so much an alternative to contraception as it is a subsidiary method of birth control, to be used when the primary method fails—as it often does.

The woman *is* pregnant: this is the base level at which the moral decision begins. If she is pregnant against her will, does it matter to society whether or not she was careless or unskillful in her use of contraception? In any case, she is threatening society with an unwanted child, for which society will pay dearly. The real alternatives facing the woman (and society) are clearly these:

---

[9] Lawrence Lader, *Abortion,* Indianapolis: Bobbs-Merrill, 1966.
[10] Alan F. Guttmacher (ed.), *The Case for Legalized Abortion,* Berkeley, California: Diablo Press, 1967.
[11] Garrett Hardin, "A Scientist's Case for Abortion," *Redbook* (May 1967), p. 62.

abortion————*compulsory pregnancy*
When we recognize that these are the real, operational alternatives,
the false problems created by pseudo-alternatives vanish.

Is Potential Value Valuable?

Only one weighty objection to abortion remains to be discussed,
and this is the question of "loss." When a fetus is destroyed, has
something valuable been destroyed? The fetus has the potentiality
of becoming a human being. A human being is valuable. Therefore
is not the fetus of equal value? This question must be answered.

It can be answered, but not briefly. What does the embryo
receive from its parents that might be of value? There are only
three possibilities: substance, energy, and information. As for the
substance in the fertilized egg, it is not remarkable: merely the
sort of thing one might find in any piece of meat, human or animal,
and there is very little of it—only one and a half micrograms, which
is about a half of a billionth of an ounce. The energy content of
this tiny amount of material is likewise negligible. As the zygote
develops into an embryo, both its substance and its energy content
increase (at the expense of the mother); but this is not a very
important matter—even an adult, viewed from this standpoint, is
only a hundred and fifty pounds of meat!

Clearly, the humanly significant thing that is contributed to the
zygote by the parents is the information that "tells" the fertilized
egg how to develop into a human being. This information is in the
form of a chemical tape called "DNA," a double set of two chemical
super-molecules each of which has about three billion "spots" that
can be coded with any one of four different possibilities, symbolized
by A, T, G, and C. (For comparison, the Morse code offers three
possibilities in coding: dot, dash, and space.) It is the particular
sequence of these four chemical possibilities in the DNA that
directs the zygote in its development into a human being. The
DNA constitutes the information needed to produce a valuable
human being. The question is: is this information precious? I have
argued elsewhere[12] that it is not:

> Consider the case of a man who is about to begin to build a
> $50,000 house. As he stands on the site looking at the blueprints
> a practical joker comes along and sets fire to the blueprints. The

---

[12] Garrett Hardin, "Blueprints, DNA, and Abortion: A Scientific and
Ethical Analysis," *Medical Opinion and Review*, 3:2 (1967), p. 74.

question is: can the owner go to the law and collect $50,000 for his lost blueprints? The answer is obvious: since another set of blueprints can be produced for the cost of only a few dollars, that is all they are worth. (A court might award a bit more for the loss of the owner's time, but that is a minor matter.) The moral: *a non-unique copy of information that specifies a valuable structure is itself almost valueless.*

This principle is precisely applicable to the moral problem of abortion. The zygote, which contains the complete specification of a valuable human being, is not a human being, and is almost valueless. . . . The early stages of an individual fetus have had very little human effort invested in them; they are of very little worth. The loss occasioned by an abortion is independent of whether the abortion is spontaneous or induced. (Just as the loss incurred by the burning of a set of blueprints is independent of whether the causal agent was lightning or an arsonist.)

A set of blueprints is not a house; the DNA of a zygote is not a human being. The analogy is singularly exact, though there are two respects in which it is deficient. These respects are interesting rather than important. First, we have the remarkable fact that the blueprints of the zygote are constantly replicated and incorporated in every cell of the human body. This is interesting, but it has no moral significance. There is no moral obligation to conserve DNA—if there were, no man would be allowed to brush his teeth and gums, for in this brutal operation hundreds of sets of DNA are destroyed daily.

The other anomaly of the human information problem is connected with the fact that the information that is destroyed in an aborted embryo *is* unique (unlike the house blueprints). But it is unique in a way that is without moral significance. A favorite argument of abortion-prohibitionists is this: "What if Beethoven's mother had had an abortion?" The question moves us; but when we think it over we realize we can just as relevantly ask: "What if Hitler's mother had had an abortion?" Each conceptus is unique, but not in any way that has a moral consequence. The *expected* potential value of each aborted child is exactly that of the average child born. It is meaningless to say that humanity loses when a *particular* child is not born, or is not conceived. A human female, at birth, has about 30,000 eggs in her ovaries. If she bears only 3 children in her lifetime, is there any meaningful sense in which we can say that mankind has suffered a loss in those other 29,997 fruitless eggs? (Yet one of them might have been a super-Beethoven!)

People who worry about the moral danger of abortion do so because they think of the fetus as a human being, hence equate feticide with murder. Whether the fetus is or is not a human being is a matter of definition, not fact; and we can define any way we wish. In terms of the human problem involved, it would be unwise to define the fetus as human (hence tactically unwise ever to refer to the fetus as an "unborn child"). Analysis based on the deepest insights of molecular biology indicates the wisdom of sharply distinguishing the information for a valuable structure from the completed structure itself. It is interesting, and gratifying, to note that this modern insight is completely congruent with common law governing the disposal of dead fetuses. Abortion-prohibitionists generally insist that abortion is murder, and that an embryo is a person; but no state or nation, so far as I know, requires the dead fetus to be treated like a dead person. Although all of the states in the United States severely limit what can be done with a dead human body, no cognizance is taken of dead fetuses up to about five months' prenatal life. The early fetus may, with impunity, be flushed down the toilet or thrown out with the garbage—which shows that we never have regarded it as a human being. Scientific analysis confirms what we have always known.

The Management of Compulsory Pregnancy

What is the future of compulsory pregnancy? The immediate future is not hopeful. Far too many medical people misconceive the real problem. One physician has written:

> Might not a practical, workable solution to this most difficult problem be found by setting up, in every hospital, an abortion committee comprising a specialist in obstetrics and gynecology, a psychiatrist, and a clergyman or priest? The patient and her husband—if any—would meet with these men who would do all in their power to persuade the woman not to undergo the abortion. (I have found that the promise of a postpartum sterilization will frequently enable even married women with all the children they can care for to accept this one more, final pregnancy.) If, however, the committee members fail to change the woman's mind, they can make it very clear that they disapprove of the abortion, but prefer that it be safely done in a hospital rather than bungled in a basement somewhere.[13]

What this author has in mind is plainly not a system of legalizing abortion but a system of managing compulsory pregnancy. It

---

[13] H. Curtis Wood, Jr., "Letter to the Editor," *Medical Opinion and Review,* 3:11 (1967), p. 19.

is this philosophy which governs pregnancies in the Scandinavian countries,[14] where the experience of a full generation of women has shown that women do not want their pregnancies to be managed by the state. Illegal abortions have remained at a high level in these countries, and recent years have seen the development of a considerable female tourist trade to Poland, where abortions are easy to obtain. Unfortunately, American legislatures are now proposing to follow the provably unworkable system of Scandinavia.

The drift down this erroneous path is not wholly innocent. Abortion-prohibitionists are showing signs of recognizing "legalization" along Scandinavian lines as one more roadblock that can be thrown in the way of the abolition of compulsory pregnancy. To cite an example: on February 9, 1966, the *Courier*, a publication of the Winona, Minnesota Diocese, urged that Catholics support a reform law based on the American Law Institute model, because the passage of such a law would "take a lot of steam out of the abortion advocate's argument" and would "defeat a creeping abortionism of disastrous importance."[15]

Wherever a Scandinavian or American Law Institute type of bill is passed, it is probable that cautious legislators will then urge a moratorium for several years while the results of the new law are being assessed (though they are easily predictable from the Scandinavian experience). As Lord Morley once said: "Small reforms are the worst enemies of great reforms." Because of the backwardness of education in these matters, caused by the long taboo under which the subject of abortion labored, it seems highly likely that our present system of compulsory pregnancy will continue substantially without change until the true nature of the alternatives facing us is more widely recognized.

---

[14] David T. Smith (ed.), *Abortion and the Law*, Cleveland: Western Reserve University, 1967, p. 179.

[15] Anonymous, *Association for the Study of Abortion Newsletter*, 2:3 (1967), p. 6.

William Masters
Virginia Johnson

The Clitoris

1. Anatomy and Physiology

The clitoris is a unique organ in the total of human anatomy. Its express purpose is to serve both as a receptor and transformer ✓ of sensual stimuli. Thus, the human female has an organ system which is totally limited in physiologic function to initiating or elevating levels of sexual tension. No such organ exists within the anatomic structure of the human male.

Conceptualization of the role of the clitoris in female sexual response has created a literature that is a potpourri of behavioral concept unsupported by biologic fact. Decades of "phallic fallacies" have done more to deter than to stimulate research interest in

From: William Masters and Virginia Johnson, *Human Sexual Response,* Boston: Little, Brown and Company, 1966. Reprinted by permission.

clitoral response to sexual stimulation. Unfortunately, the specific roles previously assigned clitoral function in female sexual response were designated by objective male consideration uninfluenced by and even uninformed by female subjective expression.

In the past, anatomic dissection, microscopic examination, and surgical ablation of the clitoris have established the organ as a homologue of the male penis. The clitoris consists of two corpora cavernosa enclosed in a dense membrane primarily of fibrous-tissue origin. This capsule has recently been shown to contain elastic fibers and smooth-muscle bundles. The fibrous capsules unite along their medial surfaces to form a pectiniform septum which is well interspersed with elastic and smooth-muscle fibers. Each corpus is connected to the rami of the pubis and ischium by a crus. The clitoris is provided (as is the penis) with a suspensory ligament which is inserted along the anterior surface of the midline septum. In addition, two small muscles, the ischiocavernosus muscles, insert into the crura of the clitoris and have origin bilaterally from the ischial rami.

The dorsal nerve of the clitoris is very small and is the deepest division of the pudendal nerve. It terminates in a plexus of nerve endings within the substance of the glans and the corpora cavernosa. Dahl described both myelinated and unmyelinated fibers of the somatic and vegetative nervous systems. Pacinian corpuscles are distributed irregularly throughout the autonomic system nerve fibers both in the glans and the corpora but usually have greatest concentration in the glans.

The pacinian corpuscles are concerned primarily with proprioceptive stimulation. The blood supply to the clitoris is derived from the deep and dorsal clitoral arteries, which in turn are branches of the internal pudendal artery. The arterial supply to and venous return from the clitoris follow the distribution patterns described for the penis. Although the blood supply has distribution patterns similar to that of the penis, clitoral vascularity obviously is accomplished from vessels of smaller capacity for fluid volume.

Anatomic dissection was supplemented by reported clinical mensuration of the female phallus only forty years ago. Clitoral glans size has been established at an average of 4 to 5 mm. in both the transverse and the longitudinal (less accurate) axis. One hundred adult females were used in Dickinson and Pierson's first sample. Dickinson later described clitoral position with relation to the distance between the crural origins on the anterior border of the symphysis and the urethral meatus. A mean of 2.5 cm. was reported. Marked variation has been recorded in the length of the clitoral body (glans and shaft). Frequently overlooked has been the possibility of an endocrine source for instances of hypertrophy of the organ observed clinically. Exact descriptions of points of origin of the clitoral crura on the anterior border of the symphysis or of any constant relation of crural origin to urethral meatus are an anatomic impossibility.

Aside from academic interest, Dickinson's expressed purpose in accumulating these data was to encourage clinical attempts to establish the physiology of clitoral function in female sexual response. In order to amplify his pioneer efforts, certain fundamental questions of clitoral reaction to sexual stimuli must be answered: (1) What anatomic changes occur in the clitoris during periods of sexual stimulation? (2) Are there consistent physiologic patterns of clitoral response that can be related to the descriptive framework of the four phases of the cycle of sexual response? (3) Does the clitoral body develop different response patterns during coition as opposed to those resulting from manipulation of the mons or other erogenous areas or to pure psychogenic stimulation? (4) What clinical application can be developed from the basic material accumulated to answer the first three questions? (5) Are clitoral and vaginal orgasms truly separate anatomic and physiologic entities? The questions relating to anatomy and physiology (Nos. 1-3) are approached immediately following, and the clinical questions (Nos. 4 and 5) are approached in Part 2 of this chapter.

The first two questions will be explored in sequence in order to define clitoral anatomic reaction and physiologic response to sexual stimuli within the descriptive framework of the four phases of the female cycle of sexual response.

It should be reemphasized that there normally is marked variation in the anatomic structuring of the clitoris. Clitoral glandes frequently have been measured at 2 to 3 mm. in transverse diameter, yet a glans measuring 1 cm. in transverse diameter is still within normal anatomic limits. There also is marked variation in points of origin of the crural and suspensory ligaments. These ligaments originate on the anterior surface of the symphysis but vary from the lower to the upper border. The clitoral shaft (crura and corpora) may be quite long and thin and surmounted by a relatively small-sized glans, or short and thick with an enlarged glans. Frequently the reverse of these shaft-and-glans combinations

134

has been observed. Clinical mensuration of clitoral shaft length has been so unreliable that results will not be reported.

The first pelvic response to sexual stimulation is the production of vaginal lubrication. This material appears on the walls of the vaginal barrel within 10 to 30 seconds from the onset of any form of sexual stimulation. Clitoral reaction does not develop as rapidly as the production of vaginal lubrication. Consequently the widespread belief that the clitoris responds to sexual stimulation with a rapidity equal to that of penile erection is fallacious. This physiologic misconception may have developed from the realization that anatomically the clitoris is a true homologue of the penis. It was a natural error to assume that similar anatomic structures would demonstrate parallel response patterns in a relatively equal time sequence.

The rapidity of clitoral response depends upon whether the stimulative approach is direct or indirect. The only direct approach is manipulation of the clitoral body or the mons area. There are numerous indirect stimulative techniques: manipulation of other erotic areas, coition, fantasy. If, for example, only breast or vaginal stimulation is employed (without direct clitoral contact), clitoral response will follow established patterns. However, there is a distinct delay in the onset of these patterns as opposed to the rapid reaction developed from direct stimulation of the clitoral body or the mons area.

Excitement Phase

There is a clitoral response to sexual stimulation which occurs in every responding female during the excitement phase regardless of whether there is clinically obvious tumescence of the glans. The superficial integument of the unstimulated clitoral glans is wrinkled and moves without restriction over the underlying glans tissue in manner similar to the integument of the unstimulated glans penis, but with less freedom than the integument of the scrotum. When any form of sexual tension develops, the clitoral glans always increases in size to a degree sufficient to develop close apposition between the subjacent tissues and the loosely applied, superficial integument. The vasocongestive reaction is of such finite nature that it usually cannot be noted by unsupported clinical observation. This anatomic response to increasing sexual tension has been established with aid of colposcopic magnification (6–40×). Microscopic tumescence of the clitoral glans always develops with sexual tension, regardless of whether this vasocongestive process continues into a clinically observable (macroscopic) tumescent reaction.

There is no way of anticipating from observation in an unstimulated state whether or not a clitoral glans will develop a clinically obvious tumescence under sexual influence. When increase in size of the glans does occur, this reaction pattern develops with total consistency. Variations in tumescent reactions relate only to the rapidity and extent of increase in size of the glans in response to direct manipulation, as opposed to slower and less extensive glans tumescence in response to breast manipulation, active coition, or fantasy.

More than half of the study subjects did not develop clinically obvious tumescence of the clitoral glans. When macroscopic tumescence does occur, the degree of vasocongestion ranges from a barely discernible increase in diameter to a twofold expansion of the glans. This tumescent reaction of the glans has been confused with the penile erective process and has been mistermed "erection of the clitoris." Total clitoral-body erection has not been observed unless there has been an obvious pathologic hypertrophy of the organ in its unstimulated state. Generally, the smaller the clitoral glans, the less frequently there is a clinically demonstrable tumescent reaction. However, some of the smaller organs have demonstrated the greatest relative size increases, while many of the larger clitorides have provided no gross evidence of a tumescent reaction.

When observable tumescence of the glans occurs, it does not develop until sexual tensions have progressed well into the excitement phase of the sexual response cycle. The clitoris engorges in a time sequence that parallels that of vasocongestion of the minor labia. It may be recalled that the minor labia of the sexually responding human female increase in size to a minimum of twice their unstimulated diameter and provide external extension for the expanding vaginal barrel. A similarly responding male has long since achieved full penile erection and, quite possibly, a moderate degree of elevation of at least one testicle.

Once observable tumescence of the clitoral glans develops, the engorgement persists throughout the remainder of the sexual cycle, or for as long as any significant degree of sexual stimulation is maintained.

As the anatomic structuring of the corpora cavernosa would suggest, the shaft of the clitoris also undergoes an excitement-phase vasocongestive reaction. There is definitive increase in diameter of the shaft which is a constant development regardless of shaft size. The vasocongestive increase in shaft diameter occurs simultaneously with the development of any macroscopic tumescent reaction of the glans. However, the clitoral shaft increases in diameter whether or not the glans reacts with clinically obvious tumescence.

In addition to a constant diameter increase, shaft elongation can occur. However, most clitorides go through vasocongestive glans reactions without developing clinically observable shaft elongation. Although objective observation admittedly is very difficult, an elongation reaction of the clitoral shaft has been firmly established in less than 10 percent of the observed orgasmic cycles. Shaft elongation develops only after the normal vasocongestive increase in shaft diameter has been stabilized. Elongation of the shaft has been observed only during direct manipulation of the mons area and not in response to the stimulation of other erotic areas of the body, fantasy, or active coition. It also should be emphasized that shaft elongation is confined to excitement-phase levels of sexual response, as discussion of plateau-phase clitoral response patterns will make evident.

Plateau Phase

The most significant physiologic reaction of the clitoris to effective sexual stimulation occurs in the plateau phase of the sexual cycle and develops with universal consistency. The entire clitoral body (shaft and glans) retracts from the normal pudendal overhang positioning. The crura and suspensory ligaments of the clitoris have major anatomic functions in this pattern of physiologic response. The ischiocavernosus muscles also contribute actively to retraction of the clitoral body, as opposed to their function during male ejaculation. It should be emphasized that the exact roles of the crura, suspensory ligaments, and various muscle bundles in clitoral retraction have not been determined with total conviction.

Clitoral reaction to plateau-phase levels of sexual tension occurs in a constant pattern. The shaft and glans of the clitoris withdraw from normal pudendal-overhang positioning and retract against the anterior border of the symphysis. Any portion of the clitoral glans that normally projects from the clitoral hood in a sexually unstimulated state is withdrawn deeply beneath the protective foreskin as the retraction reaction progresses. In the immediate preorgasmic period the clitoral body (shaft and glans) is extremely difficult to observe clinically. At this time the retraction of the clitoral shaft normally is so advanced that there is at least a 50 percent overall reduction in the length of the total clitoral body. The degree of individual clitoral-body retraction has been estimated with the aid of direct colposcopic observation.

During the plateau phase, clitoral-body retraction develops in relation to mode and effectiveness of sexual stimulation. During coition or breast manipulation, clitoral retraction develops late in the plateau phase as an indication of preorgasmic levels of sexual tension. With manipulation of the mons area, retraction of the clitoral shaft develops more rapidly, frequently early in the plateau phase, and may indicate sensate response to tactile stimuli rather than imminence of orgasmic experience.

Obviously, psychic components of sexual response patterns cannot be equated objectively for each orgasmic cycle under investigation. However, it would be a major mistake to presume that psychogenic influences do not contribute to either degree or rapidity of clitoral response to effective sexual stimulation. No woman who can fantasy to advanced plateau stages of sexual tension has been available to the investigation, so there is no information as to the degree of clitoral retraction possible in response to purely psychosexual stimulation.

Retraction of the clitoral body during the plateau phase is a reversible reaction. If high sexual tension levels are allowed to fall by deliberate reduction or withdrawal of stimulative techniques, the retracted shaft and glans will return to the normal pudendal-overhang position. With return to effective sexual stimulation, clitoral-body retraction will recur. This clitoral reaction sequence may develop repetitively during long-maintained plateau phases. Such a situation would exist when a woman who cannot quite achieve orgasmic expression insists on long-continued or repetitive return to stimulative activity in attempts to obtain release from her demanding sexual tensions.

Orgasmic Phase

No specific orgasmic-phase reaction of the clitoris has been established. In fact, due to the severity of the normal clitoral retraction beneath the minor labial hood, the clitoral glans has never been available to direct observation during an orgasmic experience.

Resolution Phase

After an orgasmic episode the return of the clitoris to normal pudendal-overhang positioning occurs within 5 to 10 seconds after cessation of orgasmic platform contractions. Retraction of the clitoral body is reversed even more rapidly than detumescence of the orgasmic platform and as swiftly as the sex-skin discoloration disappears from the minor labia. To provide further concept of this rapid clitoral-body "release," a parallel might be drawn to the male reaction pattern. The relaxation of the retracted clitoral shaft and the return of the glans to the normal pudendal-overhang positioning occurs in a parallel time sequence with the primary-stage involution of male penile erection after ejaculation.

When an observable tumescence of the clitoral glans has developed during the excitement phase, subsequent resolution-phase detumescence of the glans is a relatively slow process. This is particularly true for the individuals who demonstrate as much as a twofold vasocongestive increase in glans size. Although termination of the clitoral retraction reaction occurs very rapidly, continued tumescence of the glans and vasocongestion of the shaft frequently have been observed to last 5 to 10 minutes after orgasmic expression. Occasionally some women have demonstrated continued venous engorgement of the clitoral shaft or glans for 15 to 30 minutes after an orgasmic experience.

Those individuals who achieve plateau-phase levels of sexual response but do not obtain orgasmic-phase release of the accumulated sexual tensions occasionally maintain venous engorgement of both clitoral shaft and glans for a matter of hours after termination of all sexually stimulative activity.

Patterns of Clitoral Response

With the answers to the first two questions established and available as anatomic and physiologic baselines, the third question may be approached with more security. Does the clitoris develop different response patterns during coition as opposed to manipulation of the mons or other erogenous areas or to pure psychogenic stimulation?

Clitoral response was observed during natural coital activity in three positions: female supine, superior, and knee-chest; during artificial coition in female supine and knee-chest positions; and during both manual and mechanical manipulation of the mons and other erogenous areas. In female supine position, during natural coition, it was impossible to establish accurate observations of clitoral reaction patterns. The information returned from female supine positioning was developed by artificial coital techniques. Conversely, artificial coition was a technical impossibility in female superior coital positioning, so information of clitoral-body reaction patterns in this position was returned only from natural coital activity. Regardless of positioning and type of coition, or erogenous areas manipulated, the reactions of the clitoris to successful sexual stimulation followed the physiologic response patterns detailed in preceding portions of this chapter.

When women developed clinically obvious tumescence of the clitoral glans subsequent to mons manipulation, they achieved similar degrees of vasocongestion during coition in the three described positions. Conversely, none of the female study subjects developed glans tumescence during coition without demonstrating similar or more severe degrees of glans vasocongestion during mons area stimulation. When the mons was manipulated directly, the observable tumescent reaction of the glans occurred earlier in the excitement phase than when this vasocongestive reaction developed during coital activity.

Vasocongestive increase in diameter of the clitoral shaft occurs in all women regardless of the presence or absence of an observable glans tumescence. This reaction developed earlier in the excitement phase when direct mons area manipulation was employed than when the study subjects were responding to coital stimulation. The presence or absence of a clitoral shaft-elongation reaction could not be determined during active coition.

Three women were able to achieve orgasmic response by breast manipulation alone, in addition to their ability to react with orgasmic success to mons manipulation and to coition. Only one of the three women demonstrated an observable excitement-phase tumescent reaction of the clitoral glans during mons manipulation, coition, or breast stimulation. There was obvious delay in this secondary vasocongestive reaction during breast automanipulation when compared with the rapid development of glans tumescence during direct manipulation of the mons area.

As anticipated, the retraction reaction of the clitoral body (glans and shaft) developed during the plateau phase for all three breast manipulators. The reaction paralleled in time sequence that achieved during intercourse (late plateau, preorgasmic phase) and obviously was delayed as compared to the more rapid response patterns (early plateau phase) elicited by direct mons manipulation.

Unfortunately, as mentioned earlier, study subjects available to the investigation did not include individuals who could fantasy to orgasm. Therefore, observations of clitoral-body reaction patterns subsequent to psychogenic sexual stimulation have been limited to excitement-phase levels of sexual response. This level of sexual tension has been created frequently by providing suggestive literature for the study subjects. A clinically obvious tumescent reaction of the clitoral glans could be demonstrated in only a few of the women who normally developed this reaction during somatogenic stimulation. When clinical tumescence of the glans did occur, it developed long after there was obvious production of vaginal lubrication and paralleled a vasocongestive increase in the size of the minor labia. A minimum of a half-hour of exposure to stimulative literature was necessary to produce an observable glans tumescence in any woman.

The microscopic vasocongestive reaction of the clitoral glans which provides close apposition between integument and underlying glans tissues occurred in approximately 75 percent of the women who were exposed to suggestive literature. Fewer than one-third of the responding women produced a demonstrable increase in clitoral shaft diameter and no shaft-elongation reaction was observed.

The only variations in clitoral response developed from psychogenic forms of sexual stimulation, natural or artificial coition, and manual or mechanical manipulation of the mons or other erogenous areas have been in the rapidity and intensity of physiologic reaction.

2. Clinical Considerations

Clinical error has dominated the assignment of clitoral function in sex tension increment for the human female. Therefore, a detailed consideration of the dual capacity of the clitoris, as both a receptor and transformer of sexual stimulation, is in order. The definitive role of the clitoris in sexual response must be appreciated if female sexual inadequacy ever is to be treated effectively.

Five questions have been raised and must be answered if the role of the clitoris in human female sexuality is to be established. Three of these five questions have been discussed in Part 1 of this chapter. Two questions remain: (4) What clinical application can be developed from the basic material accumulated to answer the first three questions? (5) Are clitoral and vaginal orgasms truly separate anatomic and physiologic entities? Attempts to answer these two questions have directed investigative interest toward a clinical evaluation of clitoral influence upon female sexual response.

While the literature contains innumerable discussions of the role of the clitoris in female sexuality, authoritative opinion has reached essential accord only in the view that the primary function of the organ is to stimulate female sexual tensions. In order to accomplish its clinical purpose, the clitoris functions in the dual capacity of both receptor and transformer of sexual stimuli regardless of whether these stimuli originally have been somatogenically or psychogenically oriented. This concept will be discussed later.

In the past, attempts have been made to assign to clinical variants in clitoral anatomy and physiology specific influence on the total of female sexual response. Eleven years of investigation have failed to support these concepts. Both the size of the clitoral glans and the total clitoral body's positioning on the anterior border of the symphysis have been assigned roles of major influence in female sexual response. However, Dickinson and Pierson originally expressed the conviction that there is no relation between the size of the clitoris and the effectiveness of its role in female sexual stimulation. Direct observation of thousands of sexual response cycles has confirmed their opinion.

Historically, the anatomically oriented concept that clitoral size has a direct relation to the effectiveness of the individual female's sexual performance has been fostered by our "phallic fallacy" literature and has no foundation in fact. The diameter of the unstimulated clitoral glans measured at the juncture of the glans and shaft has varied in the study-subject population from 3 mm. to 1 cm. In this group there has been absolutely no relationship established between the size of the glans and the rapidity and intensity of the individual's ability to respond to effective sexual stimulation. Conversely, there also has been similar variation in clitoral glans size among women treated for inadequacy of sexual response during the past seven years. Regardless of the type of somatogenic or psychogenic approach to sexual stimulation, clitoral glans size has played no definitive part in the effectiveness of the individual's sexuality.

Consideration of the anatomic positioning of the clitoris has paralleled any discussion of clitoral size in relation to degree of sexual response. Clitoral placement on the anterior border of the symphysis has been assigned a role of major influence on female response during coition. A low implantation has been presumed to improve the sexuality of the individual female due to the possibility of increased direct contact between the penis and clitoral glans. Regardless of clitoral-body positioning the penis rarely comes in direct contact with the clitoral glans during active coition. In fact, clitoral retraction, which always develops during the plateau phase and elevates the clitoral body from its normal pudendal-overhang positioning, further removes the glans from even the theoretical possibility of direct penile contact.

Specific physiologic reactions, like anatomic variants of the clitoris, also have been assigned major roles in elevating female sexual tensions. Studies in depth of both the study-subject population and women undergoing treatment for sexual inadequacy have failed to support these contentions. Whether the clitoris develops an obvious tumescence of the glans or elongation of the shaft has little to do with the degree of the individual woman's response to effective sexual stimulation. Tumescence of the glans and shaft elongation have been observed in women during multiple orgasmic sessions as well as in women who have not been able to achieve orgasmic levels of sexual tension. Clitoral-body retraction occurs during the plateau phase whether or not an orgasmic experience is to follow. In brief, sexually responding women achieve orgasmic levels of sexual tension without regard to variables in the basic anatomy and physiology of the clitoris.

Dickinson insisted that women with histories of decades of masturbatory activity did not develop a consistent hypertrophy of the clitoris. While this general concept certainly is acceptable, there are minor exceptions that should be noted. Observations of individuals over the past decade have removed any doubt that frequent, severe masturbatory activity occasionally may produce measurable increases in the diameter of the clitoral glans and questionable increases in the length of the clitoral shaft. When recordable clitoral glans hypertrophy develops over a period of years, the women usually are found to employ extensively one or more of the mechanical methods for clitoral stimulation. Obviously, long-continued androgenic influence (adrenal hyperplasia, testosterone ingestion, etc.)must be ruled out first in these cases.

It may be recalled that there are reports of African tribes that measure female sexuality in terms of clitoral length and labial hypertrophy. From infancy, female members of such tribes deliberately are manipulated for countless hours to stimulate the development of these artifacts. These girls have been reported to obtain an obvious hypertrophy of the clitoris and the labia, if not by puberty, at least during their early teens. Although the fact of manipulative hypertrophy is established, there is no reliable information relating the hypertrophy directly to excessive levels of female sexuality. It is possible that methods used to attain a culturally desirable condition of adornment can simultaneously increase individual sexual responsiveness.

Although anatomic placement and physiologic reaction preclude any consistency of direct clitoral glans stimulation during coition, the significant influence of secondary stimulation should not be overlooked. The fact that the clitoral glans rarely is contacted directly by the penis in intravaginal thrusting does not preclude the coital development of indirect clitoral involvement. Clitoral stimulation during coitus in the female supine position develops indirectly from penile-shaft distention of the minor labia at the vaginal vestibule. A mechanical traction develops on both sides of the clitoral hood of the minor labia subsequent to penile distention of the vaginal outlet. With active penile thrusting, the clitoral body is pulled downward toward the pudendum by traction exerted on the wings of the clitoral hood. However, there is not sufficient excursion developed by coital traction on the clitoral body to allow direct penis-to-clitoris contact.

When the penile shaft is in the withdrawal phase of active coital stroking, traction on the clitoral hood is somewhat relieved and the body and glans return to normal pudendal-overhang positioning. However, the rhythmic movement of the clitoral body in conjunction with active penile stroking produces significant indirect or secondary clitoral stimulation.

It should be emphasized that this same type of secondary clitoral stimulation occurs in every coital position when there is a full penetration of the vaginal barrel by the erect penis. Anatomic exceptions to this statement are created by any significant pathologic gaping of the vaginal outlet, such as might be occasioned by childbirth injury. If the vaginal outlet is too expanded to allow strong traction on the minor-labial hood by the thrusting penis, minimal clitoral excursion will occur and little if any secondary stimulation will develop.

Only the female superior and lateral coital positions allow direct or primary stimulation of the clitoris to be achieved with ease. In these positions the clitoris can be stimulated directly if apposition between male and female symphyses is maintained. There also remains the constant factor of secondary clitoral stimulation provided by traction on the minor-labial hood during active coition in these positions. The influences of both direct and indirect stimulation are essentially inseparable in these coital positions. Clitoral response may develop more rapidly and with greater intensity in female superior coition than in any other female coital position.

In the knee-chest coital position no direct stimulation of the clitoris is possible. Yet glans tumescence, when it occurs, and clitoral-body retraction, which is a constant factor, occur in the response patterns established for the supine or superior coital positions. The intensity of physiologic reaction usually is less pronounced than in either supine or superior coital positioning.

Obviously, active coition develops psychogenic as well as physiologic response patterns, both of which contribute to indirect or secondary clitoral stimulation. It will remain for more sophisticated methods of neurophysiologic and psychologic investigation to assign individual spheres of influence to these multiple influences which create the total picture of indirect stimulation of the receptor organ developed by active coition.

In essence, stimulation of the clitoris (receptor organ) developing during active coition is the secondary or indirect result of penile traction on the minor labial hood. This traction occurs regardless of female coital positioning, anatomic variations in clitoral size, or crural origin on the pubic rami.

The importance of development by marital units of specific coital techniques to facilitate clitoral stimulation has been emphasized repeatedly in the literature. The clinical fallibility of these suggestions now is obvious. Unless the male partner makes a specific effort to bring the shaft of the penis in direct apposition to the total mons area, the clitoris is not stimulated directly by penile thrust with the female in the usual supine position. An overriding coital position is difficult for the male partner to maintain as sexual tensions increase, particularly if the female does not have parous relaxation of the vaginal outlet. The nulliparous woman may not be able to retain the penis in an awkward pelvic override position without complaining of vaginal outlet or rectal discomfort.

An additional objection to the male-override position is that it precludes full vaginal penetration at the apex of the penile thrust. Thus the mutual coital stimulation of vaginal engulfment for the male and cul-de-sac distention for the female are lost to the sexual partners. Intensity of vaginal exteroceptive and proprioceptive response can be dulled for the female partner by any awkward attempt to provide direct clitoral glans contact.

The primary focus for sensual response in the human female's pelvis is the clitoral body. The clitoris responds with equal facility to both somatogenic and psychogenic forms of stimulation, and is truly unique in the human organ system in that its only known function is that of serving as an erotic focus for both afferent and efferent forms of sexual stimulation. How, then, does the clitoral body function in its role as receptor and transformer to sexually invested stimuli?

At the outset it should be made perfectly clear that although stimuli are characterized as somatogenic or psychogenic in origin and the roles of the clitoris as receptor and transformer, this does not imply that any form of stimulation is or can be purely somatogenic in character. All stimuli are appreciated, delineated, and referred by higher cortical centers. The term *somatogenic* relates only to physical activity. This form of clitoral stimulation can vary from heterosexual manual manipulation to automanipulative use of bedding material or thigh pressure. Thus the use of the terms *somatogenic stimuli* or *transformer role* connotes initiation or approach rather than any concept of discriminatory ability.

Sexual stimuli may be derived from either somatogenic or psychogenic origins. The clitoral response patterns will vary depending upon the initial involvement of either afferent or efferent pathways. When the clitoral body reacts directly to automanipulative techniques or secondarily to coital activity, these stimuli (initially somatogenic but with an obvious psychogenic overlay) are received through the afferent nerve endings in the clitoral glans and shaft. Clitoral-body response to this type of stimulation could, from a clinical point of view, be termed *receptor* in character.

The pacinian corpuscles within the large nerve bundles conceivably play an important role in relaying afferent impulses created by somatogenic forms of stimulation. As Krantz so ably has shown, there is marked variation in quantity and quality of nerve endings and in the number of pacinian corpuscles located within the individual clitoral glans and shaft. Since the assigned role of the pacinian corpuscles is that of proprioceptive response to deep pressure (receptor role), the great variety in female automanipulative techniques ranging from demand for severe pressure to insistence upon the lightest touch may be explained.

Little is known of the neurologic pathways that lead from stimulated afferent nerve endings in the clitoral body. Although a reflex center in the sacral portion of the spinal cord has been

identified in the male animal by Semans and Langworthy, no
similar response center has been described for the human female.
It may be that the entire reflex arc involving the spinal cord and
the higher cortical centers constantly is caught up in the continuum
of response to dominantly somatogenic forms of sexual stimulation.
Particularly is this concept plausible when it is realized that regardless of the effectiveness of the somatogenically oriented stimuli, the
psychogenic overlay inherent in any approach to female sexual
stimulation is of constant import. Therefore, the possibility of a
pure reflex-arc response to afferent stimulation is reduced with
the realization that psychogenic stimulation of the higher cortical
centers and the resultant direct, efferent, transformer response in
the clitoris is an undeniable factor in the sexual response of the
human female.

The clitoral body functions as a receptor organ in an objective
expression of sensual focus, as well as the subjective end-point
(transformer) of neurogenic pathways. The result of efferent
stimulation of the clitoris, be it psychogenically or somatogenically
initiated, has been recorded in the detailed consideration of the
anatomy and physiology of the clitoral body's response to varying
intensity of sexual stimulation (see Part 1 of this chapter). However, the functional role (that of serving clinically as a transformer
or subjective organ of sensual focus) has not been considered
previously.

The subjective, or transformer, response of the clitoris to any
form of effective sexual stimulation, such as reading of pornogra-
phy, direct manipulation, coital connection, etc., has been vocalized
by women in many ways. Some vocally identify a subjective sensation of deep pelvic fullness and warmth (possibly vasoconcentra-
tion), others a feeling of local irritation, expansive urge, need for
release, etc. (possibly glans enlargement). The clinical or functional response of the clitoris as a transformer of efferent forms
of stimulation is to create in turn a subjective urge or tension
increment and, ultimately, a higher cortical need for release. It is
impossible to delimit this functional clitoral role of sensual focus
because vocalization of the sensual response patterns varies from
woman to woman. The transformer role also differs between
clitoris and penis. Suffice it to say that the clitoris, serving as a
receptor and transformer organ, has a role as the center of female
sensual focus, and the functional response it creates easily is
identifiable by any sexually oriented woman.

Any clinical consideration of clitoral response to effective sexual
stimulation must include a discussion of masturbation. The tech-

niques of and reactions to direct manipulation of the clitoral body (glans and shaft) or the mons area vary in each woman. Observations of higher animal patterns of foreplay first sensitized investigators to the clinical importance of effective autostimulative techniques by emphasizing the obvious response that such effective foreplay can develop in the female of the species.

Marriage manuals discuss at length the importance of clitoral manipulation as the basis of adequate coital foreplay. Most discussions of initiation and elevation of female sexual tensions have included the questions of why and when to stimulate the clitoris. To date there has been little consideration of the infinitely more important questions of how to manipulate the clitoris and how much stimulation usually is required. Direct observation of hundreds of women using mechanical and manual masturbatory techniques through repetitive orgasmic experiences has emphasized the fundamental importance of the questions, "How?" and "How much?"

No two women have been observed to masturbate in identical fashion. However, there is one facet of general agreement. Women rarely report or have been noted to employ direct manipulation of the clitoral glans. In those isolated instances when the technique is used it is limited to the excitement phase only and frequently a lubricant is applied to this normally quite sensitive tissue. Additionally, the clitoral glans often becomes extremely sensitive to touch or pressure immediately after an orgasmic experience, and particular care is taken to avoid direct glans contact when restimulation is desired.

Those women who manipulate the clitoris directly concentrate on the clitoral shaft. Usually they manipulate the right side of the shaft if right handed, and the left side if left handed. Occasionally, women have been observed to switch sides of the shaft during stimulative episodes. A relative degree of local anesthesia may develop if manipulation is concentrated in just one area for extended periods of time or if too much manipulative pressure is applied to any one area.

Women usually stimulate the entire mons area rather than concentrating on the clitoral body. Regardless of whether the clitoris is stimulated by direct means or indirectly through mons area manipulation, the physiologic responses of the clitoris to elevated sexual tensions are identical. Most women prefer to avoid the overwhelming intensity of sensual focus that may develop from direct clitoral contact. Instead, mons area manipulation produces a sensual experience that although somewhat slower to develop is, at orgasmic maturity, fully as satiating an experience as that result-ing from direct clitoral shaft massage. Mons area manipulation also avoids the painful stimuli returned to many women when the clitoris is manipulated directly either with too much pressure or for too lengthy periods of time.

The concept of the mons as an area of severe sensual focus is supported by the clinical observation that after clitoridectomy, masturbation has been reported to be as effective a means of sexual stimulation as before surgery. Manipulation usually has been con-fined to the mons area, although sometimes concentrated on the scarred postsurgical site.

Evidence of the extreme tactile sensitivity of the entire peri-neum in addition to the clitoral body and the mons area has been presented by the Institute for Sex Research. During the Insti-tute's gynecologic observation, the minor labia were determined to be almost as perceptive to superficial tactile sensation as the cli-toral glans. The Institute also considers the minor labia to be fully as important as the clitoris or mons as a source of erotic arousal. While the tactile sensitivity of the minor labia is without question, stimulation of the labia does not provide the human female with the extremes of sensual stimuli that massage of the clitoral shaft or mons area produces.

Another observation of female automanipulative technique should be considered for its clinical import. Most women continue active manipulation of the clitoral shaft or mons area during their entire orgasmic experience. This female reaction pattern parallels their coital pattern of demand for continued active male pelvic thrusting during the woman's orgasmic experience. This female demand for continued stimulation during the actual orgasmic ex-pression is in opposition to the average male's reaction to his ejaculatory experience. Most males attempt the deepest possible vaginal penetration as the first stage of the ejaculatory response develops. They maintain this spastic, deep vaginal entrenchment during the second phase of the ejaculatory experience rather than continuing the rapid pelvic thrusting characteristic of preorgasmic levels of sexual tension.

The human female frequently is not content with one orgasmic experience during episodes of automanipulation involving the cli-toral body. If there is no psychosocial distraction to repress sexual tensions, many well-adjusted women enjoy a minimum of three or four orgasmic experiences before they reach apparent satiation. Masturbating women concentrating only on their own sexual demands, without the psychic distractions of a coital partner, may enjoy many sequential orgasmic experiences without allowing their sexual tensions to resolve below plateau-phase levels. Usually physical exhaustion alone terminates such an active masturbatory session.

There is a specific clitoral-body reaction to effective sexual stimulation that has created a state of confusion for the average male sexual partner. This physiologic response to sexual tension has been termed the *retraction reaction*. The entire clitoral body is elevated high on the anterior border of the symphysis (away from its normal pudendal-overhang positioning) during both the plateau and orgasmic phases of the female sexual response cycle (see Part 1 of this chapter).

This physiologic reaction to high levels of female sexual tension creates a problem for the sexually inexperienced male. The clitoral-body retraction reaction frequently causes even an experienced male to lose manual contact with the organ. Having lost contact, the male partner usually ceases active stimulation of the general mons area and attempts manually to relocate the clitoral body. During this "textbook" approach, marked sexual frustration may develop in a highly excited female partner. By the time the clitoral shaft has been relocated, plateau-phase tension levels may have been lost. Not infrequently the female partner, frustrated by male ineptitude, may not recover from her psychophysiologic distraction sufficiently to avoid the frustrating, vasocongestive pelvic distress occasioned by orgasmic inadequacy.

It is important to reemphasize the fact that the retracted clitoral body continues to be stimulated by traction or pressure on the protective clitoral hood. Once plateau-phase clitoral retraction has been established, manipulation of the general mons area is all that is necessary for effective clitoral-body stimulation.

Most marriage manuals advocate the technique of finding the clitoris and remaining in direct manual contact with it during attempts to stimulate female sexual tensions. In direct manipulation of the clitoris there is a narrow margin between stimulation and irritation. If the unsuspecting male partner adheres strictly to marriage manual dictum, he is placed in a most advantageous position. He is attempting proficiency with a technique that most women reject during their own automanipulative experiences.

As stated previously, no two women practice automanipulation in similar fashion. Rather than following any preconceived plan for stimulating his sexual partner, the male will be infinitely more effective if he encourages vocalization on her part. The individual woman knows best the areas of her strongest sensual focus and the rapidity and intensity of manipulative technique that provides her with the greatest degree of sexual stimulation.

Finally, a brief consideration of the fifth and last of the questions raised about the role of the clitoris in female sexuality: Are clitoral and vaginal orgasms truly separate anatomic entities? From a biologic point of view, the answer to this question is an unequivocal No. The literature abounds with descriptions and discussions of vaginal as opposed to clitoral orgasms. From an anatomic point of view, there is absolutely no difference in the responses of the pelvic viscera to effective sexual stimulation, regardless of whether the stimulation occurs as a result of clitoral-body or mons area manipulation, natural or artificial coition, or, for that matter, specific stimulation of any other erogenous area of the female body.

With the introduction of artificial coital techniques, the reactions of the vagina during coition became available to direct observation and repeatedly have been recorded through the medium of cinematography. These vaginal reactions first had been observed during sexual response cycles stimulated by manipulation of the mons area and clitoral body. During artificial coition the reactions of the vaginal barrel initiated under direct stimulation conformed in exact detail to the vaginal response patterns which developed subsequent to the indirect stimulation of mons area or clitoral-body manipulation.

Three study subjects available to the investigative program have demonstrated the facility of orgasmic response to breast stimulation alone, as well as to coital, clitoral-body, or mons area manipulation. Identical vaginal response patterns were observed for these three study subjects from all the above-described modes of stimulation.

Conversely, what of clitoral-body reaction to direct or indirect stimulation? The physiologic responses that develop in the clitoral glans and shaft during the four phases of the sexual cycle are the same regardless of whether the clitoral body is responding to direct or indirect stimulation. For research purposes the definition of indirect or direct clitoral-body stimulation has been oriented to clinical considerations alone.

Direct stimulation results from manual or mechanical manipulation of the clitoral shaft or glans. Indirect stimulation develops from mons area manipulation or the stimulation of any other erogenous area of the female body, such as the breasts. In addition, the clitoral body may be stimulated indirectly by natural or artificial coition with the female partner in the supine, superior, or knee-chest position. All these techniques have been used in order to record clitoral-body response patterns. These patterns are identical and vary only in intensity of reaction to the effectiveness of the stimulative technique, regardless of whether this technique is described clinically as direct or indirect.

There may be great variation in duration and intensity of orgasmic experience, varying from individual to individual and within the same woman from time to time. However, when any woman experiences orgasmic response to effective sexual stimulation, the vagina and clitoris react in consistent physiologic patterns. Thus, clitoral and vaginal orgasms are not separate biologic entities.

Frank Caprio

The Problem of Impotence

Definition

Impotence is an all-encompassing term for a functional sexual ✓ *inadequacy* in the male. It is a symptom complex and is not confined specifically to a man's inability to get an erection. On the contrary it includes *various* types of sexual difficulties—semierections, hasty ejaculations (premature ejaculation), unreasonably delayed ejaculation, inability to enjoy the sex act, a lack of sexual desire for the opposite sex (sexual apathy), failure to ejaculate during intercourse (coitus sine ejaculatio), complete inability to

From: Frank Caprio, *The Sexually Adequate Male,* New York: Citadel Press, Inc., 1959. Reprinted by permission.

attain an erection (impotentia paralytica), difficulty in sustaining
an erection following penetration, and many other manifestations
of sexual inadequacy.

The most comprehensive definition of impotence I have encountered in literature is the one given by Dr. Benjamin Karpman
in his article, "Psychic Impotence," in the Psychoanalytic Review:

"He is impotent, for whatever reason, the desire for the opposite
sex is absent or is so weak as to never result in any attempt
towards meeting the partner; and he is also impotent who although willing, midway creates obstacles of his own which prevent
him from realizing the original attempt. He is impotent who with
a strong erection is unable to realize the act because of the rapid
precipitation of the orgasm, and he is doubly impotent whose erection is confined to a small degree of function or who can neither
erect nor get pleasure out of it, that is, is anesthetic. He is impotent in whom the climax, instead of producing the tremendous
physical sensation that normally is orgasm, is followed by either
absence of the same or by an indefinite, tasteless, and sometimes
painful, even agonizing sensation. He is impotent in whom the
urge asserts itself with relative rarity and, strangely enough, we
must also regard as impotent the man who driven by an obscure, but insatiable sexual urge repeats the act with great excess
and in frequent succession, thus revealing a fundamental lack of
satisfaction with each act; for it is in the nature of the sexual act,
as it is with other physiological processes, that it too must reach
a point of saturation followed by a period of physiological relaxation which period must increase in length as the frequency of the
act is repeated. And finally he is impotent who, although having
performed the act with apparent satisfaction finds himself on its
completion unsatisfied and unrelieved."

Impotence therefore involves a disturbance in the requisites of
normal potency, namely (1) Libido; (2) Erection; (3) Coitus
proper; (4) Voluptas-pleasure during coitus and preceding orgasm
(prepleasure); (5) Ejaculation and (6) Orgasm and the relationship in quality and time to each other.

General Considerations

One would surmise from such a definition of impotence that
every man at one time or other has experienced one or more of
the above manifestations described. It is a logical and correct as-

sumption. In other words, the penis in its *normal* state is flaccid and pendulous and not *erect*. The erection is caused by physiological or psychological stimulation. For example, when a man is normally aroused sexually by a woman and he is in the proper receptive mood to allow himself to become stimulated, an impulse is generated in the brain and is conveyed by the nervous system to the sexual organs. This can be likened to the turning on of a switch which sends the current of electricity from the brain to the penis via a nerve pathway from the brain down the spinal column to the penis.

During sex play between the husband and wife, if the latter stimulates the male organ (manually or orally), it creates added excitation which enables the husband to perform even more adequately. The so-called "reflex arc" becomes complete. The original stimulus from the brain to the penis returns back to the brain by means of this added excitation by the wife, and the erection becomes more sustained. Inserting the penis into the vagina adds to his pleasure and speeds up the stimuli traveling in the form of a circle from the brain to the penis, to the vagina, back to the brain again.

This current can be short-circuited by an uncalled-for remark, a gesture of rejection, or a distraction from without or within. The ringing of the telephone during coitus or children knocking on the bedroom door can have this effect. A distraction from within may be caused by a man thinking unduly of matters other than sex. For example, a man may be overconcerned about his golf score or the effect which intercourse will have on his heart condition, or on some imagined illness. All this may result either in a premature ejaculation, a sudden loss of an erection or inability to ejaculate at the time of the wife experiencing her orgasm. Any frustration during lovemaking may create sufficient anxiety to cause a break in the so-called "reflex arc." The man will either want to achieve a hasty climax, fearing he will be interrupted again, or his original stimulation or desire for coitus may be displaced by a disturbing emotion. He may become so angry at his wife's tactlessness for having made the wrong remark, or become so enraged at the person who called him on the telephone that his hostility prevents him from getting back into his original mood for lovemaking. He may decide not to resume his sexual lovemaking, leaving his wife weeping and unsatisfied.

Sensitivity of this kind is fatal to good lovemaking. A man who wishes to be sexually adequate must be mature enough to understand that situations are bound to occur in the course of time that tend to detract from lovemaking. He adapts himself quickly to some unforeseen interruption, and is able to carry on where he left off without consequences to himself or his partner. To desensitize himself to advantage, he must realize that it is his own selfishness that makes him react with hostility to that which interferes with his physical pleasures. It is usually the man who takes himself too seriously that is more apt to become a sexual casualty. Men with a sense of humor can make light of their frustrations, confident in the knowledge that their ability to perform well will depend upon their mental attitude.

It facilitates matters if a wife would restimulate her husband when he has lost his erection, *without being asked*, to a point where he becomes sufficiently potent to continue in his lovemaking. Many husbands, unfortunately, because of their male pride, are too embarrassed to ask their wives to do that which may be required to enable him to regain his erection—manual or oral stimulation of the penis.

The sexually adequate male includes his wife within this stimulation-response cycle by training himself to wait for certain signals before he proceeds to ejaculate. His wife may tell him or indicate to him during the heat of passion that she is experiencing her climax, and wants him to join her with his orgasm. But if he concentrates solely on the pleasurable sensations within his penis during coital movements, the stimulation-response cycle includes only the nerve impulses going from his brain to the penis and back to his brain, thereby failing to encompass his wife's need for satisfaction. It is this lack of understanding of the physiological and psychological cycle of stimulation and response that causes the majority of impotence and frigidity disturbances.

Since civilized man has developed a certain sensitivity to that which offends his esthetic tastes, it is understandable that he may not react to every kind of sexual stimulation. For example, it might be considered *normal* for a man not to respond sexually to a prostitute who is unclean and unattractive. Likewise it may also be normal for a man to become impotent under certain circumstances—such as being *surprised* in an illicit relationship by the knock at the door of a returning husband. There are many situations wherein failure of a man to become aroused sexually may not always be regarded as abnormal. Every case of impotence therefore must be carefully studied and evaluated per se. At any rate, problems of sexual inadequacy should be referred to the psychiatrist for proper diagnosis and treatment.

Incidence

The extent of sexual incompetency in the male has already been mentioned above. Freud lends added support to the prevalence of impotence as evidenced by his statement: "I assert that physical impotence is far more widespread than is generally believed, and that a certain degree of this is characteristic of the love life of civilized man." Freud, very significantly, went on to say ". . . that the attitude of the man to love in our modern civilization bears the impress of psychological impotence. The emotional and sensual elements are very rarely merged to the proper extent among the educated classes; the man in his sexual activity nearly always feels embarrassed by his respect for the woman, and only manifests his potency completely when confronted with a debased sexual object which again is partly due to the fact that there is a perverted component in his sexual aims which he dare not attempt to satisfy on the respected woman. He only derives complete sexual satisfaction when he can abandon himself to that object regardless of anything else, and he dare not do this, for instance, with his virtuous wife."

The above, of course, is not applicable to every case of impotence. In fact, in some instances, as I already mentioned, the opposite is true—that a man becomes *less* potent with the "debased sexual object." Nevertheless the problem of impotence is a very complex one, mainly because there are many varieties and degrees of impotence. Sexual behavior varies according to the individual situation and the particular set of circumstances involved.

Types and Causes

Impotence may be classified under two main headings, Organic Impotence and Psychic Impotence.

The former is caused by *physical* factors such as venereal diseases (gonorrhea or syphilis), glandular deficiencies, tumors of the sexual organs, prostate gland trouble, infectious diseases resulting in general debility, etc. The excessive use of drugs or alcohol may also cause disturbances in sexual function. Physical exhaustion may contribute to a temporary state of impotence. Certain physical conditions in a woman such as vaginismus (spasm of the muscles of the vagina), inflammations of the vagina, or a thickened hymen requiring surgical incision, may all contribute to the development of impotence in the man.

However in the *majority* of cases, impotence is due to *psychological* factors. It may represent the symptom-consequence of some deep-seated unresolved conflict, or may be the result of inhibitory influences, bashfulness, sex-ignorance, fear, guilt feelings, disgust, unhappiness, sudden indisposition, inability to love, insecurity, faulty attitudes toward sex, self-pity, masochism or psychic invalidism, homosexual repressions, bisexual conflicts, penis inferiority, fear of causing a woman pain, fear of making a woman pregnant, dislike of contraceptives, sadism (desire to punish the partner), preoccupation with fantasies involving sexual deviations, incestuous attachments to a mother or sister, fallacies about masturbation, fear of being seen or interrupted during the sex act, conflicts involving religious or parental censure, jealousy, hostility and numerous other causes.

In my experience, I have found premature ejaculation far more common among men who were *inexperienced* and *inhibited* because of *fear* of one kind or another. Kenneth Walker, author of "Physiology of Sex," found that three out of every four men treated for impotence stated that they either had no sex education at all or else they were brought up to believe that all sexual manifestations were shameful or evil.

Premature Ejaculation

This is the most common type of sexual inadequacy. It involves the involuntary expulsion of semen long before the woman has had an opportunity to experience her orgasm. Some husbands ejaculate before insertion of their penis in the vagina (Ejaculatio Ante Portas); others reach their hasty climax shortly after intromission (Ejaculatio Post Portas).

Dr. G. V. Hamilton, in his classic study, "What Is Wrong With Marriage?" found that out of every one hundred husbands he interviewed, fifty-five stated that they ejaculated too quickly for their wives' satisfaction. And when the wives were asked the question, "Do you believe that your husband's orgasm occurs too quickly for your own pleasure?" forty-eight answered "Yes." Dr. Edwin Hirsch claims that between fifty and seventy-five percent of men have suffered from premature ejaculation.

Coitus is successful when it results in the mutual gratification of the husband and wife. When sex relations leaves the woman unsatisfied, there is something wrong. Every husband should learn to control his urge to ejaculate prematurely and give his wife the amount of preliminary love play and stimulation she requires in order to prepare herself for an orgasm during coitus. Such husbands can *train* themselves to *postpone* their ejaculation. The man who ejaculates too quickly is more than likely concentrating on the pleasurable sensation he is experiencing at the time and is thinking of his own gratification *only*. We sometimes refer to this "two minute" type of coitus or ejaculation following a few frictional movements as "masturbation per vaginam." "Progress cannot be made in treating the sexually inexperienced," Dr. Hirsch writes, "until they are made to realize that coitus is not masturbation within a vagina."

The husband should keep his mind focused on a desire to please his wife as well as himself and enable her to achieve an orgasm. Kissing passionately with eyes closed during intercourse increases the ability of the partners to *concentrate* and enhances their chances of reaching a simultaneous orgasm.

By concentrating on giving his wife ecstatic pleasure during the sex act, he will not be depriving himself of any real enjoyment. Rather, he will be enjoying sexual relations in its fullest sense, and through the knowledge that he is able to make his partner thoroughly enjoy the experience, gain a greater respect for himself and earn the love and admiration of his wife.

The husband may try resorting to what we might call "distraction technique," which may enable him to control his ejaculation for a longer period of time, such as thinking about an unpaid bill or his income tax.

Psychoanalysts have advanced various plausible theories to explain some of the deeper mechanisms involved in the psychology of this specific type of sexual disorder.

According to Abraham (a pupil of Freud) premature ejaculation is the result of a hypersensitive urethra. He claims that when a little semen gets into the urethra, a rapid ejaculation takes place because the urethra is hyperexcitable and tends to expel the semen as soon as it is stimulated. His clinical observations have led him to the conclusion that men who suffer from "ejaculatio praecox" were bed wetters and had difficulty in bladder control. As to his psychological explanation, he interpreted the disorder as an unconscious wish on the part of the male to defile the woman, expressing his disgust with her.

I have treated several patients in which this theory definitely applied. When the unconscious sadism was brought to the level of conscious appreciation the patients were able to control their ejaculation.

In the following case a fairly intelligent and educated young man fell ardently in love with a beautiful girl whom he idolized and worshipped. He described how he had assumed in his own mind that she had never been intimate with any man (The Madonna Complex). However, as the courtship progressed, and he spoke to her of marriage for the first time, he noticed that she behaved in a restless manner, and began manifesting a number of psychosomatic symptoms—headaches, nervous indigestion, fatigue. She would remark, "I have a terrible headache. Do you mind driving me home early this evening?"

As the day approached when he planned to present her with an engagement ring, she informed him that she had something very important to tell him. She told him that she had been made pregnant seven years before by a man whom she did not profess to love. She attributed the pregnancy to a mistake on her part, and to his carelessness, during a night of drinking. She added that she had a son who was being raised by an aunt as she did not feel at the time that she wanted to have an abortion. But she knew that if she married she would have to reveal the truth. She would prefer to have the prospective husband take her child, born out of wedlock, into their home.

Naturally, this was a great shock to him. On the one hand, he wanted to forgive and marry her; on the other, he was afraid the child would always remind him of the past indiscretion. He finally decided to marry her, believing that he would master the problem.

He noticed, much to his amazement, that when he attempted sexual relations, he was able to get an erection, but upon inserting his penis, he ejaculated in a matter of a few seconds. This same thing took place with each intercourse, leaving his wife unsatisfied which, in turn, made her irritable and quarrelsome. Never having had sexual relations prior to marriage, because of his idealization of the opposite sex, and the shock or psychic trauma of having married an ideal who had previously been deflowered, he became a victim of an unconscious conflict which he could not understand or cope with.

Analysis plus corroborative dream material gave the clue. The key dream was the one in which he urinated over his wife's body (particularly her face, mouth and hair). The dream illustrated what psychoanalysts call a displacement from below to above which, in this case, meant that he wanted to urinate into her vagina (mouth), the hair representing the pubic hair, as an act of contempt, thereby gratifying a sadistic wish to defile her as had already happened in her past life.

The premature ejaculation was interpreted to him as an expression of urethral sadism—an unconscious wish to soil her with his semen (urine substitute), and also sadistically to leave her unsatisfied. When he realized, for the first time, that he had been making a game of the sexual act, and that he had also become the unhappy victim of his own unconscious doings, this insight by itself enabled him to resolve the essential conflict of his sexual neurosis, and with time and practice, he succeeded in becoming an adequate sexual partner.

Stekel on the other hand attributed premature ejaculation to a conflict between the urge to gratify one's sexual desires and an opposing force—the inhibition of such an urge. Stekel discovered that fear played a predominant role—fear of religious censure, fear of women, fear of infection, fear of hurting a woman, and fear of sexual failure. He believed also that the key to the cure of premature ejaculation was to be found in the dictum "Love conquers all things"—that when a woman is frigid she influences detrimentally her husband's sexual performance.

Several years ago I encountered just such a case. The wife's frigidity proved to be responsible for her husband's *hasty ejaculation*.

To uncover the psychodynamic factors involved in the sexual incompatibility of this particular couple, one had to go back to the early backgrounds of both husband and wife in order to appreciate the predisposing factors in their childhood and adolescence that led to the development of the wife's unresponsiveness or *orgasm-incapacity* and the husband's *premature ejaculation*.

Mary's father had been an alcoholic over a period of many years. He was a week-end drinker. From Monday to Friday he managed not to let his drinking interfere with his job. However, on week ends he would indulge in alcoholic sprees, making himself obnoxious around the house. On many occasions Mary witnessed her father assaulting her mother. She developed a strong antipathy toward the father and always came to the rescue of her mother whenever there was a quarrel. Being an only child, this incompatibility between the parents accounted for much of Mary's early unhappiness. During her high school years, she became very defensive and feared the opposite sex. Whenever she accepted a date and attended a dance, she had a tendency to be sarcastic. Invariably her boy friend would become discouraged and showed no inclination to invite her out a second time. During this age period (15 to 17) her feelings of hostility towards her father increased. She became more and more attached to her mother who, incidentally, made the tragic mistake of instilling in her a distrust of the opposite sex. She conveyed the idea that all men were selfish and that they would attempt to seduce her if she let the barriers down. The mother made the added mistake of confiding in her daughter, stating that her father was sexually inadequate, inclined to be brutal in his approach and that she had never enjoyed sexual relations with him. Unknowingly, the mother was already planting the seeds of her own *frigidity* in her daughter, to the extent that Mary developed a preconceived idea that sex relations following marriage were to be *tolerated* rather than *enjoyed*.

When Mary reached her seventeenth year her parents obtained a divorce. She lived with her mother and limited herself socially so that she had little opportunity to make new friends with the opposite sex. At her place of work, one day, she met Harry whom she liked well enough to date frequently and who eventually became her steady boy friend. As we might expect from the background, Mary was quite *prudish* and although she wanted to respond to Harry's lovemaking, she felt *inhibited*. She began to experience for the first time the kind of conflict Stekel describes —a strong sexual urge on the one hand and the repression of that urge on the other. As long as such a conflict was to persist, she was almost doomed to develop a case of *frigidity*.

Harry had his own sexual problems. He was an only child and came from a very happy family. But he was handicapped by not having matured sufficiently to develop a healthy detachment from his parents. He admired his father greatly and worshiped his mother. His mother was a kind, feminine, submissive type of woman and inclined to be oversolicitous, catering to her son's every wish. As close as Harry was to his father he never received any sex instruction or advice from him. He was completely in the dark regarding the fundamental facts about sex. On the few occasions that he masturbated he experienced extreme feelings of guilt and manifested numerous psychosomatic symptoms during late adolescence as a result of his *masturbation-guilt*.

This background affected Harry's relations with Mary. He, too, became a victim of a strong conflict between his desire to become sexually intimate with Mary and the feeling that it was wrong to engage in sexual relations prior to marriage. Whenever they indulged in so-called "light petting" Harry would apologize stating, "This is wrong I know, but I can't seem to help myself. I promise to control myself the next time." But instead, the petting continued and took on a more passionate quality. It was a case of two young people very *inhibited* battling with opposing forces within themselves—the force of moral censorship was struggling against the force of physical desire (a mind-body conflict).

As often happens in many cases of this kind, young lovers often compromise and settle for so-called substitute-gratifications. Harry attempted to achieve sexual relief by rubbing against Mary's body in such a way as to bring about an ejaculation. This masturbatory practice of obtaining relief by body-friction (frottage) tends to favor the development of *premature-ejaculation*. The repression of the sexual urge and the frustration of not being able to have intercourse often sets up tension and anxiety in a man to the point that he becomes *overanxious* to relieve himself sexually. When such a situation arises, any gesture of rejection or manifestation of fear and anxiety on the woman's part will very likely precipitate reactions of *impotence* in the male.

Many young unmarried couples who experience problems of this kind involving sexual frustrations believe that they can be solved by indulging in sexual intercourse. They fail to realize that there is no guarantee that consummating the sex act prior to marriage will resolve the sexual conflicts involved. If anything premarital coitus sometimes results in increased feeling of guilt which in turn interferes with the enjoyment of the sex act. The same guilt may cause a man to lose his erection or experience premature ejaculation. In the case of Mary and Harry, they decided not to have intercourse until after they had been married. The initial honeymoon coitus frightened Mary because of the pain she experienced. Harry's fear of hurting her made him even more anxious with the result that he developed increased *sexual inadequacy*. He would achieve his climax a few seconds after inserting his penis in the vagina leaving Mary unsatisfied.

The sexual incompatibility continued. They finally decided to seek guidance from a physician friend who sent them to me for help.

It was a question of having each of them appreciate their respective backgrounds, the nature of their premarital inhibitions and the relationship of their fears and anxieties to the development of their sexual difficulties.

Harry has learned to relax and is successfully able to delay his ejaculation until his wife achieves her orgasm. He was given advice regarding the technique of the ideal relationship which I will discuss below. Mary was also given the necessary advice she required in order to bring about a more harmonious and cooperative relationship between them.

Hirsch, in his clinical experience attributed premature ejaculation to the fact that the average male is incompetent because he was never or poorly prepared for the process. He shows how the voluntary control over the elimination of urine is brought about by adequate training. In my experience with patients, while many of them were inexperienced and untrained, the majority of them suffered from *inhibitions* or conflicts of the kind Stekel describes, some traceable to neurotic incestuous fixations to a mother or sister.

To illustrate, this patient, aged thirty-four, of healthy heredity, married and the father of one child, complained of his inability to satisfy his wife sexually because of his *hasty ejaculation*. Whenever he failed in an attempt at coitus he blamed it on his being fatigued from overwork at the office. His wife induced him to take a vacation, and when this produced no response, he became worried and sought psychiatric treatment. The patient was shy as a child. He had had little premarital heterosexual experience, and boasted that he accorded women the same respect he showed his sister.

He had a strong attachment to his sister whom he idolized. She was very affectionate and demonstrative in her love for him to the extent that his wife could no longer tolerate these unnecessary scenes of brotherly and sisterly affection. The wife and sister, incidentally, were of opposite types. His dreams betrayed his unconscious fixation to his sister, and he presented a number of masturbation fantasies in which his sister played a dominant role.

In cases of impotence the psychoanalyst is on the defensive, the patient evaluates the success of the analyst in terms of physiological results. The fact that this patient, through his acquired insight, was able to delay his ejaculation until such time as his wife achieved an orgasm, was proof that his sexual disorder had been caused by an intrapsychic conflict. His premature ejaculation, in the language of the unconscious, represented his anxiety to get the sex act over quickly as though he were having sex relations with his sister. His wife assumed the role of a sister-surrogate. In other words, in many of these cases of quick ejaculation, the man is torn between the conflict of having to fulfill his duty by having sexual relations which is expected of him, and a force at the unconscious level which may remind him that he is doing something forbidden or taboo; what psychoanalysts refer to as the unconscious incestuous barrier. Stekel has found many cases of premature ejaculation caused by this mother or sister fixation.

I once treated a patient, thirty-one years of age, who also suffered from premature ejaculation and had been referred to me by his physician because of "enuresis" (the inability to control one's bladder). On many occasions he would wet himself while conversing with a young lady. A genito-urinary checkup revealed an absence of any physical disorder.

The patient's father was extremely neurotic. The mother died when the patient was an adolescent. He had been much attached to his mother and became very depressed following her death. Although he was quite introverted as a child, he became more so in later years. The father remarried and the patient found that he did not like his stepmother too well. He also harbored repressed hostility toward the father. The incontinence represented an unconscious regression to infancy (what the French call a retour a l'enfance). The urethral erotism (pleasure in the act of urination) represented a disguised form of masturbation. Through his enuresis he was expressing his hostility toward his father (what a psychoanalyst would call "urethral sadism"—an unconscious wish to urinate on his father to show his contempt for him). Fear and anxiety were the two emotions involved in his premature ejaculation. Insight-therapy eliminated the hostility toward his father which in turn lessened the anxiety responsible for the inability to control his bladder. He realized for the first time also that his "urethral erotism" was a *masturbation equivalent*. When he attempted sexual intercourse following the completion of his analysis he experienced for the first time an ability to retard his ejaculation to the point of satisfying his partner.

This next patient, a young man, age twenty-seven, experienced *premature ejaculation* every time he attempted sex relations. He

came from wealthy parents, was spoiled by having had things given
to him all of his life and soon developed in early life a devil-may-
care attitude toward responsibilities. His father gave him the opportunity to attain a college education, but he soon found that
it required too much work and deprived him of pleasures which
he was constantly seeking. Feeling guilty for not having made a
success at school, he made some endeavor to find a position that
would meet his requirements. But here again he failed. Nothing
seemed to suit him. He was easily bored. He then concluded
that since he did not make good at college and achieved no success in any occupational endeavor, what he needed was the love of
a woman who would inspire him to become a success at something.
He argued that a man needed inspiration and needed a goal-life
and that the right kind of a woman would give him the happiness
that he was seeking, which would be the foundation for a successful future.

One naturally would expect him to exercise neurotic judgment
in the selection of a mate, with such a background. He did this
very thing. He fell in love with a young girl, attractive physically,
but who was a dominating type, frustrated and unhappy. When
asked why he selected such a mate he informed me that he wanted
to find someone whom he could help, that he would serve as an
amateur psychiatrist and would be able to cure her of her emotional conflicts. The marriage turned out to be a very unwise
one and was doomed to fail. Shortly after the wedding ceremony
he complained that he was unable to fulfill his physical relations
adequately, and developed a severe anxiety neurosis associated
with his premature ejaculation. His wife became increasingly neurotic as a result of being sexually unsatisfied. The marriage went
from bad to worse. He took a very irresponsible attitude toward
his treatment, and soon discontinued, with the hope that he would
eventually solve his own problems.

An analysis of this case revealed that he was the victim of a
very dominating mother for whom he developed strong feelings
of ambivalence (love-hate emotions). Unconsciously, he was pro-
jecting the same ambivalence toward all women, particularly the
woman he married. His sexual disorder represented an unconscious
protest against feminine domination. The marriage was a fraudu-
lent one, since he was neither sexually nor emotionally prepared
for marriage.

His wife, neurotic as she was, at least was smart enough to
realize the hopelessness of the situation and saved herself by
starting divorce proceedings. When a wife finds herself married

to a man who is very immature, gets no security of any kind, economic or emotional, and who proves to be sexually impotent, there isn't much point in remaining in a marriage that is destined to bring greater unhappiness.

A divorce in this case was much like an operation on a gangrenous limb that is urgently recommended as a life-saving measure.

In this next case, the marriage was *salvaged*. The husband's sexual inadequacy (*premature ejaculation*) was remedied and the relationship between the husband and wife improved immeasurably.

This particular husband was a very brilliant man, had received a doctor of philosophy degree from a leading university and had married a very beautiful woman. He stated that he had had premarital sex relations with other women but had never experienced to his knowledge any difficulty in satisfying them. However, following his marriage, he found he was unable to control his impulsive ejaculation several minutes after starting the sex act. His wife was naturally frustrated as she was deprived of satisfaction. Her attitudes and responses were normal. There seemed to be no apparent explanation for the sex incompatibility until in one of his sessions he asked me if the following would have any possible bearing on the development of his sexual disorder.

His wife told him during their courtship that when she was sixteen she had been made pregnant by a neighbor's boy and she had to have an abortion to avoid a scandal in the community. Her parents at the time were unaware of her condition. She managed to make a prolonged visit to a friend on the West Coast and in that way succeeded in taking care of the situation.

Not being able to harbor the secret any longer, she broke down and told him the details. Although he seemed grateful to her for having had the courage to be honest with him, he never quite felt the same toward her. The disillusionment haunted him. His idealistic image had been shattered. But he succeeded in suppressing his disappointment, forgave her and married her. Consciously he denied any connection between his sexual disorder and this "psychic trauma" caused by the wife's confession of her past sexual transgression. In the language of the unconscious, he was expressing his inner conflict by having the sex act over with as *quickly* as possible.

When the buried conflict was brought to the level of conscious understanding, he resolved what was definitely a "complex" regarding her past vita-sexualis. The proof was in the pudding. He regained his potency, developed a new and healthier attitude toward his wife and was able to satisfy her adequately.

An unconscious sadistic wish to leave a wife unsatisfied because of some deep-seated frustration has been found by many psychoanalysts to lie at the root of various forms of impotence.

Many frustrated husbands feel too guilty to deny their wives sex relations so they make the attempt, fail and blame their failure to a disorder they cannot understand. They apologize, believing they will do better the next time, but the failure only repeats itself.

I generally tell impotent husbands that there are times when a cinder is so lodged in a person's eye that it takes an eye specialist to extract it. In the same way sex must sometimes be resolved with the assistance of the trained specialist.

Sexual Apathy

Sexual apathy or sexual indifference in men is not too uncommon.

I have run across a good many husband-patients who were married to beautiful women and had *infrequent* sex relations with them.

In many instances these husbands were found to be suffering from "latent homosexuality." Their lack of sexual appetite was symptomatic evidence of their "psychic impotence." The marriage is often motivated by an unconscious desire on the part of the husband to enlist flattering remarks from men admirers relative to their wife's pulchritude.

You may have seen the cartoon of a beautiful woman in a black lace negligee with a disappointed look on her face lying next to a husband in bed who prefers to read a book on some technical subject. It describes the situation perfectly.

Some husbands use the male menopause as an excuse for their loss of interest in coitus.

In the following case, the husband developed neurotic health ailments which he used as an alibi for his sexual apathy. When the health symptoms are subjective in origin and have no organic basis, the condition is sometimes referred to as "psychic invalidism."

Harold came under this category. He began calling his doctor, telling him he suffered from indigestion, irritability and general nervousness. His doctor found nothing wrong with him physically, but he continued to complain of tension, and thought that he was about to suffer a nervous breakdown because of overwork. Actually, he had little responsibility at work and had plenty of time in the evenings to relax. Inquiring into his sex life I learned that Harold had a tendency to deny any connection between his sex life and the way he felt physically. He stated:

"My sex life is all right, doctor. Of course I don't have sex relations with my wife as frequently as I did and I notice that at times I am unable to sustain an erection, but this doesn't seem to bother my wife, and I have no conflicts about my diminished virility."

As soon as I showed him that what he was suffering from was not the fear of a nervous breakdown, but a fear of increasing impotence and that his health complaints were a manifestation, unconsciously, of his anxiety concerning his potency, he then began to make a change for the better. When he was assured that potency is a matter of mental attitudes he resumed regular sex relations and his symptoms began to disappear.

Many fat men develop sexual apathy. They find greater pleasure in eating. Their libido or sex hunger becomes displaced in eating, by a greater desire for food. Excess food and alcohol become substitutes for sexual pleasure. Of course there are exceptions, particularly those obese bon vivants who include women with their food, wine and song.

"Condom Impotence"

There are thousands of men who suffer from what I would like to call "condom impotence"—the inability to sustain an erection because of not wanting to use a condom. These men who have come to me with this problem claimed that they simply cannot perform unless they engage in sexual relations without being hampered by the wearing of a contraceptive; that they have tried to use a condom on several occasions, and failed each time to maintain an erection.

This "condom complex" is the result of a combination of frustrated attitudes towards the use of a contraceptive and bad technique in its use. For example, these husbands will say, "Doctor, wearing one of those damn rubbers is like taking a shower with your socks on." They also claim that the pleasurable sensation is diminished with the use of a condom.

I generally tell such patients that it is normal for a man to want his sexual enjoyment unimpeded, but he must discipline himself by making the necessary sacrifice so that his partner need not be subjected to the risk of unwanted pregnancy. I attempt to convince them that any normal man with the right attitude and proper technique can function normally even though he wears a condom. There is overwhelming evidence to prove this as manifested by the fact that it is the most widely used contraceptive. And justly so, for it is the safest.

The neurotic, selfish husband who becomes "condom conscious" is thinking only of his own pleasure. His impotence represents an unwillingness to sacrifice even a small pleasure he believes he is entitled to. I have found that men who experience "condom impotence" are inadequate in other aspects of the sexual relationship. This same selfishness manifests itself in their technique of lovemaking. Many of these men prefer to resort to *coitus interruptus* (withdrawal of the penis prior to ejaculation) which causes their wives to be tense and nervous, fearing that the withdrawal will not take place in time. This, in turn, invites the development of frigidity in thousands of women. How often have I heard a woman patient say to me, "Doctor, my husband always promises to pull out in time, but the result is always the same. I wind up becoming pregnant."

In reëducating men who have this "condom complex," it is necessary to eliminate various errors in technique which tend to cause impotence reactions. To illustrate: a husband may engage in spontaneous lovemaking with his wife, and may successfully arouse her and himself, but is suddenly reminded by his wife that he should take precautions before entrance. The husband then proceeds to search frantically for the condom, and becomes angry with his wife when she is unable to remember where he had placed them. The conversation may run something like this:

"Darling, I believe you put them in the top drawer behind the socks. Remember you said you didn't want Johnny to run across them."

The husband's anger generally increases when he discovers that the condom is not where he had hoped to find it. He becomes more frustrated, takes his anger out on his wife, and destroys the entire mood for lovemaking. When he finally does find the package, opens it, returns to bed, and attempts to proceed, he discovers that he has lost his erection and his wife her desire.

After a few such disastrous experiences, these husbands come to the erroneous conclusion that they simply cannot function properly with a condom. I invariably prove to these victims of a "condom complex" that with an improved technique, they can learn to eliminate the frustration and anxieties that are responsible for the loss of the erection. For example, I advise all husbands that prior to the beginnings of lovemaking, they should have the condom ready for use within arm's reach. The husband can then engage in an amount of foreplay which will stimulate him sufficiently to achieve an erection. (And in this respect, the wife can do much to help her husband to attain an erection.) When he is ready for entrance and his wife is ready to receive him, he can quickly roll on the condom which requires a matter of seconds, and can lubricate the end of the contraceptive with his own saliva. After this he can proceed to achieve his orgasm, keeping in mind, of course, that he must attempt to delay his ejaculation until such time as his wife is able to achieve her own orgasm.

The Castration Complex

Excluding the minority of cases of impotence due to some organic condition, impotence for the most part is associated with a condition known in psychoanalysis as the "castration-complex." This occurs among males who are highly *sensitive* and suffer from some deep-seated emotional conflict.

For example, an overt male homosexual is able to attain an erection when he makes advances to some member of his own sex. But when he attempts to have sex relations with a woman he develops a reaction of impotence. Physiologically there is nothing wrong with his sexual apparatus. But psychologically, he harbors neurotic fears associated with the sex act, which figuratively speaking, is equivalent to a feeling of no longer possessing a penis or of it being amputated. In many cases *guilt* is the predominant factor involved. The homosexual may be so attached to his mother or sister that when he makes love to a woman, it is almost like making love to his mother or sister. Incestuous thoughts are common to homosexuals. We say their unconscious guilt "castrates" them. They often come to the false conclusion that they are permanently impotent insofar as women are concerned. They fail to realize that the "castration" is psychological in origin and brought on by their own unconscious conflicts. Hence we speak of it as "autocastration" or self-imposed impotence.

We have a better example of this, when a wife makes a statement in the bedroom such as—"If you insist on having a party, let's get it over with. I'm tired and want to go to bed." If the husband was previously aroused sexually, he loses his desire immediately and if he forces himself to go through with it, may fail in his attempt to sustain an erection. There are many husbands who are castrated by their wives because of their behavior or some remarks they make at the wrong time.

Revenge may be a motive, particularly if the wife has committed adultery or has done something to incur the displeasure of the husband.

Feelings of inferiority can also bring about this same "castration phenomenon."

I have found among married couples, that the husband who is most apt to suffer from impotence reactions is the one who is married to a "Virago"—a wife who is masculine, dominating and inclined to become abusive. I tell such neurotic wives that every time they insult their husband, it is equivalent to short-circuiting the current, resulting in the fuse burning out. Some men have learned to insulate these wires or nerves leading to their sexual apparatus and are protected against these castration influences. The opposite also holds true of course. Men who are abusive to their wives cause in them reactions of frigidity.

The intelligent couple is aware of the importance of personality compatibility in relation to sex incompatibility. They are wise enough to realize that sex begins in the mind—that better sex comes from harmonious living.

The following case involves a rather unusual combination of a husband suffering from impotence caused by "psychic castration," married to a women suffering from frigidity. On the surface one would think there was no problem—that both partners would reconcile themselves to each others' sexual inadequacy. This, however, was not the case.

The wife, although suffering from frigidity, threatened to divorce her husband unless he agreed to psychoanalytic treatment. She also decided to sue for a divorce in the event that her husband failed to respond to psychotherapy.

At the time the husband was courting his wife she had been going with a rival suitor. She claimed she loved this other person and considered him the more eligible candidate for marriage. The husband however, succeeded in persuading his wife to make the decision in his favor. On the wedding night she began to cry, and began thinking of the other person. She humiliated her husband and went so far as to confess that she had been intimate with her former lover, and that his technique of lovemaking was superior.

The husband, of course, upon learning of this prior to an attempt at coitus, became impotent. Things went from bad to worse. They quarreled over trifles which led to a threatened separation.

The wife belonged to the masculine-protest type as described by Adler. She was aggressive, and extremely career-minded up to the time of marriage. She psychologically castrated her husband by sadistically confessing her premarital intimacy prior to a honeymoon coitus. The husband, on the other hand, was weak, passive and infantile. He was more masochistic than sadistic. He idealized women, and was greatly inhibited and inexperienced. However, there was a sadistic component at work in his impotence, for he unconsciously gained revenge satisfaction by leaving his wife out on a limb, so to speak. His penis was insulted and it behaved accordingly. When he began to regain his potency, she developed "vaginismus" which I felt served as an outlet for her sense of guilt arising from her psychic infidelity. There was also one other potential explanation, namely she wished to restore her virginity psychologically by bringing about the difficulty of penetration found in virgins. This clue was gathered from a statement she made relative to her premarital chastity.

Analysis of both husband and wife revealed the psychological causes of their sexual inadequacies. Their relationship improved to a point where they decided to remain together. Their marriage had been definitely a competitive one, emotionally and sexually.

One young man I treated had an overpowering fear of marriage, especially in its sexual aspects. He used this fear as the vehicle for fantastic imaginings concerning what would happen to him if he indulged in sexual acts, and of course the content of these imaginings were a poor substitution for a normal married sex life, which he wanted so greatly. His trouble was that he was afraid any real experience would prove him impotent. We speak of such a fear as part of this same castration phenomenon described above.

Treatment and Cure

Impotence or sexual inadequacy may be responsible for a multiplicity of psychosomatic complaints. It also influences the personality and disposition of the individual.

Impotent men generally turn out to be "health neurotics" or "sexual hypochondriacs." They go to many doctors, frequently suffering from a variety of ailments—insomnia, fatigue, depression, lack of appetite, indigestion, headaches, nervousness and tension, etc. Men who are impotent are also difficult to get along with. They project their inner unhappiness onto others.

General practitioners of medicine today are aware of the relationship between impotence problems and psychosomatic disturbances. When they suspect that the health symptoms which fail to respond favorably to medication, represent in the language of the unconscious, disguised evidence of sexual inadequacy, they refer such patients to a psychiatrist.

Psychiatrists first determine if the impotence is due to any physical or organic causes. A genito-urinary checkup by a competent urologist can rule out quickly any disease or condition that requires medical treatment.

Anything that builds up the physical vitality of the person (good food, fresh air, rest, vitamins, etc.) all help to favor the restoration of potency. Narcotics and the excessive use of alcohol must be discontinued.

In impotence caused by glandular deficiencies, some doctors have prescribed injections of a substance known as "testosterone propionate." However results have not always been encouraging.

When it has been established that the impotence is psychological in origin, the next step is to inquire whether or not the wife is suffering from a physical condition that needs the attention of a gynecologist, particularly a condition that causes intercourse to be painful. Many husbands lose their erection if they feel their wives are made uncomfortable during the sex act. The wife may also require specific information as to what she can do to eliminate errors in technique on her part and how to build up her husband's sexual confidence.

For example, Dr. Edwin Hirsch advises that "shyness, coyness, apparent sensitivity and all the other attributes born within woman to augment her attractiveness are gradually to be shed in the marital bed." He states also that "the active participation of the female helps the male overcome his sexual fear and thus she promotes sexual courage within the male who previously felt inferior because of supposed weakness."

Cases of psychic impotence that are caused by factors deeply rooted in the unconscious require rational psychotherapy. The prognosis is essentially good if the individual concerned manifests a genuine "will to be cured." The duration of treatment depends on each individual case. Some cases of impotence respond favorably to a short-term analysis while others require deep psychological therapy over a prolonged period of time.

Many husbands have to be educated in sex matters, particularly in lovemaking technique. I generally recommend that they read several books on the subject, books preferably written by physicians who are considered authorities in the field.

The practice of withdrawal prior to ejaculation (coitus interruptus) should be discouraged. Anxieties and fears of various kinds generally yield to psychotherapy and can be eliminated.

Lubricants have a tendency to make the male organ less sensitive and enables the husband to prolong the coital act.

Small quantities of alcohol in the form of a glass of wine or one or two cocktails generally relaxes the nervous system and makes the sexual partner less inhibited. It also acts as an aphrodisiac (sexual stimulant).

Improving the relationship between husband and wife—making the marriage more harmonious—aids us to achieve our therapeutic goal.

In conclusion I can safely say that psychoanalysts, as a result of having learned much about the problem of impotence, are encouraged by the large number of impotent men who are responding successfully to psychotherapeutic treatment. Here is what Dr. Benjamin Karpman says:

"Barring a certain number of cases of impotence which have a physical basis, the larger number of cases of impotence are of psychological causation. Diagnostically, the condition should be regarded as an hysterical conversion reaction. In the majority of cases, psychotherapy offers the only reasonable approach and many cases can be cured or improved within a short time."

Husbands who suffer from impotence feel quite guilty that they are not able to adequately satisfy their wives. They are embarrassed and humiliated when their attempts end in failures.

Therefore wives are cautioned not to berate, ridicule or humiliate their husbands because of their sexual inadequacy. Reactions of disappointment only makes matters worse and makes the husband feel more inferior, inadequate and guilty, which in turn enhances his impotence.

Marie N. Robinson

Sexual Surrender

The ability to achieve normal orgasm can be called the physical counterpart of psychological surrender. In most cases of true frigidity it follows on a woman's surrender of her rebellious and infantile attitudes as the day the night. It is the sign that she has given up the last vestige of resistance to her nature and has embraced womanhood with soul *and* body.

The achievement of orgasm, usually is the *last* step in the process of growing up. If one reviews in one's mind the actual orgastic experience it is not difficult to see why this is so.

For a woman orgasm requires a trust in one's partner that is absolute. Recall for a moment that the physical experience is often so profound that it entails the loss of consciousness for a period of time. As we know, in sexual intercourse, as in life, man is the actor, woman the passive one, the receiver, the acted upon. Giving oneself up in this passive manner to another human being, making oneself his willing partner to such seismic physical experiences, means one must have complete faith in the other person. In the sexual embrace any trace of buried hostility, fear of one's role, will show clearly and unmistakably.

But there is even more to the psychic state necessary for orgasm than faith in one's partner and readiness to surrender. There must be a sensual eagerness to surrender; in the woman's orgasm *the excitement comes from the act of surrender*. There is a tremendous surging physical ecstasy in the yielding itself, in the feeling of being the passive instrument of another person, of being stretched out supinely beneath him, taken up will-lessly by his passion as leaves are swept up before a wind.

There can, it is clear, be no crossed fingers about such yielding, no reservations in such surrender. As one thinks of it one can certainly feel why, of all the steps in the process of yielding, of surrendering, the orgasm should be the last. To those who are moving toward it the experience often remains for a time elusive because its very totality, its uncompromising demand that the whole being be swept up in the experience, remains somewhat frightening.

Orgasm, as I have said, is the physical aspect of surrendering. However, while there are similarities between the physical and the psychological experience, there is also an important difference between the two.

The difference is that orgasm cannot be sought entirely rationally. It will arrive when it will arrive, as the end process of a total change in a frigid woman's deepest psychological attitudes. It cannot be sought separately or as an end in itself. Indeed, to seek it directly, to wait upon it, to try to force it are the surest possible ways of postponing its arrival.

The idea that orgasm can be forced is typical of the thinking of a frigid woman. We have seen that, because she is basically frightened, basically mistrusts her husband's love of her and her own femininity, she has to feel that she is "in control" all the time. The trouble with that standpoint is that in real orgasm a woman must be out of control; must willfully, delightedly desire to be entirely so.

The delusion that the orgasm can or should be sought as an end in itself and not as the result of a deep change . . . has been fostered by many of the books which have dealt with the problem of frigidity or with the role or responsibility of woman in marriage. One recent book counseled the conscious contraction of certain muscles during intercourse, holding that this would heighten sexual pleasure. Other books emphasize the importance of position during intercourse. Their tacit or stated contention is that orgastic potency can be achieved by mechanical means.

The simple fact is that concentrating on one's sensations during intercourse, wondering if one is feeling the "right" feeling, can destroy real sexual passion more completely than any technique I can think of. We know this from scores of patients. Such a clinical and objective attitude toward local sexual sensations merely reflects the frigid woman's need to be in control of a situation and her fear of surrendering herself to her man. She can get little more from this obsessive scrutiny of her sexual reactions than an even more frustrating experience than usual.

Is there, then, an attitude one can take toward orgasm before one has achieved it? Yes, there is, and we have found it a helpful and productive one. This attitude may be summarized in this fashion: If one has truly pursued the goal of self-surrender, uprooting and exposing attitudes left over from childhood and youth, the ability to achieve orgasm must inevitably arrive. Until that time, and particularly during intercourse, *one must put the matter out of one's mind entirely.*

The growth of a woman's ability to have orgasm is a natural growth. It has been impeded by her psychic attitudes; it resumes its development when these attitudes changes. It is as natural a move as the move from winter to spring. Gradually she finds herself allowing her new tenderness and concern for her husband to become a part of the meaning of her sexual embrace. She sees and feels the pleasure her sexual thawing brings him, and this process becomes circular, his increased pleasure giving her more pleasure. And with his pleasure in mind she now seeks out more and more those things that please him, and her exploration leads inevitably to the discovery that what pleases him most, outside of his own sensations, is her pleasure. This mutual spiraling of feeling ultimately climaxes in her unconscious decision to give him the greatest psychological pleasure of all, her total surrender to the delights he can bring her.

For many women the ability to surrender physically comes rather swiftly; to others it is a very gradual process, as though the unconscious mind needed to build up a reserve of reassurances before it felt perfectly secure. In either case, but particularly in the latter, they can be forewarned of one important thing: sexual thaw will not proceed uninterruptedly; there is no straight line from frigidity to true womanhood. I should like to explain this more fully.

When, in the sexual embrace, a woman allows herself to experience more pleasure as her physical sensations increase, a part of her unconscious mind very frequently takes alarm and causes her to draw back from any further immediate advance.

If you stop to ponder this point you will find it readily understandable in terms of our former discussions. The experiences and relationships upon which frigidity is based took place a long time ago, often in very early childhood. They occasioned fear in the child, fear of sexuality, of surrender to one's sensual impulses, or powerful guilt. Now, as one starts to move toward a resumption of one's sensuality, it is almost certain that these irrational, buried fears will try to reassert themselves.

In most cases it is not necessary to uncover the childhood incidents upon which these fears were based. If one will insist on pursuing the techniques for inner change I have described here, these fears will finally become inoperative in the sexual area. It is, however, necessary to know that you *are* experiencing such fears. Generally speaking, they do not show themselves directly. A woman will not say to herself: "That new sensual experience I had last night is causing me alarm."

The fear separates itself from the sensual experience and expresses itself indirectly. The woman may find herself once again becoming quarrelsome, critical of her husband; old feelings of deprivation or of inferiority may reassert themselves with apparently new vigor. And the new sensual capacity may retire once more from view. The reason: the old defenses are protecting one against the new femininity.

Such anxiety reactions, I wish to make clear, should not give any real cause for concern. Indeed, one does not have to analyze them or to investigate them. One merely has to be *aware* that they *are* the result of the new advance in sensuality, the new ability to surrender oneself a bit more completely than formerly. Advance of this kind is never lost in any final sense.

Let me give you an example of a typical reaction to such an advance. The patient was of the type I call the clitoridal woman. Her orgasm had been exclusively clitoral. Together we had covered the ground that I have presented in this section. She had been able to air her feelings about men and about woman's lot; she had corrected her view of men and, in a very real way, had begun to view her husband with the eyes of a loving woman. Then one day she came to me in great excitement. It was unmistakable, she told me; during last night's love-making she had felt, for the first time in her life, distinctly pleasurable vaginal sensations.

But in the next session her attitude was entirely different. She had had a quarrel with her husband over some trivial matter, and she forthwith launched into the kind of tirade against men I had not heard from her for several sessions.

After letting her air her feelings, I pointed out to her the possible connection between her new sensual experience and her regression to her old defenses. She was incredulous and remained so until, a week later, the episode repeated itself in its entirety: vaginal sensations and delight, followed quickly by a quarrel and ill feelings toward her husband. Forewarned, she was now on guard for such negative reactions, and when they did appear, knowing their significance, she was able to handle them, prevent herself from actually acting out her irrational feelings by quarreling with her husband.

In making the above point I do not wish to be misunderstood or thought to be contradicting myself. I am not advising women to fixate obsessively on their new sexual sensations. However, noticing such new experiences will be unavoidable, and I am simply saying that it is helpful to know that they may be followed by minor neurotic regressions.

The above observations now lead me to a closely related matter which I consider to be of central importance.

In the move toward womanhood there comes a juncture in most cases which can be called "the danger point." When a woman is working with a therapist on her problem, the danger when she reaches this point is minimized by the fact that her therapist is aware of the problem and can usually help her to handle it when it arises. If a woman is working on her problem by herself, however, she should be strongly forewarned of her potential reaction.

This danger point generally comes when a woman who has suffered frigidity has at last allowed herself to experience orgasm for the first time. Her immediate reaction is one of tremendous relief. But this is almost always followed by the same kind of regression I have described above; only this time the pull-back from her own advance and from her husband is far more powerful. We have seen in some . . . case histories . . . just how dangerous this period can be to the entire relationship. Indeed, the wife may at this point precipitate a crisis of such severity that the marriage itself is endangered.

The form the difficulty takes is always individual; it is usually an exaggerated version of the particular woman's most typical neurotic characteristic. If she is argumentative, she is apt to start a fight of proportions heretofore undreamed of. If her tendency is to become depressed, her melancholy can become very, very profound indeed. If she is critical and carping, she can make Craig's wife appear to be a normal, healthy woman.

I am not exaggerating. It is not impossible that many divorces are caused by wives who, by the natural reassurance that marriage to a tender husband often brings, have moved close to their true natures all unwittingly. They achieve orgasm; and then, without the benefit of any insight, the intense anxiety reaction sets in, causing a powerful desire to flee from the frightening situation.

The pull-back, of course, is caused by an exacerbation of early fears brought on by the orgasmic experience. But again I must emphasize that the chief danger during this period of reaction lies in the fact that the woman sees no connection between her emotional upset and the successful sexual experience she has just achieved. Why should she see such a connection? Orgasm is what she has been consciously waiting for, has it not? It would only be surprising if she did see a connection between the two experiences.

Her emotional outburst represents, at this point, an inner panic. Consider this: in the course of growing up it took her years to construct a defensive system against a feminine sensuality which she had learned was dangerous or wicked. Though this defensive system (her frigidity, her psychological rejection of men, etc.) had deprived her of much, it had at least allowed her to feel secure in some deep manner; she has maintained her defenses in order to hold onto her feeling of unconscious security.

And now, with orgasm, she feels all these defenses swept away in a moment. She feels exposed, guilty, naked to her imaginary enemy, tempted to surrender to him completely. In her panic she forgets the advance she has been making, the revaluation of her attitude toward men, children, womanhood.

She cannot admit the irrational nature of her unconscious fear, even to herself, so she represses it and creates an exterior diversion. Real trouble is always an excellent defense against insight.

In the case histories I have given of frigid women you will recall that the discovery of true feminine sexuality within her often brought a woman to therapy. In a sense the therapist, at the beginning, represents a safe harbor, a protection against the woman's frightening femininity. Coming for help is, in part, a kind of flight in itself; a search for a place to hide.

When women do not understand the nature of their actions in such cases, the flight can take a potentially harmful direction. I have known some who "fall in love" with another man at this juncture. Others feel that they have really discovered just how incompatible their husbands are and think seriously of divorce. Still others develop somatic difficulties, sometimes serious ones. I know two women who had had tuberculosis during adolescence and both broke down again during this "danger point." In both cases their disease had been considered totally arrested.

I realize, of course, that such reactions sound alarming to a reader. However, my intention in stating the facts here is not to frighten but to forewarn. There is nothing in *reality* to be alarmed about. Feelings are not reality. But a woman must be certain that she does not act upon her feelings. The only danger is that she might.

But, I am often asked, how can one cope with such fears, fears so deep one does not even dare to let them into the conscious mind? The answer is that, generally speaking, you do not have to cope with them in any active way. They will pass. All you have to do is to sit tight, so to speak. The unconscious will in fairly short order (a week, a month) calm down.

Reality, a good reality, can prove to the infantile unconscious that it has nothing to fear. When one has quieted again, resumed the straight line of progress one had been pursuing, orgasm will occur again. This time the reaction of alarm is generally far less. By the third and fourth times it has become virtually nonexistent. The neurotic, defensive portion of one's mind has then been permanently disarmed.

All frigidities are basically related. We could prescribe no general approach that would be helpful if this were not so. However, I have found that there are specific measures that can be of great value if applied to the individual kinds of frigidity. Indeed, if these measures are omitted, the return to full feminine maturity can be slowed down dramatically or even stopped, at least on the sexual level.

I must warn once again, however, that one should be careful to put no reliance on these techniques if they are not combined with the "feeling through" and revaluative processes I have described. With this in mind, then, let us examine these measures that can be taken by individual types.

First let us look at the *masculine type*. As we have seen both in our abstract description and in our case-history approach to this type, the only method of gratification possible for this woman is clitoral. She achieves climax through self-masturbation or through masturbation by her husband. She has few if any vaginal sensations during intercourse, and her orgasmic reactions are confined entirely to the clitoris. This is so even if she is able to establish contact between her clitoris and her husband's penis in intercourse. In most cases vaginal entrance of the penis is a matter of indifference to such women; to some it is actively disliked.

We have seen how women establish this erotic primacy of the clitoris. Because of early fears connected with becoming women they have firmly rejected the vagina. They have held onto infantile and pubertal masturbation long past the point when it is normal for a girl to give it up.

Now, with a new evaluation of the meaning of feminine sexuality, with a new tenderness and warmth toward their husbands available to them, the time at length comes when it is possible for them to switch from clitoral sensations to vaginal. However, the pathways for satisfaction have been set up for many years, the "habit" of clitoral climax has been deeply established. What should they do?

We have found that, if the clitoridal woman wishes to achieve a more mature form of sexual satisfaction she may be aided in reaching her goal if she can give up the form of gratification she now employs. This form of gratification still symbolizes an attachment to the earlier form of sexuality. For that reason, of course, it is a defense against the type of sexuality that stands for psychic maturity. The simple decision to abandon the less mature form of gratification often signifies a deep decision within a woman: the decision to take the final step toward womanhood.

On the other hand, many women experience the abandonment of clitoral gratification as a keen deprivation and deeply resent it. In such cases the resentment signifies that they have not sufficiently "felt through" their childhood defenses against femininity.

Obviously there are only two possible steps to take: one can continue the practice of masturbation or one can examine the resentment that is caused by giving it up. If a woman decides on the first step, progress toward the goal of vaginal orgasm may be slowed down or halted completely.

If, however, one decides to examine the resentment more closely, using the "feeling through" technique I have described, the bases upon which the resentment rests may be discovered and disposed of, just as resentments against men and against motherhood were disposed of. Indeed, many of the same feelings, though now more specifically related to sexuality, often come out.

Let me give an example. A patient with a clitoridal fixation had worked through many of her negative feelings toward her husband; she had seen that these feelings had been based on an irrational envy and fear of men and a depreciation of women. Her progress, however, seemed to halt completely when she attempted to give up clitoral masturbation.

All of her early feelings toward men returned, only now they referred to the act of intercourse. Men were the lucky ones; they were on top. Just as in life. Woman's classical sexual position in our civilization (on the bottom) was "degrading and humiliating." It represented her position vis-à-vis men in life. As in life, men were the ones for whom irresponsible enjoyment was designed; no wonder they could enjoy sex so much; and they couldn't get pregnant; they didn't have to menstruate, etc., etc.

She aired these irrational feelings quite completely and saw them for what they were. She saw that they were a recapitulation, in sexual terms, of the negative feelings she had expressed earlier toward men. She realized, too, that her feeling that it was humiliating and degrading to be "on the bottom" really showed her deep distress, fear of, and underlying depression about what she took to be woman's role in life.

The patient was rather surprised to see these irrational feelings reappearing. However, because of her earlier work on her psychological defenses, it was not too difficult for her to dispose of these negative attitudes toward the sexual act and to integrate her positive feelings about womanhood with woman's sexual role. At that point she was not far from achieving vaginal orgasm. Within a month or so she had achieved it.

When a woman consciously abandons clitoral gratification in favor of her search for a deeper and more abiding joy, the switch from clitoris to vagina usually takes place gradually. I have known cases in which it has happened rather quickly, but it is more frequently a matter of two, three, or even more months.

One further word on this type: the clitoridal woman may discover that she cannot take the final step to vaginal primacy alone. She may need direct and expert counsel. This should in no way discourage her. The problem is a deep-seated one, but it almost certainly can be resolved. If after a few months of trying to handle the problem alone one finds out that too little progress is being achieved, I strongly urge that outside help be sought.

I have heard the therapy for *total frigidity* described as "a problem in rearing." Recalling the case history of Patricia Agnew, one can easily see why this phrase is so apt. The causes of this kind of frigidity go back to infancy. Punishment for infantile masturbation and/or an overly strong early fixation on the male parent causes the child to repress her sexual feeling entirely. She does not go through, in any complete way, the normal stages of psychosexual development; a part of her, the sensual and sexual part, remains frozen in the bud.

In my opinion, psychotherapy is frequently indicated when the frigidity is of this total type. The sexual aspect of the problem is sometimes too deeply seated for the individual to handle alone.

However, I know of several women who, when therapy was not possible, were able to make great strides toward truly feminine values and behavior by adopting the procedures described in this section. Though some of them were not able to achieve orgasm, the psychological change they were able to effect in their personalities added greatly to their general happiness and security in marriage. A few even were able to achieve orgasm.

For women with this form and degree of frigidity who wish to or must attempt to approach their problem without outside aid, I should like to point out that if general sexual development is resumed it will tend to recapitulate the stages of psycho-sexual growth we have described. Thus we find that when such women through insight, are once again able to experience sensual feeling they sometimes go through a period of self-masturbation. Recall that this stage had been omitted in their development.

I should like to emphasize that, in terms of the final resolution of her sexual frigidity, this masturbation is perfectly normal for this kind of woman—just as it is contraindicated for the masculine or clitoridal woman. The totally frigid woman is making up for phases of development she had missed in growing up. Guilt feelings about masturbation in such cases are harmful, and the ego of the individual can be put in the service of overcoming such emotions. For those who have moral feelings against masturbation it is some times helpful to realize that modern scientific findings indicate that societal prohibitions against it were partly based on insufficient and incorrect information. It was believed for centuries that pubertal or infantile masturbation was harmful physically and mentally. It has now been clearly demonstrated, however, that the only harm of any kind that can come from masturbation is the psychological harm that is caused by guilt feelings connected with it.

The fact is that, in attempting to establish her lost sexuality, the totally frigid woman may be helped by encouraging any sensuality, however meager, she may discover in herself, whether it is psychological or physical. The sensuous feelings engendered by sun-bathing, of the press of the earth under one when lying down in a field or under a tree, the soft beauty of the moon on a hazy night, the warmth and coziness of a fireplace as the rain beats upon the roof —if she will allow her body and mind to enjoy these kinds of things, they can help to awaken her dormant sensuality, can help her to move back from her dusty sensationless condition toward a reappreciation of the glory of the senses.

Some women may discover (if they can consciously dispense with their inhibitions or with a hindering sense of propriety) that they are able to experience sensual feelings of a moderately keen nature in areas which are secondarily erotic. During our work together one woman suddenly discovered that she enjoyed having her back stroked by her husband. Another discovered that though she could not enjoy kissing her husband if she was in bed with him she could if she remained fully clothed in the living room. A third was able to respond quite strongly to clitoral stroking if she had a drink of liquor with her husband beforehand. In each case the sensual capacities described in these women preceded their work with me. But it was only when they realized that they possessed unexplored potentialities and that these could be used to enrichen their sensual lives, to move them closer to the ultimate experience of love, did they dare to take their first tentative steps toward maturity.

As we have observed, *partial frigidity* includes those degrees of frigidity that lie between total frigidity and normalcy. This includes such a large range of sexual reaction (or the lack of it) that it would not be possible to describe specific measures that would be helpful in all cases.

However, those who find they are closer to total frigidity on this scale than to normalcy often discover that the general techniques just described are helpful. Many of these, if they persevere, will find that they will ultimately achieve orgasm without requiring psychotherapy. Others, after determining the distance they can go on their own, may wish to seek outside help.

For those who lie closer to normal feminine sexual reactions it is usually sufficient to persist in the techniques for self-discovery and self-realization described earlier in this section.

As we saw when we examined *psychic frigidity*, it seemed to be the exception that proved the rule. Women of this type are able to have orgasms that are apparently normal. But they cannot form a relationship with any man that will endure. They frequently select ineligible men as partners or, if by chance the man happens to become eligible, they will then flee the relationship. If they cannot flee it they become sexually frigid.

We have found that women with this type of frigidity can help themselves by denying themselves the easy gratification to which they are accustomed. Their facile sensuality is a red herring used to disguise their real fears from themselves. They can come to grips with these fears only when they allow themselves to enter a close psychological relationship with an eligible member of the opposite sex.

I have called the steps by which a woman moves from frigidity to emotional and sexual maturity a "process." Once really started, it tends, almost by inertia, to complete itself, needing only a kind of minimal guidance from one's intelligence and a few specific facts.

For the sake of clarity, then, let us review what the steps in this process are.

It is launched by the surfacing of negative emotions and fantasies from which the frigid woman has been hiding. These emotions and fantasies reflect an underlying attitude toward the opposite sex which is based on early childhood fears and misunderstandings and which is seriously affecting one's ability to love. As the emotions are exposed to full view they lose their power for harm, for it is only when they are partially or totally hidden from oneself that their primitive force is dangerous. When they are exposed to the light of intelligence and judgment, their power over one can at first be greatly reduced and finally can be disposed of entirely.

When all or most of one's negative daydreams and emotions have been exposed, step two can be taken. This is a revaluation of the male in terms of his real nature and real goals. We saw that his real nature is basically aggressive, and one of his chief aims in life is to put this aggression to work for his wife and family. Viewed from this standpoint, man's differences from woman are seen in their true light. The frigid woman, from this revaluation, learns that she can now let down her defenses, knowing that her husband, far from being hostile or wishing to enslave or exploit her, is her loving ally. She sees that his once-feared aggression is the very thing that makes it really safe for her to be a woman.

From this realization, on a deep level of her personality, the next step follows naturally. She first achieves a tranquillity and then a serenity she had not known before. This is followed by an acceptance of and a surrender to her real role—that of a loving and wise wife who glories in her womanly functions and in her man's love.

The last step was seen to be the achievement of orgasm as a natural sequel to her psychological maturation. This part of the process we saw was attended by a resurgence of early anxiety when orgasm finally occurred. This anxiety caused a desire to flee from the newly acquired ability to love. However, the only danger at this juncture was seen to be the possibility that the anxious woman might act upon her fears. Forewarned of this reaction, she is forearmed, and by seeking further insights and waiting out the anxiety she will find that it will gradually subside completely.

These general steps, then, outline the process that can lead to recovery. I can add little to them. I have seen this method work for many women and I know of no other that will.

Patience and faith are the prime requisites for emotional maturation. Nobody can name the time it will take for any given individual to cross the bridge to womanhood. But that most women can cross it, there can be no doubt. Those who have gone before make that point ultimately clear.

Milton R. Sapirstein

Outcasts from Eden: The Paradox of the Marriage Manual

A good way of wrecking a new marriage is to present either or both of its partners with a marriage manual. . . . Paradoxical? Yes . . . Wildly exaggerated? Not really. The truth is that these solemn treatises, written though they are with all the good will in the world, make unreliable guides for the young people who consult them. Much of their advice is based on erroneous assumptions about men and women and the standards they set are rarely attainable. In doing so, they may create emotional strains which aggravate the very problems they are designed to solve.

Unless they are protected by a sense of humor, even quite settled couples may feel a sense of unease, of dissatisfaction with themselves and each other, when exposed to the counsels of perfection in the manuals. Measured against so glowing an ideal, the reasonable happiness they have achieved seems tame and flat, somehow unworthy. I can fancy them, those earnest couples, gazing at each other with a wild surmise. Would life have been richer, more meaningful, with somebody else? Or are they both lacking, dull clods forever condemned to mediocrity? A couple thus jolted out of its accustomed serenity might well agree with the poet who said:

"Never, being damned, see Paradise.
The heart will sweeten at its look;
Nor hell was known, till Paradise
Our senses shook." *

It is, indeed, a sense-shaking paradise to which the manuals beckon the true believer in their precepts. And, as I said before, unattainable, men and women being what they are. Perhaps I should make one point clear at the outset. When a couple, in spite of the most heroic efforts, fails to achieve the idyllic and continuous bliss described in the *vade mecum*, both husband and wife are apt to feel guilty and defrauded. But, in the majority of cases, it is the husband who feels most guilty, the wife most defrauded. To understand why, we must go back to the latter part of the nineteenth century and the pioneering studies in sexual psychology written by Havelock Ellis.

The reason we must do so is that contemporary marriage manuals, even the most recent, are all in greater or less degree variations on a theme first made explicit by Ellis. And that theme, in turn, was predicated on the kind of marriage and the kind of sexual relations within marriage which were the rule in Victorian England. Ellis, whose mind was both stimulating and generous, was an ardent feminist, as eager to wake women from the sexual torpor of centuries as others were to see her take a place in the world at large. It was the duty of men, he felt, to make that awakening glorious. As late as 1933, when a short version† of his massive "Studies" was published, he declared:

"The chief reason why women are considered 'frigid' lies less in themselves than in men. It is evident throughout that while in men

---

* Leonie Adams, *Those Not Elect*. New York, Robert M. McBride & Co., 1925.
† *Psychology of Sex*. New York, Emerson Books, 1933.

the sexual impulse tends to develop spontaneously and actively, in women, however powerful it may be latently and more or less subconsciously, its active manifestations need in the first place to be called out. That, in our society, is normally the husband's function to effect. It is his part to educate his wife in the life of sex; it is he who will make sex demands a conscious desire to her. If he, by his ignorance, prejudice, impatience or lack of insight fails to play his natural part, his wife may, by no defect of her own, be counted as 'frigid.' "

While Ellis was probably the first Anglo-Saxon of note to place his *imprimatur* upon this theory, and while he was primarily responsible for its subsequent wide circulation, similar views had long been expressed by continental writers, notably Balzac and Stendhal. (The latter, incidentally, in his "De l'Amour," proved no mean feminist himself, a champion of women's rights at a time and in a country where women themselves displayed little interest in the subject. Among the reasons which motivated his attitude, not the least was his belief that genuine love is only possible between two free human beings, not between master and slave.)

Let me repeat: Ellis and the other writers who shared his views were arguing within the framework of a specific cultural setting— the patriarchal society which was still dominant in the Western civilization of their day and whose origins go back to the earliest period of the Judaeo-Christian era. In such a society, sexual desire and sexual pleasure were regarded as masculine prerogatives; the majority of women were anaesthetic and the majority of men content to have them so. Faced with this overwhelming fact, reformers like Ellis not unnaturally generalized on the basis of the existing situation. This led them to overlook certain fundamental realities about men and women which are determined, not culturally, but by biological and psychological laws. It will be the purpose of this chapter to explain those laws and to show why the marriage manuals, which also largely ignore them, may do more harm than good.

But first let us set our problem in context. What is the purpose of marriage, in particular of monogamous marriage? Why was the institution adopted at all? In terms of instinctual sexual gratification, it certainly serves no vital need; it is quite possible and sometimes more agreeable to find such gratification outside of marriage. Other animals do very well without it and there are primitive human societies where the kind of marriage we are speaking of is unknown.

A brief note on animals is in order, if only for the benefit of sentimentalists. Where they have a family organization at all, the unit consists only of mother and children. The male parent is either absent altogether or around on a strictly temporary basis. Each litter, except where human beings intervene, has a new father. As for insects, the attempt to find in their lives analogies to the family as we know it bogs down hopelessly, since what organization they have is confined to communal groups. We may add that there is little basis for the popular belief that true love exists among birds; the belief itself is merely a projection of our romantic ideals. In sub-human primates, on the other hand, we do often find the kind of close attachment between individuals which approximates our fond desires. Nothing in their relationships, however, approaches the stability of the monogamous family unit.

There must be some very basic reason why human beings have formed this very special type of social organization. The reason, which also accounts for so many other complexities of human behavior, is to be found in the long period during which the human infant is helplessly dependent on others for its very survival.

There is in all nature, probably, no more profound relationship than that which exists between the human mother and her child. That it should be so is a vital necessity; without that extended and reciprocal attachment, the race would die. The child's need for the mother is obvious. Not so obvious, but equally important, is the mother's need for the child. Bearing a child, caring for it, supervising its growth, are deeply satisfying experiences for a woman. In a sense, she is dependent on her child's dependence for her own full development.

Occasionally one comes across human females—powerful, instinctually archaic creatures—for whom their mate's function is over when once he has succeeded in impregnating them. But they are the exceptions. Most women feel unable to cope single-handed with their reproductive task; they need in their environment a supporting male figure who will provide, not only shelter and food and care, but emotional sustenance as well.

Women's preference for such a stable association is thus not hard to explain. But what about men? By entering into a monogamous relationship they seem to hamper themselves unnecessarily, limiting their freedom to roam and make love where they please, shouldering economic burdens, even, in times of great stress, diminishing their capacity for individual survival. Why do they do it? What prompts them?

Well, men were babies themselves once. Human babies. The prolonged dependency of that period in their lives, the deeply-rooted attachment to one woman—the nourishing and reassuring mother image—are never entirely outgrown. However swaggering and confident they are, however male, they cannot be altogether free and self-sufficient. Infantile memories haunt the depths of their being, memories of helplessness, of fear and pain and warmth and love, of home.

As I said before, there are many primitive peoples who know nothing of our kind of marriage. Their family groupings, while often complex, lack the cohesion and stability found in more developed and successful societies. From the cultural standpoint, they are weeds, persistent but valueless. Every major culture, every branch of the human species which has left its mark on the face of the earth, has been characterized by strong fixed family units. The strongest of them all, monogamy, reached its high point in the Judaeo-Christian culture of the West which ultimately imposed itself on the greater part of the world. Its energy should not surprise us. The more secure children are, the more effective will be their achievement in maturity. And monogamy provides maximum security for both mother and child.

But such security depends on the loyalty of the father and for that loyalty he exacted a price. It was woman who, in the interest of her maternal role, paid it. Not too willingly, perhaps, but in the course of long centuries of educational and social pressure, without too much protest. The price was, until very recently, the surrender of herself as a person and, more particularly, the renunciation of her capacity for sexual enjoyment.

Why was such a fantastic sacrifice demanded of her? Submissiveness is all very well but why should any man regard frigidity in his wife as a value rather than a liability? Is it simply to keep her from temptation, to insure that her children cannot possibly have any other father than himself? Probably not. A woman can be chaste and virtuous without being cold. Is he still hunting then, perhaps, for the lost mother image, the woman who, in his infancy, seemed to belong only to him, who gave everything and asked nothing in return?

That hopeless unremitting search may be a factor in the situation but it does not tell the whole story. Underlying the strange preference of the patriarchal male is his awareness—rarely acknowledged, not conscious even, but existing just the same—of a basic biological fact, the fact that women have a far greater sexual potential than men. If he wakes the sleeping giantess, she may prove too much for him. Asleep or somnolent, on the other hand, she is no threat.

The average healthy female—even in our own culture, where she is still relatively repressed—is capable of much more sexual activity than she can possibly experience with any one man. She can function repeatedly, having no need, as he does, to manufacture fresh seminal and testicular fluid. Moreover, whether she is interested or not, she is always anatomically ready for the act of intercourse; nature has thriftily arranged that the one egg she produces per month should have every chance of being fertilized.

Man's lot is much more difficult. Before he can get going at all, he must first have an erection, and that in itself is a very complex phenomenon, with nothing automatic about it. Recent animal experiments indicate that, in males, sex performance depends upon the integrity of the entire nervous system. A small cerebral lesion is enough to cause impotence. On the other hand, relatively massive lesions in the female will not prevent her from functioning.

The difference in sexual potential is less apparent among animals because, in them, desire is closely linked to the reproductive function and determined by hormonal action which reaches its peak at periodic intervals. During the breeding season, the sexual desire of animals is almost uncontrollable; in between, it is at a minimum. Among human beings, desire has been divorced from reproduction and is largely dependent on psychic rather than hormonal influences. Many women, indeed, experience heightened desire after their menopause when they are no longer capable of bearing children.

To refute my thesis that women have by far the greater sexual potential, objectors will point to an indubitable fact: the existence of male polygamy, more precisely polygyny, among a large number of cultures less sexually inhibited than our own.

Let's take a brief look at these cultures. What strikes us immediately is that, while the possession of multiple wives may be socially approved, few men actually have more than one. The custom is usually restricted to the ruling groups, among whom it is a sign of prestige, or determined, as in China, by the desire for additional male progeny where the first wife has failed to fulfill it. An authority on the subject, Lowie, has this to say: "The sexual factor pure and simple is of course not to be wholly ignored . . . but everything goes to show that its influence on the development of polygyny is slight."*

Another writer, Linton, remarks: "A man who can support a conjugal group without help must be richer and more able than the average. Conversely, in a polygynous society, monogamous unions may mean loss of prestige. If a man has only one wife, it will be tacitly assumed that he is too poor to buy or support a second."†

Another argument generally cited to bolster belief in the sexual superiority of the male grows out of women's ability to endure, without difficulty, long periods of complete sexual deprivation. It is true, also, that orgasm, the summit of sexual pleasure, is more easily inhibited in women than in men.

True, at least, in our society which is still, in many ways, bemused by its past. The great weight of the patriarchal tradition has by no means been altogether lifted. It conditions the thinking and emotional attitudes of even the most enlightened among us and never does it lie more heavily than when we are engaged in making love. Women, of course, are particularly oppressed by it. Let us not forget that, for thousands of years, the dominant male tried to convince his mate that she wasn't really interested in sex. Home, school and church cooperated in making the lesson stick. So, as a matter of fact, did the medical profession.

Listen, for a sample of its views, to Acton, an English physician generally regarded in his day as an expert on the subject. In the year 1875, less than a century ago, he made this astonishing assertion: "The majority of women, happily for society, are not much troubled with sexual feelings." It was, in his opinion, a "vile aspersion" to suppose women capable of desire. Moreover, he declared sternly, only "lascivious women" took any pleasure in the sexual act. Acton, we must assume, was a conventional scientist. But he spoke for his kind and in line with commonly accepted belief.

Women, generally, would have been the last to challenge his statements. With such pressures impinging upon her from every side, the lustiest wench could not help being intimidated. She would do everything in her power to still the excitement of her

---

* R. H. Lowie, *Primitive Society*. New York, Liveright, 1920.
† R. Linton, *The Study of Man: An Introduction*. New York, Appleton-Century, 1936.

body, to deny its claims and conceal them from others. The penalty for failure, after all, was social ostracism, exclusion from the ranks of respectable womankind.

Most women, probably, never had to face this painful issue. Human beings, like plants, can be twisted into strange shapes if their training begins early enough and is vigilantly supervised. They will accept their deformation as the natural state of affairs and even take pride in it, as Chinese women once did in their crippled feet. The sexual impulse is so peculiarly plastic that it lends itself readily to the educational process. Especially when that process is universal, affording no grounds for comparison or envy. Unrecognized, deprivation loses much of its sting.

Moreover, patriarchal society offered its women some very genuine advantages in return for their docility. Since they were helpless creatures by definition, some man had to look out for them—father, husband, brother, brother-in-law or remote cousin, as the case might be. They did not have to spend agonized hours wondering, as so many women do today, about their place in the scheme of things. Their role was clearly marked out for them and it involved no abrupt changes in mid-stream, from a career to domesticity or vice versa. No choice, no doubts, no internal struggles. Marriage, a home and children were at once every woman's goal and the only excuse she needed for existence. To get a husband required little individual effort on her part and, once she got him, she was pretty sure to keep him. He might stray but only as a tethered goat strays; it was a rare man who dared to break the chain of convention that bound him to home and family. The same society which denied women any joy in sex also set limits to the sexual activity of men. In doing so, it fulfilled its major purpose— to provide a stable environment and the utmost protection for children.

Were men content in such a cultural setting? Could they achieve sexual satisfaction with a partner so deeply repressed? Apparently. We must remember that they expected no response from the woman and would probably have been alarmed and disgusted if they got it. A response would have seemed to them unwomanly, if not indeed "unnatural." A man so conditioned does not think of the sex act as a means of impressing the woman or ingratiating himself in her eyes. The pleasure he derives from it is a private pleasure, exclusively his own, and he will seek it as often and in such manner as his needs dictate.

Biologically, and to some extent psychologically as well, this kind of sexual pattern is in many ways suited to the male constitution. When the man's desire is alone consulted, when he sets the sexual pace, undistracted by the effect he may be making on the woman, he is able to function to the best of his capacity. Under these circumstances, psychic impotence is practically non-existent and other defects in performance are of no great consequence, either to the man himself or his mate. As far as she is concerned, sex is a burden anyway and whatever mitigates it so much gain. Thus the man's unconscious dependency on the woman is not threatened; he can proceed on his lordly way without the fear that she may become disgruntled with him and, perhaps, look elsewhere for satisfaction.

This, in broad outline, was the relationship between the sexes when Havelock Ellis began his work. Major changes were impending, caused by shifts in the general culture, but their manifestations were as yet sporadic, their implications hardly conceivable. Psychoanalysis was in its infancy; many of its most searching insights were still buried under assumptions hoary with age and never critically appraised because they were embedded in the mentality of the researchers themselves. Nobody, to return to our subject, questioned the superiority of the male sexual impulse. How, indeed, could there be any doubt of it when women were so very passive, so much its mere victims?

To Ellis, this female thralldom seemed both repugnant and unnecessary. Correctly assessing the importance of social factors in the situation, he associated himself with the feminist movement of his time. Women, he agreed, should be given the opportunity to play a more active and meaningful role in society. But it was with their sexual liberation that he was primarily concerned and here he drove home forcefully the individual man's responsibility to his mate. "It is his part to educate his wife in the life of sex; it is he who will make sex demands a conscious desire to her." Ellis, we may concede, was right on this point which still retains considerable validity. But he also said: "As desire is usually more irregular and more capricious in the woman than in the man, it is the wife who may properly be regarded as the law-giver in this matter and the husband may find his advantage in according her this privilege." Will he? There's the rub.

Women are no longer the beaten and submissive creatures they once were. They are capable of earning their own living, they vote, they think for themselves and they expect to find pleasure in sexual experience. For the great majority of them, marriage has not ceased to be the supreme goal, but it is a very different kind of marriage from that of their grandmothers. It can hardly be called a patriarchal institution any more; the husband's absolute predominance is a thing of the past. Nor is it, for the woman, an all-absorbing career. Modern contraceptive methods have made it possible to limit the number of her children; in caring for them, schools have taken over many of her previous responsibilities; a host of ingenious devices reduce the burden of house-keeping. She has time and energy for outside activities. And if marriage itself becomes a kind of prison-house, the door of divorce is wide open.

All these changes are reflected in the sexual relations between men and women. They are freer and warmer than they were, more deeply significant for both partners. But it would be foolish to claim that they are better in every respect. Certainly, marriage is not as solidly based as it was formerly and this instability alone creates many problems.

Some of the difficulties faced by married couples today are no doubt due to the fact that, sexually as in other respects, we live in an age of transition. Our values are confused, and old, outmoded habits of thought cling to them like burrs. In training our children, for instance, we tend to be uncertain; while boys and girls are not as restricted sexually as they were before, as oppressed by mysterious taboos, they are still somewhat alienated from the sensations of their developing bodies. In progressive homes, there may be a good deal of verbal freedom but behavior patterns have altered very slightly, if at all. Sexual functioning is discouraged by even the most enlightened parents for some years after it has become biologically possible. I am not saying these restrictions are unnecessary. They do, however, make it very hard for young people to adjust to the kind of adult sexual life which has now become the ideal.

Take the young girl. She is a little less ignorant of the facts of life than her grandmother was but, emotionally, she may be just as inhibited and her apprehensions are apt to be considerably keener. There is, after all, so much more expected of her in a world where the vital, passionate female has become every man's dream, and where a transcendent image of her is celebrated by all the persuasive devices of mass communication. The inhibited girl must somehow resolve herself into a reasonably convincing facsimile of that image. Timidity is out of fashion; coolness and excessive reserve deplored. The emphasis is on the "warm" woman.

Nowadays the most inexperienced girl is aware that some sexual interest on her part is necessary if she wants boys to find her desirable. Unless she can manage, at the very least, to pretend eagerness, she is likely to be left out in the cold. Her first encounters may be rather frightening; she has to cope simultaneously with the adolescent male and her own childhood fears, a battle on two fronts for which she is not well equipped. If, after a number of experiences, she remains unresponsive, a new fear assails her: is something lacking, is she cold, as a woman a potential failure? Such a fear, in our times, induces much the same kind of shame which her grandmother would have felt had she been considered "fast." A girl who has never been sexually responsive enters marriage with a good deal of trepidation.

If, on the other hand, she is easily aroused, her disturbance may be even greater. Our morality is still heavily weighted against premature sexual adventures. The too responsive girl may fear, with some justice, that her emotions will get out of control and doom her to a life of promiscuity.

In any case, and whatever the nature of her premarital activity, the girl cannot in any genuine sense prepare herself for marriage. Her sexual role in that relationship will be entirely new and largely dependent on the character and reactions of her husband.

He, too, we must remember, was an inhibited child. Like his sisters, like the woman he will one day marry, he has forgotten the intense drama of those early days, with its overweening desires, its terrors and the inevitable defeat which was its climax. If it emerges into consciousness at all, it will be in the form of obscure guilts and anxieties, irrational compulsions, a pervasive feeling of insecurity. Only those whom we call neurotic are incapacitated by these ghostly visitations but all of us are troubled to a greater or less extent.

That is true especially during the critical periods of our development. One of those periods is adolescence. Primitive peoples, closer to the instinctual sources of behavior, take great pains to prepare their boys for manhood, for the duties, sexual and otherwise, of their adult lives. We leave sexual indoctrination to the whim of the individual parent. So it is not surprising that a boy's first contacts are usually fumbling and unsatisfactory, marked by such deficiencies in performance as loss of erection or premature ejaculation.

There are men in whom these deficiencies persist, who, through fear or lack of opportunity, fail to achieve sexual confidence.

Most men, however, make a tolerable adjustment, gaining experience in one way or another, through a series of affairs, a relationship with an older woman or, *faute de mieux*, with prostitutes. Exposed as they are to our sex-glorifying civilization, they are under considerable pressure to become adequate lovers before venturing into marriage. They know that the girl of their dreams will expect it of them. They themselves expect to derive much of their sexual enjoyment from gratifying her and comparing their capacity to do so with that of other men. It is at this stage in a young man's life that, lacking the counsel of more experienced contemporaries, he may turn to the manuals for advice.

If he does, he will undoubtedly encounter a much-quoted dictum of Balzac's: "In love—quite apart from the psychic element—woman is a harp who only yields her secrets of melody to the master who knows how to handle her."

Incentive enough, one might think. But Van der Velde, the Dutch gynecologist who wrote the most successful of all manuals, "Ideal Marriage," adds his own gloss to the text: "Who can play this delicate human harp aright, unless he knows all her chords, and all the tones and semitones of feeling? Only the genius—after long practice and many discords and mistakes." Should the young man become discouraged and abandon all thought of marriage, he is hardly to be blamed.

One further note before we take up the case of Ted and Sally, two young people in love with each other, newly married and fairly conversant with the literature. The average young man we have been discussing is convinced that his sex drive is superior to that of most females. In this conviction he has the support of tradition and of his own premarital experiences. Almost always, the sexual initiative is his; he pursues while the girl of his choice retreats or, at least, pretends to. Her greater reserve is partly the result of more profound inhibitions, more stringent taboos, but it is reinforced by her unwillingness to take social risks involved in sexual activity outside of marriage, as well as by her wish to offer the man an incentive for marriage. Virginity still carries a premium.

Let us turn now to our young couple. They are attractive, popular and reasonably sure of themselves; both have hurdled successfully the trials, disappointments and dangers which are the lot of youth. Ted has had, over a period of years, some gratifying adventures. Though they were casual, short-range relationships, he has no real reason to question his sexual capacity. However, a trace of insecurity remains, aggravated at the moment by the fact that he is very much in love. He cannot bear the thought that he might, just possibly, not come up to Sally's expectations.

Sally has doubts of her own. For one thing, she is a virgin and, while she is eager to put an end to that state, she now wonders whether it would not have been better to do so earlier. Were her motives for abstaining valid, is she really as passionate as she thinks she is? And what about Ted? During their courtship, he has stirred her intensely but will he be able to fulfill her long-deferred dreams? These mixed reactions, half fearful, half pleasurable, Sally keeps to herself. She loves Ted, and whatever happens, she has no intention of hurting him.

Both Sally and Ted, as I said before, had dipped into the manuals. Thus they did not expect too much of their wedding-night and, in any case, things went rather well. Ted was gentle and Sally grateful. They felt very close to each other. They were sure that, before the honeymoon was over, they would reach the peaks of mutual exaltation they both so ardently desired.

But they didn't. While Sally was as responsive as any man could desire, she failed to reach orgasm. And, since they had agreed to be honest with each other, she confided this fact to Ted. He, in turn, remembering his homework, gave more and more time to the preliminary sexual play which the manuals recommend for bringing the wife to the proper pitch of excitement.

It was no use. They returned from a fairly protracted honeymoon still very much in love but deeply disturbed by what they assumed was a failure in their relationship, an inadequacy on the part of one or the other. Ted developed a tendency to brood, as well he might. The manuals place most of the blame on him. As, for instance, to quote Ellis again: "One fears that there is still too much truth in Balzac's saying that, in this matter, the husband is sometimes like an orang-utang playing a violin. The violin remains 'anaesthetic' but it is probably not the violin's fault." Nevertheless, Ted could not help feeling occasional flashes of resentment. There were those other women he had made love to in the past, after all. They had not been so hard to satisfy.

Sally, meanwhile, also found something to mull over, a liberally quoted statement of Stendhal's which reads: "A 'cold' passionless woman is a woman who has not yet met the man she is bound to love." Sally was not cold, of course, far from it. She was a warm, sweet, loving woman and her greatest desire, at this potentially critical moment in her marriage, was to reassure her husband. So she devised a stratagem. By deliberately overacting, by pretending transports which she did not feel, she succeeded in making Ted believe that she was now reaching orgastic climax.

In Sally's case, the deception had unexpected results. She did finally have an orgasm, as she would probably have done earlier if she had not been so anxious. It was not her pretense that turned the psychological trick but the fact that, by concentrating upon her husband and the pleasure she could give him, she forgot to worry about herself. The reaction is both as simple and as complicated as that.

We could leave our hypothetical young couple at this point—united in their new happiness, slowly adjusting to each other and their life together—were it not for the marriage manuals. Ted and Sally took them seriously, very seriously indeed. They were determined to achieve nothing less than the "ideal marriage" Van der Velde writes about. It was not enough to enjoy making love and for Sally to have occasional orgasms. She must have them every time, and moreover her climax had to coincide with Ted's. As Van der Velde puts it:

"In normal and perfect coitus, mutual orgasms must be almost simultaneous; the usual procedure is that the man's ejaculation begins and sets the woman's acme of sensation in train at once. The time it takes for the sensation received by the woman to reach her central nervous system and translate itself into supreme delight is less than a second. Such is the marvellous rate of nervous transmission."

Now this, I submit, is nonsense. A lotus dream, infinitely appealing, the goal of all desire—but nonsense just the same. It is a poet speaking, not a scientist, not anybody who deals soberly with the limits of what is possible. To the best of my knowledge, the standard of mutual simultaneous orgasm—described as "normal" by Van der Velde—is attained, if at all, only in the rarest, most fortuitous circumstances. There are a great many happily married couples, men and women whose sexual relations are completely satisfactory, who have never once experienced it. Nor, I may add, felt its lack. For one thing, as any honest woman will admit, the onset of the man's orgasm does not set her own "in train at once." It just doesn't work that way. She has to have her orgasm before he does or, as least, to begin having it. In the latter case, the peak of sensation for each *may* coincide. But one does not, if one is wise, stake one's happiness on such chances.

Let us return to Ted and Sally, who have set their hearts on achieving this delirious consummation without knowing what pitfalls beset their path. Earnestly, though with some embarrassment —they were rather shy young people, temperamentally not inclined to excess—they embarked on a career of erotic experimentation which might have been suitable for the nymphs and satyrs of mythology but which was rather too strenuous for a rising young advertising executive and his mate. They were encouraged in this course by the manuals which uniformly urge the most complete freedom and "abandon" on the young couple, backing up their argument that unlimited variation is normal and "good" with all sorts of impressive data gleaned from biology, anthropology, ancient history and literature.

During those early hectic months, Ted played to the hilt the legendary role of the rampant male and Sally, for her part, abetted him at every turn. Not only did she respond eagerly to his slightest overture; she would often initiate the love-making, having been told by the manuals to forego modesty and do everything possible to stimulate herself and her husband. No houri in the Moslem paradise could have been more artful, more enticing. These were times when Ted looked back, with astonishment and wistfulness, to the days of their honeymoon. The new untrammeled Sally was marvellous but he could hardly recognize in her the girl he had married. He couldn't always keep up with her either.

He tried hard, of course. Uppermost in his thoughts was the desire to please her, to gain the approval of this lovely and astonishing creature. Not only affection but what Van der Velde calls a "husband's interest and honor" dictated that he should, on every occasion, give her as much gratification as she gave him. The mentor's words, in this connection, are very solemn: "I would impress on all married men that every erotic stimulation of their wives that does not terminate in orgasm represents an injury, and repeated injuries of this kind lead to permanent, or very obstinate, damage to soul and body."

As time went on, however, Ted was less and less able to carry out the implied injunction. Disturbing things began to happen to him; he had bad headaches and his nights were haunted by distressing dreams. Dreams in which he missed trains perpetually or failed in some vital examination. He was gallant with Sally, he showered her with compliments and extravagant presents, he took

her out dancing as he had done in their courtship but he could not
for long cover up the change in himself and he avoided intimacy
as much as he could. Her attempts to stimulate him only made
things worse; the harder she tried, the more reluctant was his
response. Sally cried often these days and was glad they had put
off having a baby. She was sure Ted didn't love her any more, at
least not *that* way. One day, shortly after their first anniversary,
she borrowed some money, packed her bags, and took a plane for
Reno. Ted did not attempt to stop the divorce. Wretched as he
was, he could see no alternative. Deep down, he was even relieved.

What happened to our young couple? Why did their marriage go
on the rocks? They were healthy, in love, compatible in temperament and filled with the best intentions toward each other. All the
ingredients of a successful marriage were present in their case. Yet
they failed. It was an unnecessary failure, based on ignorance of
natural laws and compounded by bad advice, like a ship sailing
into uncharted seas with a defective compass.

There is room for democracy in marriage but, as nature has
arranged matters, the husband's enjoyment of the act has to take
precedence over his efforts to please his wife. Otherwise, sooner or
later, neither of them will have any pleasure at all. (The problem
is peculiar to a long-term relationship where the partners share
the same home and have regular contact with each other. It may
not arise in extramarital affairs, whose circumstances give the man
much more leeway. If he is not in the mood for dalliance, he can
always find a pretext to break the date. Moreover, such affairs
usually involve a high degree of sexual tension on both sides, a
tension maintained by infrequency of contact, need for concealment and a variety of other factors.)

Why should the husband's pleasure be so crucial? Because, unless
he is assured of it, the mechanism of the sex act is impeded and
may even break down altogether. The man cannot simply give in
to desire as the woman can; he must feel it actively if he is to set
in motion the chain of nerve impulses which lead to erection, and
if he is to maintain the erection long enough to enter the woman.
As I said earlier, it is a complex process, involving the entire
nervous system. Once a man is sufficiently aroused, however, he
will almost invariably complete the sexual experience which culminates for him in the orgastic release of ejaculation. At that point,
his partner's interest, or lack of it, no longer concerns him. Getting
started is the difficulty.

It is true that his desire can be stimulated. But not at all times nor in all circumstances. The assumption, implicit in the manuals, that the male sex drive is unlimited is—and I cannot repeat this too often—untenable, a hangover from the days when the majority of women were genuinely frigid. Actually, the drive has very definite limits. In a situation of physical danger to the organism, it becomes inoperative. Or it may wither away, as Ted's did, under the blight of anxiety.

Let us review Ted's case. The anxiety, residually present in him as it is in most men, first became activated during his honeymoon. Sally's failure to achieve orgasm, not uncommon in an inexperienced girl, was blown up out of all proportion in their minds, shadowing the delight they might have found in each other. To Ted, it was especially damaging since it led to doubts about his sexual prowess and thus lowered his self-esteem. But a quicker reaction on Sally's part would only have postponed his troubles; he was in any case, as subsequent events proved, a candidate for anxiety.

Let us be fair. The manuals were not wholly to blame for Ted's plight though they certainly aggravated it. Given the sexual mores of our time—between which and the manuals there is a reciprocating relationship—any well-disposed man is similarly a candidate for anxiety. That is because, to win approval from his mate, to ingratiate himself with her, he has subordinated his pleasure in the sex act to hers. The test of success is then *her* gratification, a hazardous undertaking at best since it places the man on trial and induces the kind of defensive reaction which may end by paralyzing desire. But the situation becomes much worse when the woman's enjoyment is, as it were, standardized, when an almost impossible state of simultaneous ecstasy is made the criterion of gratification. Inevitably, the ideal collapses against the stubborn realities imposed by nature. Crushed under the ruins, not infrequently, is the man's desire.

The woman's does not succumb so readily. Once aroused, as it was in Sally, it can take on anything a man has to offer and more. It is interesting that Van der Velde, who places so great a burden on the man, nevertheless concedes the superior sexual potentiality of women: ". . . the sexual vigor, efficiency (and technically *tolerance*) of the healthy, erotically awakened woman is very great; decidedly greater, indeed, than the potency of the average man."

There, in those few words, is the explanation of what happened to Ted and Sally. She simply had more of what it takes than he had. Their mutual failure to achieve the ideal did not overwhelm her; she would have kept on trying indefinitely. As it was, she tried too hard. Following the advice of the manuals, she never denied herself to him, never begged off even when she was not in the mood. It would have been better for Ted if she had. He would have felt less guilty and incompetent, less like an honorable dwarf mated with a giantess.

Instead, ashamed to admit that his sexual interest didn't match hers, he allowed Sally to set the pace in their relations. Temporarily, that is, since in the final analysis the pace-maker has to be the man's sexual potential. When it gives out, to put it crudely, there ain't nothing. Ted drove himself to the point where he could hardly function at all. That precipitated the disaster. Had he been honest and confided in Sally, they might still have worked things out between them. In the circumstances, how could she guess that, when he avoided her embraces, he was motivated by fear of failure, rather than indifference? So, being young, ignorant and fairly insecure herself, Sally could only conclude that he no longer loved her. The feeling of being unloved saps a woman's confidence in the same way that a man's is sapped by the feeling of sexual inadequacy.

The saddest part of the story is that Sally would have been willing, at all times, to settle for less. She enjoyed the sex act, with or without orgasm; she had done so from the beginning. The sense of closeness, the deep satisfaction of being wanted, possessed, by the man she loved, were of extraordinary value to her. They induced contentment and that relaxation of nerves and muscles which, according to the manuals, is only possible with orgasm.

The manuals are mistaken. Most happily married women would admit that orgasm, while delightful, is not always essential to their enjoyment of intercourse. A few say it is and, moreover, insist that they invariably reach it. I am inclined to regard such claims with considerable skepticism. In my experience, they don't stand up under really close questioning. Among the women who make them are some, as a matter of fact, who don't even know what an orgasm is. Others, in their anxiety to be considered "normal," deliberately misstate the case.

Nevertheless, the whole issue does raise an interesting question. Why is orgasm, admittedly the high point in sexual experience, so very much less frequent in women than in men? In discussing the question, it will become clear why the goal of mutual simultaneous orgasm is, for all practical purposes, unattainable.

The first and most basic reason it that the mature woman is always *physiologically* prepared for intercourse. But she does not have to be psychically prepared since lack of desire imposes no veto on function. Thus, her participation in the act may be purely passive, without interest or expectancy. In this connection, the manuals stress the crucial importance of preliminary sexual play, variations in position and so forth. There are times when they do serve to arouse the woman, but there does not seem to be any real correlation between such activities and orgasm. Experienced women often develop a "feel" about this culminating moment; they can almost predict in advance whether or not they will experience it on any particular occasion.

It is possible that hormonal as well as psychic factors determine the degree of response. Research in this field indicates that desire fluctuates during the menstrual cycle, that the woman's sexual receptivity is influenced by the hormonal changes which take place at different stages of the cycle. Some workers maintain that receptivity is greatest when fertilization is most probable—around the time of ovulation between the menstrual periods. While these findings seem plausible from a biological standpoint, many women contradict them. They claim their desire is most intense during or immediately before and after menstruation, the period of least fertility. Nor do the findings explain the heightened desire felt by so many women after they have passed the menopause. All we can say at this time is that the matter is not yet fully understood.

Another reason why women have fewer orgasms than men is the difference in orgastic pattern between the sexes. The male pattern is reflex; with very rare exceptions, orgasm accompanies ejaculation. Nor is sexual intercourse necessary for release. The same reflex pattern—ejaculation plus orgasm—obtains in involuntary nocturnal emissions, masturbation and a variety of perversions. Moreover, as Kinsey has reported, the pattern is established early in life, reaching a peak of frequency during adolescence and thereafter declining slowly.

For the woman, on the other hand, orgasm appears to be an induced reaction, a complicated matter involving a shift of psychic attention and what can only be described as a learning process. It may take years to achieve and some women never achieve it at all.

That is not, in the circumstances, surprising. For one thing, and it
is not unimportant, the woman has far less opportunity for sexual
practice than the man. She is usually more strictly inhibited, both
in childhood and adolescence. Her genitals are less available for
inspection and manipulation. She possesses at least two, and possibly more, primary erogenous zones and the problem of transferring
orgastic sensation from clitoris to vagina may bedevil her all her
life. According to Kinsey, her frequency curve does not reach its
peak until she is in her late twenties. At this age, his statistics
indicate, the average man and woman are approximately equal in
orgastic capacity.

At this age, however, most men and women have been married
for some time. The man is also, as a rule, some years older than his
wife. Suppose she is twenty-two when they marry and he twenty-
seven. She has only begun the slow upward climb to her peak
while he, though already on his way down, is far ahead of her in
orgastic capacity. But, by the time she reaches the peak, he is
thirty-four years old and no longer, in the majority of instances, a
match for her. At almost no point is it possible for their frequency
curves to coincide. Taking this and all the other factors into consideration, it is apparent that the goal of mutual simultaneous
orgasm is unlikely of attainment this side of paradise.

Giving up a dream, particularly so radiant a dream, is never easy.
We cling to it wistfully, hoping that somehow we can make it come
true. The demand for perfection lurks in us all, a relic from those
infantile days when our wishes were magically gratified, when
desire and fulfillment were one. But it is better to be realistic. In
the long run, we shall be happier.

I may have given the impression that, men and women being
what they are, happiness in marriage is a very risky proposition. It
need not be if both partners face the biological facts of life and are
honest with each other. Let us return for the last time to Ted and
Sally, those casualties of the quest for an ideal marriage. How
should they have handled their sexual problem?

In the first place, by not making it such an all-absorbing problem. Self-consciousness is the death of spontaneity and, without
spontaneity, there is no delight. When young people are in love,
they can learn to adjust to each other without continually taking
notes and measuring themselves against an abstract formula. Bed
is not the place for intellectual exercises.

All they had to know really is that orgasm in women is not an
imperative, and that its absence will not damage the woman in any

way nor, indeed, prevent her from enjoying intercourse. If Ted and Sally had realized this, they would probably have stopped worrying. Sally could have "given" Ted his pleasure, even at times when she was not in the mood, and he could have accepted her compliance without guilt. His performance, incidentally, would have improved greatly, to Sally's benefit as well as his own. His confidence in himself might have been built up to the point where he could occasionally engage in the sex act because *she* wanted it. But he would never have felt ashamed to confess that he wasn't up to it and Sally would not have regarded such a confession as weakness or inadequacy on his part. It would be acknowledged between them that the pace of their relations must be set by him. But it would also be acknowledged that Sally did not always have to give in to his desires and that her refusal did not imply that she was either "cold" or unloving. With such an understanding between them, they could have found deep satisfaction in each other and placed their sexual relations securely within the context of their mutually dependent needs.

Ted and Sally were not predestined casualties. They might have had a good life together.

James L. McCary

Sexual Attitudes
and
Sexual Behavior

"Our sexual behavior is essentially the result of our attitudes towards sex; and these attitudes, in turn, are a product of how we have been brought up." And, as pointed out earlier in this text, sex education begins with the first intimate mother-infant contacts. Instruction in sexual matters, however, involves infinitely more than the interrelations between parents and child; significant roles are played by many other influences. There are not only the general demands and expectations of the specific culture in which the per-

From: James L. McCary, *Human Sexuality*, New York: D. Van Nostrand Company, Inc., 1967. Reprinted by permission.

son lives, but also the special differences in sexual ethics within that culture—differences based on such variables as the individual's, as well as the teacher's, type of religious affiliation and depth of involvement, sex, age, educational level, and socioeconomic stratum.

Sexual Attitudes

Much has been said and written in recent years about the sexual revolution that is allegedly taking place. While research findings and clinical judgments are not wholly consistent, the general consensus is that there has been no revolution of any significance since the 1920s when those women born around the turn of the century came of age and set new sexual standards. There may be no revolution at the present time, but there is more and more evidence that revolt looms on the horizon. One can hardly have escaped noticing a change in sexual attitudes in recent years, as evidenced by the growing freedom with which sexual topics are discussed in the various communication media, schools, churches, and governmental circles—as well as at cocktail parties and by the man on the street.

But *attitudes* (and the ease of discussing them) are not to be confused with *behavior*. Even those to whom a decision in the matter of a sexual ethic is most pertinent—today's college students —are bewildered and bedeviled by the dichotomy between prevailing sexual attitudes and sexual behavior. For example, although 75% of college girls express the belief that their classmates are "sleeping around" (attitude), surveys and research studies consistently point out that, actually, only 20% of all college girls experience premarital intercourse (behavior).

It should probably be underlined at the outset of any discussion of this nature that significant changes in human mores, behavior, laws, and social institutions occur only gradually. Especially slow are changes in culturally acceptable sexual behavior, because the orientation and experiences of childhood place strong limitations on the frequency, form, and freedom of such behavior in adulthood.

Cultural differences, as one might expect, produce as wide a variety of attitudes toward sexual matters as they do in other areas of human interaction. It comes as a surprise to many Americans to learn that their condemnatory views on premarital and postmarital sexual activity are not shared by the majority of the world's cultures. For example, of 158 societies investigated in one study, 70% do not condemn premarital sexual intercourse (although this permissiveness toward premarital coitus does not imply sanction of adulterous relationships).

Anthropological investigations have consistently revealed that cultures which encourage women to be completely free in their sexual expression produce sexually responsive women whose amatory reactions are as uninhibited and as vigorous as those of their men. Cultures that approve of women's having orgasms produce women who have orgasms; those cultures that do not so approve, produce women who are incapable of orgasm.

With unfortunate ease, sexual attitudes can fall under the pall of such cultural maladies as misinformation and prudery. For example, women of emancipated modern societies frequently are troubled with menstrual difficulties of one sort or another. Yet Margaret Mead's anthropological studies of the women of Samoa show that when they were questioned, only one woman of the entire population even understood what was meant by pain or emotional imbalance during menstruation, and that particular girl was in the employ of the island's white missionary family.

All people to a degree, but Americans most particularly (it would appear), are inclined to cling to their traditional ways of thinking and conducting themselves, whether in political, religious, or sexual matters. They are reluctant to accept change or to be swayed by outside influences, however rational or beneficial. This rather blind adherence to tradition is found not only in major cultures, but within specific subcultures as well.

Probably the greatest social change to occur in recent years has been the emergence of women into a position of equality in American society. The freedom and parity that women demanded and now enjoy in the United States have had a profound effect upon prevailing sexual attitudes. The traditional American attitude toward women's sexuality was an outgrowth of the Victorian ethic. Men and women were presumed to have characteristically different sexual needs and drives; and a woman, having little amatory interest in sex, participated in copulatory activity only for the purpose of procreation or to please her husband. Most women today are unwilling to accept the notion that each sex is subject to different standards in the matter of sexual desire and conduct. They expect the pleasures received from sexual activities as well as the restrictions governing them, to be equally applicable to both sexes.

An interesting side effect of this struggle for equality is that the sexual attitudes of American women are often considerably healthier than those of American men. Chroniclers of sexual histories, whether researchers or clinicians, have found that women are far more open and honest in supplying their personal data than men are. Men frequently become embroiled in the question of self-esteem, and may attempt to compensate for what they feel is a threat to their self-image by boasting, with the consequence that the data they provide are often unreliable.

Despite the recent liberalizing evolution in the realm of women's rights, certain differences between the sexual attitudes of the two sexes continue to be forged by such factors as childhood rearing, the expectations of society, and certain physiological agents. Premarital chastity, particularly for girls, is still considered an "ideal," even though, as Thomas Poffenberger says, "society no longer takes the pious position that all premarital coitus is evil and the offender should be punished." The most significant deterrents to premarital sexual activity are religious and moral codes that condemn it, family training, various fears, a desire to wait until marriage, the lack of opportunity, and the lack of desire. Fear of pregnancy was a strong deterrent in the past, but it is no longer regarded as a prime factor in premarital continence.

Other changes in sexual attitudes have their basis in the protracted period of adolescence that shifts in the American social structure have imposed on its youth. The imposition of additional educational and vocational requirements has made necessary an extended adolescence, on the one hand, yet the age of a youngster's physical maturation comes considerably earlier than it did in previous generations. Because of these two considerations, the period of social adolescence is now approximately twice as long as it was 100 years ago. During this prolonged period of youth, the two sexes begin to develop different attitudes toward premarital sexual activity. The natural feelings of insecurity which adolescence breeds and the increase in physical drives (especially in boys) make the adolescent particularly susceptible to the hawkings of Madison Avenue when it extols the supreme value of sex appeal in striving toward popularity, success, admiration, security, and the like. Boys are propagandized through the various mass communication media to believe that their masculinity (*i.e.*, success as a *man*) depends upon their success in seduction: the farther they go with girls sexually, the more masculine they are in their own eyes and from the viewpoint of their peer group.

Girls, on the other hand, are indoctrinated in the importance of being "sexy." They are exhorted to purchase an often ludicrous and useless conglomerate of products that, according to the advertisements, are guaranteed to increase sexual attractiveness. A young girl is indeed in a delicate position. She must appear and act "sexy" in order to attract as many boys and to have as many dates as possible, because these are the symbols in her all-important peer group of popularity and social success. At the same time, however, she must hold the line of propriety, because otherwise she risks losing her "good girl" status with a consequent loss of prestige. Girls too often are favorably evaluated by their peer group only in correlation with their popularity in dating (and the number of boys whom they cause to make open affectionate commitments), coupled with their ability to remain free of sexual involvements.

As boys and girls grow older, they come to adopt a more permissive sexual code of behavior. This doubtless is due in part to the fact that the younger teen-agers submit uncritically to the traditional sexual ethics of their parents; but as they grow older and think more and more independently of their parents, they come to a progressively greater extent under the influence of outside values, particularly those of their peer groups. Even with recent relaxations in sexual codes, however, changes in teen-age sexual behavior have been in the direction of increased petting rather than of increased coition.

Slightly over half of teen-age girls admit to guilt feelings if they go "too far" in petting with their dates, while only one-fourth of the boys express similar guilt. These views stand in curious contrast to statements made by the other members of the same groups (one-third of the girls and three-fourths of the boys) who are more conservative in their sexual conduct, yet indicate that they desire greater sexual intimacy on dates. Boys appear interested in petting and sexual intercourse, while their girl friends are willing to neck (mild embracing and kissing limited to face and lips), but wish to hold the line there. As the relationship becomes more serious— from dating, to going steady, to engagement—sexual behavior becomes more intimate, and guilt over sexual endearments becomes less for both sexes.

Clinical observations and the results of empirical research have frequently underlined the marked discrepancy between what parents have themselves experienced (or are experiencing) by way of sexual activity, and the code of sexual ethics they profess to their children. Psychotherapists have long detected more regret among women who were virgins at marriage for *not* having experienced premarital coitus than among those women who did experience it. The clinical observations of therapists have been upheld by the results of several investigations into the attitudes of married women toward various aspects of sexual expression. These studies show that those women who have had premarital sexual intercourse are not sorry, and maintain they would repeat their behavior if they had it to do over again; however, they expect their daughters to conform to a more conservative ethic. Essentially the same findings have been reported in yet another investigation, in this instance of highly educated, influential upper middle-class men and women.

The question naturally arises: why do these mothers behave in one way—feeling no regret about their premarital coitus, together with an assertion that they would repeat the behavior if they could turn back the clock—yet expect their daughters to behave in a contrary manner? The dynamics are rather complex, but the explanation lies primarily in the significant differences between men and women in their interpretation of the interrelationship between sexual attraction and emotional commitment. Studies indicate that for a man, love follows a sexual attraction, while for a woman, sexual involvement follows romantic attachment. (As a rule, a girl must have a strong emotional attachment before she allows herself to become sexually involved; she must be convinced that it is she, a person, who is important to the relationship, not simply her sexual potentials.) A recent investigation, for instance, demonstrated that girls enter a university with conservative sexual attitudes, then shift later in their academic life to more liberal ones, but *only* if they become engaged. The liberalizing of their attitudes would appear an outgrowth of their emotional commitment, to which the engagement bears witness.

A mother, then, in her own premarital sexual experiences may have had strong feelings regarding the significance of emotional involvement as a precedent to sexual contact, but cannot accept the fact that her daughter also recognizes the import of this sequence. Furthermore, the mother, through having defied the sexual prohibitions of her own rearing by engaging in premarital coitus, may now carry a residual of repressed guilt. This guilt can break through and be projected onto her maturing daughter in the form of disapproval of any premarital sexual experience on the part of the girl. In addition, the mother cannot identify sufficiently with the daughter to appreciate the strength of the girl's feelings when she becomes emotionally attached to a young man. Neither can she accept the fact that her daughter has perhaps evolved a liberal sexual ethic of her own because of this commitment.

The disparity between a woman's past behavior and her present preachments tends to become perpetuated. The sexually restrictive admonishments through which she attempts to indoctrinate her daughter quite likely will be no more effective than they were in her generation. But the unfortunate consequence will be the same —generation after generation of women who tend to follow their emotional and sexual inclinations, but with concomitant guilt and shame, because they have violated the sexual ethic with which they were reared.

A further example of the often curious difference between attitude and behavior lies in the fact that many people in our culture, especially men, have difficulty entering into a warm, close, loving interchange with others. Little boys are often taught that to be tender and compassionate is to show characteristics of being a "sissy"; little girls are admonished that it is "forward" to be warmly responsive. To grow up in an environment that restricts positive emotional responses makes it likely that the individual will learn to express only negative emotions, such as anger and hostility. All the same, these people grow into adulthood with the abstract knowledge that some warm emotional exchanges are vital and expected in successful sexual interaction. But since they learned in their formative years to express only negative emotional responses, these people will actually instigate quarrels or fights with their sexual partner in order to express the only type of emotionality they understand. Men who have never learned how to express tenderness, or who are afraid to do so, will often ignore the woman with whom they are sexually involved, or make belittling remarks to her. These men *want* to demonstrate their commitment, but not knowing how to use the appropriate positive emotions, they use the only emotional expression they are familiar with—the negative ones.

An adolescent form of the "princess-prostitute" syndrome, described in the section of this text dealing with sexual aberrations, is the "good girls don't, bad girls do" attitude of some youths. This attitude impels them toward intercourse with girls whom they do not care for, since they consider girls whom they respect "too good" to become involved in sexual activity. However, because of their fondness for the "good girls" and their developing emotional closeness to them, the boys may become sexually aroused. As a more intimate relationship grows, sexual behavior may well progress in some cases to sexual intercourse. As a result, the young boy often loses respect for the "good girl" who in his eyes now has turned "bad," and he may quite likely terminate the relationship; or he may develop strong guilt feelings for seducing a "good girl."

Patterns in feelings of guilt undergo a change over a period of time in both sexes, especially among the older unmarried groups. Clinicians have presented convincing arguments that many men are beset with considerably more guilt over sexual matters than women are. Their premise is that women, in nonmarital sex relationships especially, usually and understandably want reassurance that they are desired and respected for more than their sexual performance. Women also want assurance that their men will not "kiss and tell," and that they will maintain the same level of regard for them after coitus as before. A man, on the other hand, feels that as the instigator of the sex act, he is the "seducer," and that the responsibility for the girl's participation rests squarely upon his shoulders. To placate his own guilt or anxiety, therefore, he must feel either that there is love in the relationship, or that the girl is "bad." Furthermore, since he feels guilty about his "seduction" of the girl, he comes to regard her as the instigator of his guilt. He is then impelled to express his hostility and anger by quarreling or fighting with her, speaking to her in a degrading manner, or otherwise manifesting his rejection of her—the very girl who thought enough of him to share with him the most intimate of human experiences.

Women often accuse their husbands of showing affection toward them only when they have intercourse in mind; husbands deny this. What often happens is that the husband commences simply to show affection to his wife with no ulterior motive in mind. However, in the process of expressing affection, especially if his wife responds warmly, the husband may well become sexually excited. The wife then judges only in terms of the final outcome and not the initial intent of her husband.

Fortunately, both men and women can be taught to allow themselves the joy of experiencing close, warm, and loving relationships. If they have not acquired this knowledge through normal maturational processes, or through experience and observation, psychotherapy can help them gain insight into the immense value of manifestations of affection. When men and women recognize that free expression of affection is certainly nothing to fear, nor a barometer of weakness or effeminacy, all their human relationships, including the sexual one, will be much fuller and happier.

Men are considerably more upset by the extramarital affairs of their wives than women are by similar transgressions by their husbands; only 27% of all women would consider their husband's adultery sufficient grounds for seeking a divorce, while 51% of all men would regard infidelity on the part of their wives as being totally destructive of the marriage. Furthermore, women are less likely to demand virginity of their husbands at the time of marriage than men are to expect their brides to be virgins (23% of the former as compared with 40% of the latter). The more highly educated man is less disturbed today than in the past if his bride is nonvirginal, although he is likely still to prefer that she be without previous sexual experience. Because both men and women tend to regard sexual conquests and experience as indications (however stereotyped) of masculinity in a man, many women prefer that the man be nonvirginal at marriage.

Girls in their mid-teens begin to recognize that, in our society, the male is supposed to be strong and confident, and to offer security to his female. Not having the insight, tutelage, or experience to evaluate what constitutes genuine strength on the part of boy or man and, furthermore, feeling inadequate herself, the girl actually does not know what to look for by way of indicators or masculine strength, and may come to accept certain warped manifestations as qualities of manliness. These are the girls who are often impressed by the "tough guys"—the hell-raiser who is defiant of rules and of the society that makes them; the leather-jacketed thug on his motorcycle; the school drop-out committed to tobacco, alcohol, and profanity, and to little else in life; the dragster who is as reckless of human life as he is of human sensibilities. These girls have no way of assessing such behavioral patterns as being attempts by the boys to mask the marked feelings of inferiority that overwhelm and threaten them. The very things, therefore, that a young girl wishes to avoid—inadequacy and weakness in a man— are what she is unwittingly courting when she looks to the "tough guy" as an ideal. An unfortunate by-product of this twisted set of values is that the "nice" boy who attempts to treat such a girl with kindness and honesty, but who has no need to prove his adequacy by the unacceptable acting-out behavior described above, is too often ignored, if not regarded with downright contempt by her.

Other factors enter into the emotional complexities of these girls. As mentioned earlier, they are crossing the threshold into physical maturity and feel inadequate to cope with the social and sexual problems it poses. Since many girls evaluate themselves as rather worthless and insufficient beings, the boys who behave decently and compassionately toward them cannot, they reason, have very good judgment; or if the boys offer their friendship so unselfishly, they must not be of much value themselves. It follows, according to these girls' rationale, that the boys who callously ignore or mistreat them are exhibiting good judgment, and are therefore the obviously strong masculine ones, the social or sexual worthies. Furthermore, these girls have normal sexual desires and wishes, but frequently feel guilty about them; and it ensues in their thinking that, in our society, guilt demands punishment. Therefore, by selecting one of the "tough guys," such a girl is able not only to satisfy her sexual desires but at the same time to assure her punishment because, unconsciously or otherwise, she realizes that, sooner or later, she will be mistreated or rejected by this unsavory boy. It is, incidentally, a widely recognized phenomenon among psychotherapists and marriage counselors that many women marry "problem" men—for example, alcoholics—because they have an unconscious need to be punished.

As mentioned earlier, sexual attitudes and behavior differ from one culture to another and within the same culture, the determinants being such factors as religious affiliation, educational levels, socioeconomic strata, and decade of birth. One cultural or subcultural group may be so removed from another that the sexual attitudes and behavior of one may well seem perverted or absurd to the other. For example, college-educated men employed to take sex histories of men with very limited education may be overpowered at first by some of the sexual experiences of the latter— for example, one man's claim of having premarital coitus with 1000 women. On the other hand, men with grade-school education may view the oral-genital sexual behavior of the college-educated couple as being perverted and deserving of condemnation. As holds in most other cases of differences in both attitudes and behavior— whether religious, sexual, or racial—misunderstanding often could be removed and differences made more comprehensible if each group would trouble itself to become acquainted with individuals in the other group and their backgrounds.

Sexual Behavior

Human sexuality ordinarily expresses itself in six ways: masturbation, nocturnal orgasms, heterosexual petting, homosexual relations, sexual contact with animals, and heterosexual intercourse.

Throughout this section, frequent reference is made to men and women according to their levels of educational achievement. For the sake of clarity, these distinctions are intended:

Grade school (low educational group)—eight years of schooling or less

High school (middle educational group)—nine to twelve years of schooling

College (high educational group)—thirteen or more years of schooling

Masturbation

The term *masturbation* is applied to any type of self-stimulation that produces erotic arousal. It is a common sexual practice among both males and females in premarital, marital, and postmarital states. Boys and girls begin the practice at an early age, 13% of both sexes having masturbated by their tenth birthday.

Males. The incidence of masturbation to the point of orgasm among men (whether once or 1000 times) is generally fixed at about 95% of the total male population. The college group have the highest percentage (96%) of incidence; those who have only attended high school, second highest (95%); and those who only attended grade school, the lowest (89%). Slightly over two-thirds of all boys experience their first ejaculation through masturbation; about three-fourths learn how to masturbate from verbal or printed sources.

On the average, adolescent boys masturbate about two and a half times a week, although a certain number (17%) masturbate from four to seven (or more) times a week. The incidence of masturbation in men progressively declines in postadolescent years, although it frequently continues on a sporadic basis throughout adult life. About 70% of married American men who have graduated from college will masturbate occasionally (for 9% of their total sexual outlet), although the incidence is considerably lower in the married male grade-school group (29%) and in the married high-school group (42%). Approximately 25% of the married men above the age of 60 who are capable of satisfactory coitus also masturbate.

Genital manipulation is by far the most common technique of masturbation among men (95%). In 72% of the cases, fantasy always accompanies masturbation; in another 17%, fantasy is only occasionally coupled with it.

Masturbation among men occurs most frequently among religiously inactive Protestants, and least among orthodox Jews and devout Roman Catholics.

Females. Masturbation ranks second only to heterosexual petting among the erotic activities of unmarried young women (37% to 85% of total sexual outlet, depending upon the subcultural group), and second after coition among married women (constituting about 10% of their total sexual outlet). Among previously married women, masturbation accounts for 13% to 44% of total outlet, depending once more upon the subcultural group. Of all types of sexual activity among women, however, masturbation ranks first as the most successful method of reaching orgasm—in 95% of its incidence, a climax is reached. Furthermore, women reach orgasm more quickly through masturbation than through any other sexual technique (75% in under four minutes).

From 50% to 80% of all women masturbate at one time or another, the variance in figures resulting from differences in the results of several investigations into the subject. The Kinsey group reported that 34% of the women who never went past grade school, 59% of the women who had attended high school but not college, and 63% of the female college graduates masturbate. Their range of frequency is from once or twice a lifetime to 100 orgasms an hour. Of those women who masturbate to the point of orgasm, however, there is a striking similarity in frequency, regardless of age or marital status: once every two to four weeks.

Most women (57%) accidentally discover how to masturbate by exploring their own genitals. Another 40% learn techniques of autoeroticism through verbal or printed sources.

In contrast to men, who show a decline in the frequency of masturbation after their teens, the active incidence of self-stimulation to orgasm among women increases up to middle age, after which time its frequency becomes fairly constant. Of unmarried women between fifty and seventy years of age, 59% admit to autoeroticism as compared with 30% of married women in this same age group.

The large majority of women (84%) who stimulate themselves use genital manipulation as the technique, while a few others employ thigh pressure (10%), muscular tension (5%), or simply fantasy unattended by physical stimulation (2%). Fantasy is an invariable accompaniment to masturbation for half the women who stimulate themselves, but only an occasional one for a few others (14%).

Among those women who had never masturbated to orgasm before marriage, about one-third (31% to 37%) failed to reach orgasm during coitus the first year of marriage, while of those who had masturbated to orgasm, only 13% to 16% failed to have coital orgasm the first year.

Religious background influences the frequency of masturbation. The more devout the religious commitment, the lower the incidence of autoeroticism is.

Nocturnal Orgasms

It has long been recognized that men have nocturnal emissions or "wet dreams." And while women obviously cannot have nocturnal emissions, it is nonetheless true that they too have erotic dreams, frequently culminating in orgasm, although, curiously, this type of sexual outlet is persistenly ignored in studies of female sexuality. (For both men and women, however, sexual dreams often have a distressing way of stopping just short of orgasm.)

Males. Almost 100% of men have erotic dreams, and almost 85% of them have had dreams that culminate in orgasm. Erotic dreams occur most frequently to young men in their teens and twenties, but approximately 50% of all married men continue to have nocturnal emissions. This type of sexual expression constitutes 5% to 12% of the total sexual outlet for single men, 3% to 5% of the total outlet for married men, and from 4% to 6% for the previously married. Because married men of all ages have a much greater opportunity for release of sexual tension than single men do, the frequency of nocturnal emission among the married is only about two-thirds that of single men.

The incidence of nocturnal emission is considerably higher among college youths than among less educated groups, probably because college men do more petting that is not followed by orgasm, and their sexual tensions are therefore more often at a high pitch at bedtime. Over 99% of college men have sexual dreams to orgasm at some time during their lives; but only 85% of those who merely attended high school, and 75% whose education ended at grade school have nocturnal emissions. This form of sexual outlet is unique in that it is beyond the individual's conscious control. A man's religious convictions, therefore, bear little relationship to the incidence of his experiencing nocturnal emission.

Females. As many as 70% of all women have had dreams of sexual content, although only about half this group have had dreams that culminated in orgasm. Because there is no physical evidence afterwards, in contrast to men, that an orgasm has occurred, there is some question concerning the accuracy of data showing that 37% of all women actually dream to orgasm. However, there is no doubt in the minds of the women who have the dreams that orgasm has occurred.

The incidence of sexual dreams to orgasm reaches a peak when a woman is in her forties. There is an average of three or four such dreams a year for women, married or single, in all age groups. Over one-fourth of married women (28%) and more than one-third of those previously married (38%) have dreams to orgasm. These dreams constitute 2% to 4% of the total release from sexual tension for single girls, 1% to 3% for married women, and among the previously married, 4% to 14%.

There is no correlation between frequency of nocturnal dreams to orgasm and a woman's religious or educational background, although fewer women of devout religious convictions than those of less serious commitment to a religion ever have such dreams.

Heterosexual Petting

The sexual outlet termed *heterosexual petting* involves conscious, sexually oriented physical contact between persons of opposite sex that does not involve actual coitus. In the context of the present discussion, the significance of petting as a means of sexual expression will be limited to premarital petting, since petting in marriage is assumed to be a foreplay to sexual intercourse, or an outlet chosen by the partners in preference to coition as a means of achieving orgasm.

Petting is by no means limited to human beings, since many lower animals employ varying forms of it both before and after copulation. The significance of petting in relation to coitus for both man and lower animals is widely recognized. Petting is frequently practiced, and has a distinct value: it is useful not only as an arousal technique, but a means of achieving orgasm, especially during the years before marriage.

Males. There is some increase in the incidence of petting among men born after 1910 as compared with those born before then, but the increase is slight in contrast to the sharp rise in its occurrence among women.

By the age of fifteen, 57% of all boys have done some petting; by eighteen, 84% have petted, and by twenty-five, 89%. Almost all of these incidents involve erotic arousal, but only about a third of these youths ever become involved in petting to orgasm.

The often significant differences in the percentages of men who engage in a particular petting practice are directly related to the social, economic, and educational backgrounds of the boys and men sampled. There also exists a distinct correlation between the frequency of petting and educational attainments. Those men with the lowest education pet the least; men of the middle group are next; and the men of the high educational group pet most of all. The frequency with which men pet to orgasm can be as high as seven times (or more) a week, but the average incidence is three to five times a year. About a quarter of all men have five or fewer petting partners during their lifetimes, while 37% have twenty-one or more partners.

The range of petting practices is wide. Of the total male population, almost 100% engage in simple kissing; 55% to 87% engage in deep kissing; 78% to 99% in manual manipulation of the girl's breast; mouth-breast contact, 36% to 93%; manual manipulation of the girl's genitalia, 79% to 92%; and 9% to 18% of unmarried youths, in contrast to 4% to 60% of married men, orally stimulate their partner's genitalia. The two figures cited in each instance refer to men at the two extremes of educational levels.

Educational achievement correlates significantly with the occurrence of men's petting to orgasm. According to the levels of schooling reached, the lowest educational group achieve a climax through petting only 16% of the time, while the second group do so 32% of the time, and 61% of the petting in the college-level group culminates in orgasm.

Females. Almost 100% of all women have had some sort of petting experience prior to their marriage, and 90% of the entire female population, whether or not they ever marry, engage in petting at one time or another. By the age of thirty-five, 80% of those women born before 1900 had had petting experience; of those born between 1900 and 1909, 91% had petted; and of those born between 1910 and 1919, 98% had petted. The increase in percentages would seem to be an indication of the "sex revolution" which took place in the 1920s; women born after the turn of the century gradually, but steadfastly, became less sexually inhibited.

Simple kissing is engaged in at one time or another by nearly all women at all educational levels; more sophisticated methods of petting, however, are directly related to educational achievement, decade of birth, and incidence and frequency of coitus. The more advanced the level of education, the more liberal the girl is in the types of petting she engages in. Those women born after 1909 are more liberal in their petting practices than those born before 1910; and, as would be expected, frequency of coitus is directly related to freedom in petting. Furthermore, as one would also expect, at all educational levels, the more sophisticated and liberal the method of petting, the smaller the percentage of women who have participated becomes.

The type of petting that has been accepted more slowly and reluctantly than others, because of social taboos, is oral-genital contact. This form of sexual stimulation, however, is apparently rather widely accepted as an erotic outlet—and a normal, healthy one—by the majority in the higher socioeducational groups. About 65% of the younger women at the upper educational levels who have had premarital coital experience more than twenty-five times have had their genitals stimulated orally prior to marriage; 62% of these same women have orally stimulated the genitals of their partners.

Between the ages of twenty-one and twenty-five, 31% of all women have established a pattern of regular participation in premarital petting to orgasm. The average occurrence in the age bracket of fifteen to fifty-five is four to six orgasmic responses through petting a year, although the frequency may be as high as seven to ten times a week. In the sixteen- to twenty-five-year-old age group, petting affords as much as 18% of women's total sexual outlet before marriage; it consistently provides a higher percentage of the total sexual outlet for women of all ages than it does for men in comparable age groups. More than a half of all women indulge in premarital petting for a period of six years or more. The number of partners with whom women engage in petting varies from one only (10%) to twenty-one or more (19%). In excess of 33% of all women have experienced premarital petting with more than ten men.

In petting, as in most other practices in the sphere of sexual expression, women are influenced significantly by religious factors; the more pronounced the commitment to religious convictions, the more restricted the sexual behavior is. Interestingly, religion ultimately has little influence, one way or the other, on frequency of petting to orgasm, even among the most religiously devout. Once these devout women achieve orgasm through petting, they engage in such activity as often as less devout women. The rationale quite often is that petting allows a woman sexual gratification without depriving her of her virginity, a condition highly prized by many women.

Homosexual Relations

The term *homosexual relations* refers to the use of a partner of the same sex for sexual gratification. As a mode of sexual behavior in our society, it is greatly deplored, although sanctions against it are considerably more stringent for men than for women. In New York, for example, in a particular ten-year period of time, only one woman was convicted of "homosexual sodomy," while over 700 men were found guilty on the same charge. Homosexual contact among infra-human mammals is found among both males and females. Animal homosexuality is considerably more common than is popularly believed.

Males. It is generally accepted by sexologists that about 4% of all white men are exclusively homosexual all their sexual lives, 8% are exclusively homosexual for at least three years between the ages of sixteen and fifty-five, and 37% have experienced at least some form of overt homosexuality to the point of orgasm. While these data apply to white men, it has been estimated that the percentages are equally pertinent to the American Negro male population.

Educational levels bear a different relationship to the incidence of homosexuality than they do to most other avenues of sexual expression.

Homosexual Experience Among Men to Point of Orgasm

Educational Level	Single, to 35 years of age	Total male population
Grade School	50%	27%
High School	58%	39%
College	47%	34%

While the incidence of homosexuality among single men in the three educational groups is not significantly different, there is a great difference among the groups in the percentages of their total sexual outlet that homosexual practices constitute.

Homosexuality Among Single Men
Constituting Total Sexual Outlet

Educational Level	16-20 years old	21-25 years old	26-30 years old
Grade School	6.85%	8.06%	14.04%
High School	10.81%	16.31%	25.95%
College	2.43%	3.72%	8.82%

For all single men there is a gradual increase before the age of forty in the percentage of total sexual outlet that homosexuality affords, progressing from 5% to 22%. For married men, homosexuality represents less than 1% of the total outlet. For the previously married, there is also a gradual increase in total outlet, growing from 9% to 26%.

Some men who engage in homosexual practices are rather promiscuous: although 51% of them have only one or two sexual partners, 22% have over ten partners.

Generally speaking, the strength of the individual's religious convictions influences both the incidence and frequency of homosexual contacts; the more intense the commitment to religion, the less homosexual activity there is. The incidence is slightly higher among Catholic men than among the other two religious groups, the incidence among Jewish men falling behind that among Protestants.

Females. The incidence of homosexuality appears to be somewhat less among women than it is among men; the occurrence of both exclusive and partial homosexuality among women is only two-thirds of that among men.

The findings of some investigations indicate that as many as 50% of all women during their sexual life have harbored "intense feelings" for another woman or women. Most sexologists, however, agree with the more conservative conclusions of the Kinsey investigation: that 28% of women (compared with 50% of men) have experienced some sort of homosexual response. Only about 1% to 3% of the female population between the ages of twenty and thirty-five are exclusively homosexual, although an additional 2% to 6% in this age bracket are "more or less exclusively homosexual" (meaning that, very rarely, there may be a heterosexual contact). Compared with 37% of all men, only 13% of all women have had homosexual contact to the point of orgasm. In homosexual relationships, then, twice as many men as women experience some sort of sexual response short of orgasm, while three times as many men as women respond to orgasm.

In contrast to other types of sexual outlet, there is apparently no more female homosexuality (also called *lesbianism*) among those women born after 1900 than among those born earlier. The incidence of lesbianism at various educational levels differs, to be sure, but the figures do not correlate with those pertaining to male homosexuality. The percentages of women who, by the age of thirty, have experienced homosexual contact to the point of orgasm are these: those educated to the level of grade school, 6%; high school, 5%; and college, 10% (14% for women having attended graduate school). In the early years of active homosexuality, women in the two lower educational groups have a higher frequency of orgasm than college women do; but the differences subsequently disappear, and the frequency of orgasm then averages once in two or three weeks for women of all three educational levels.

Female homosexuality is largely confined to single women and, to a lesser extent, to the previously married. The incidence, as well as frequency, of lesbian contact is negligible among married women. Although 19% of the total female population have had active homosexual contact by the age of forty, when the factor of marital status is introduced, this pattern of active homosexual incidence emerges in the same age group; 24% of the women who have never been married, 9% of the previously married, and only 3% of the married women.

By the age of twenty, only 4% of the total female population have had orgasmic response through lesbian contacts; by thirty-five, the incidence of orgasmic response through homosexual outlets in the total female population has risen to 11%. The figure is 13% among women in their mid-forties. Of those women who have homosexual associations, from one-half to two-thirds experience orgasm at least occasionally.

Homosexual activity does not last long for women. About one-third have fewer than ten experiences; for many, there has been only one or two. The homosexual experiences of half the women last for a total period of one year or less, while the activity of another quarter is spread over two to three years. Half the women (51%) involved in homosexual activity limit their experience to a single partner, another 20% have only two partners, and only 4% have ten or more partners (compared with 22% of the men who have ten or more partners).

Of those women who have the most extensive homosexual experience, only 20% express definite regret. Almost 90% of all women with homosexual experience themselves declare they would keep as a friend any woman with a history of lesbianism; they are less accepting (74%) of male friends with a history of homosexuality.

In all three religious groups, the more devout adherents had less homosexual contact to the point of orgasm than the non-devout. Among women (as well as among men) only nominally affiliated with the Catholic Church, 25% have experienced homosexual contact to orgasm, while 5% of devout Catholic women have had this experience. Among Protestants and Jews, a similar correlation exists between casual or serious religious affiliation and homosexual experience.

Sexual Contact with Animals

The taboo against sexual relations with animals is well established in the Old Testament and in the Talmud. Sexual contact between humans and infrahumans (which is also called *bestiality*) has occurred since early civilization, but such behavior is highly abhorrent to most people who have not had a similar experience. The extent of such sexual activity among either men or women is extremely small, and the significance in studying it lies in its social impact rather than in its importance as a sexual outlet.

Males. As would be expected, male contact with animals, whenever it exists, is found primarily among boys reared on farms. Between 40% and 50% of all farm boys have some sexual contact with animals, but only 17% experience orgasm as a result of animal contact. About twice as many men (32%) as women (16%) are erotically aroused by seeing animals in copulation. About 15% of rural males of only grade-school achievement have some sexual experience with animals to the point of orgasm, but there is an increase to 20% of the rural high-school group, and to about 27% of the rural males who are college-educated.

Sexual contacts with animals vary in frequency from once or twice a lifetime to as high as eight times a week for some adolescent rural boys; the average for those involved is about two times a week. The period of time over which these contacts occur is ordinarily limited to two or three years; most sexual contact with animals occurs in preadolescence before the boy is capable of orgasm. Sexual contact with animals represents considerably less than 1% of the total sexual outlet for men in both urban and rural communities.

City boys have limited sexual experience with animals. Their contacts are customarily with household pets, and with animals on a farm where they might visit during vacations.

Females. An extremely low percentage of the total female population have ever had any sort of sexual contact with animals. About 1.5% of women have had sexual contact with animals during preadolescence (usually as a result of accidental physical contact with a household pet), and only 3.6% of the female sample have had sexual contact with animals after their adolescent years. Of those sexually precocious women who were able to have orgasms prior to adolescence, 1.7% experienced their first orgasm in animal contact.

Only about 16% of Kinsey's total female sample had ever been erotically aroused by witnessing coitus between animals. Out of the entire 5940 women in Kinsey's sample, twenty-nine had caused dogs or cats to stimulate their vulval area orally, and two had had coitus with dogs. In only twenty-five of these histories had women recorded being brought to orgasm by sexual contact with animals, and the method was primarily oral stimulation of their genitals. Of those women who engaged in bestiality, half had only a single experience, and a fourth had six or more contacts.

Heterosexual Intercourse

The average man or woman is more interested in coitus with a member of the opposite sex than in any other type of sexual outlet, although other methods of outlet are significant in the sexual lives of both men and women. Ordinarily, heterosexual intercourse is thought of in relationship to marriage, but premarital, extramarital, and postmarital heterosexual coitions are also to be considered in analyzing this type of sexual outlet.

Premarital Heterosexual Intercourse

The term *premarital heterosexual intercourse* is used to indicate that at least one of the heterosexual partners is single and has not been previously married. In our culture this act usually involves two single persons, although the second person may, of course, be married.

Males. In the American culture, men are generally accorded considerably more latitude in sexual expression than women are; premarital sexual intercourse is the most controversial of these sexual outlets, and is the one most often considered in discussions concerning the double standard of morality.

At some time or another before they are married, 98% of men who have attended only grade school, 84% of men who have attended high school only, and 67% of men with college education will have sexual intercourse. The decade in which they were born appears to have little or no correlation with the frequency of premarital coitus among men, in contrast to the rather sharp differences found in the correlations between birthdate and frequency among women.

Between the ages of sixteen and twenty, the grade-school group has seven times the frequency of sexual intercourse that the college group has. Furthermore, this disparity in coital frequency lessens only slightly between the groups of older single men of the same educational levels. Depending upon their ages, the college group obtains from 4% to 21% of its total premarital sexual outlet from coitus; the high-school group, from 26% to 54%; and the grade-school group, from 40% to 68%. Also, unmarried college men commonly engage in coitus for the first time at an age five or six years older than that of the unmarried men of lower educational levels when *they* first experience coition.

The correlation between premarital intercourse with prostitutes and educational level follows the same trend. Of single men at the age of twenty-five, 74% of the grade-school group, 54% of the high-school group, and 28% of the college group have had coitus with prostitutes. The total sexual outlet sought from prostitutes by single men rises, between the ages of sixteen and forty, from 6% to 23% for the grade-school group, from 3% to 11% for the high-school group, and from less than 1% to 3% for the college group. Furthermore, sexual intercourse with any woman, prostitute or otherwise, never accounts for more than 21% of the total sexual outlet of single college men, whereas coitus may constitute as much as 68% of the total sexual outlet for single men in the lower educational groups.

Among unmarried men who have coitus regularly, frequency is at its maximum during early adolescence, averaging about two contacts a week; among males in their teens and twenties, the average is about 1.4 times a week, dropping to a lesser frequency among older groups of unmarried men. The lowest education group maintains a level of two to four coitions a week—which incidentally equals the average incidence of coition among married men in the same age bracket.

The point should be made that the incidence of premarital sexual intercourse among men ranges from a single contact to such sexual activity as twenty-five or more coitions a week (the latter pattern sometimes persisting for as long as five years or more). Many men, particularly those at the upper end of the socio-educational scale, limit their premarital coition to one girl—often the girl they eventually marry; other men, particularly at the lower end of the social-educational scale, may copulate with as many as several hundred girls.

A few single men have sexual intercourse with older women—single, married, or divorced. However, almost all the coital experiences of single men are with single women, usually of their own age or slightly younger. Studies have shown that boys of a higher social stratum often sexually exploit girls of a lower social stratum but that, in college populations, young men and women will customarily have their sexual experiences with persons of an equal social class.

Religion, at all social-educational levels, has a direct relationship among men to the incidence and frequency of premarital sexual intercourse. Of Catholics and Protestants, there is much less premarital coitus among the devoutly religious than among the less devout. Interestingly, inactive Jews have less premarital coitus than do the orthodox Jews (although the incidence of experience does not differ greatly except among early pubescents up to the age of fifteen years). Kinsey speculated that this discrepancy could be a result of the strong condemnation with which the Jewish faith views masturbation; the religiously active Jew possibly feels less guilt over premarital coitus than over masturbation.

Females. Kinsey drew his conclusions about premarital coition among women from data concerned only with sexual activity after early pubescence (about 10 years of age). Any earlier coital experiences among girls would not, therefore, have appeared in his findings. In any event, most sexual behavior during these early years is merely experimentation and sex play—although, of course, there are exceptions.

Prior to marriage, almost 50% of all women have experienced coitus and 67% have experienced orgasm. However, only about 17% of the orgasms that women experience result from coition, which lags far behind masturbation as unmarried women's primary source of sexual outlet. Girls younger than sixteen have only 6% of their total orgasmic experience from premarital coitus; girls between sixteen and twenty, 15%; and those still unmarried in their early twenties, 26%. After the early twenties, coition becomes more important to single women as a source of orgasm than petting is, and it is by this time not far behind masturbation as such a source.

The high percentage of women who engage in premarital coitus surprises and disturbs many people. It should be pointed out, however, that about half the single women who are coitally active have sexual intercourse only with the men they eventually marry; furthermore, most of women's premarital coition takes place only the year or two just preceding marriage. About 50% of the women who marry by the age of twenty have premarital sexual intercourse; the same percentage holds for those who marry between twenty-one and twenty-five. Of those women who marry between the ages of twenty-six and thirty, however, between 40% and 66% have experienced coition. Except for the girls who marry quite young, premarital coitus during the early teens is relatively rare; only 3% of all girls have premarital coition by the age of fifteen. The important conclusion to be drawn from these data is that females who marry at an early age will experience any premarital coition earlier than women who marry at a later age. This fact is significant in the consideration of premarital coital activity at the various educational levels, which will be discussed later.

As is true with other types of premarital sexual activity, the frequency of premarital coitus does not reach its peak until the women involved are in their late twenties, after which it remains remarkably regular. Of those single girls under the age of twenty who engage in coition, sexual intercourse occurs on an average of once every five or ten weeks, while the frequency is about once every three weeks among older single girls. The frequency of premarital coitus among women as a group and individually often varies considerably. About 20% of the group who experience premarital coition have coitus as often as seven times a week (7% having it fourteen times in the same period), but there are usually intervals of complete (or relatively complete) sexual inactivity between the sexually active times.

Some girls who have premarital intercourse are capable of multiple orgasms from the very beginning of their coital experience. About 14% regularly experience multiple orgasms, and a vast majority have a similar capacity.

Of all women who engage in premarital coitus (whether or not they eventually marry), 53% have a single partner, 34% have two to five partners, and only 13% have six or more partners. Of married women who had premarital coitus, 87% had at least some of their coital experience with the men they eventually married, and 46% only with their future husbands. Only 13% of these women had premarital coitus with men other than their future husbands, but never with the latter.

The age at which marriage occurs has a significant impact on the incidence of premarital coition at the various education levels. At first glance, Kinsey's findings would lead one to believe that single college girls are much more coitally active than girls of the two lower educational groups: the data show that 60% of the girls who have gone to college, 47% of the girls who have finished high school only, and 30% of those girls who have not gone beyond grade school have premarital coitus. (These statistics, incidentally, stand in striking contrast to those concerning men, wherein 67% of men with college education and 98% of those with only grade-school education were found to have had sexual intercourse prior to marriage.) Despite the seemingly high incidence of premarital coition among college girls, certain facts should be borne in mind: because girls who are schooled only to grade-school or high-school level tend to marry at a considerably earlier age than college girls, they obviously have fewer prenuptial years in which to form attachments that might lead to sexual intercourse. As Kinsey pointed out, among women within a given age group *after* the age of twenty, no matter what the educational background, coital experience before marriage is about equal.

The lower educational groups begin their coital experience at an earlier age than girls with more education do; between the ages of sixteen and twenty, 38% of the grade-school group, 32% of the high-school group, and about 18% of the college group have premarital sexual intercourse. The relationship between the *frequency* with which girls have coitus and their educational level is not as consistent as is the relationship between the *incidence* of premarital coitus in the female population and educational level.

It was pointed out earlier that a rather noticeable change occurred in women's sexual behavior about 1920, affecting almost every aspect of their sexual lives. Two and a half times as many of the women born between 1900 and 1910 had sexual intercourse before marriage as women born before 1900 (36% as compared with 14%). Since that time the increase has leveled off onto a fairly consistent plateau. It is of interest to note that despite the increase in premarital coital *incidence* among women born in the decades mentioned above, the percentage of women who attained orgasm coitally before marriage remains about the same—50% at the age of twenty, 75% by the age of thirty-five—no matter which generation is under consideration. The *frequency* of premarital coital experience has also remained remarkably consistent for women of all generations.

With regard to the site chosen for their premarital coition, over half (58%) the women so involved have coitus at least some of the time in their parents' home. Furthermore, while a small percentage of girls attending college and living away from home have coition in the college town, by far the greater number have it in their home towns during visits and vacations. Almost half (48%) have some part of their coital experiences in their partner's home, 40% have some part in a hotel or in similar accommodations, and 41% have a portion of their total experiences in an automobile. Kinsey found a correlation between date of birth and site of premarital coition; automobiles, for instance, doubled in popularity as a site over the thirty-year period covered by his sampling.

Premarital coital experience for women is directly related to their degree of involvement in religion, whether Catholicism, Judaism, or Protestantism; women who are the least active religiously engage the most in premarital sexual intercourse, the moderately devout next most, and the devout the least of all. By the age of thirty-five, slightly over 60% of the Protestant and Jewish single women who are inactive in their churches or synagogues have had premarital coitus, as compared with 55% of the inactive Catholic women. Of the single devout Protestant women of the same age, about 30% have had premarital coitus, while 25% of devout Catholic and moderate Jewish women (no figures on orthodox) have had the experience. Of couples who attend church regularly, 28% have engaged in premarital coitus; the percentage increases to 48% when one of the couple is a regular churchgoer, the other not, and to 61% when neither of the pair attends church regularly.

Marital Heterosexual Intercourse

According to the legal and moral codes of our Anglo-American culture, coitus between husband and wife is the one totally approved type of sexual activity (excepting, of course, erotic dreams). It is the sexual outlet most frequently utilized by married couples; yet, as a conservative estimate, sexual relationships in about one-third of all marriages are somewhat inadequate. One reason for marital problems stemming from the sexual relationship may be that too much is expected of sex. Both the glories and the pitfalls of sexual intercourse have been part of the preachments heard by almost every man and woman. The negative aspects of sex (such as feelings of guilt, and fear of inadequacy or rejection) are expected to be dispelled as the groom carries the bride across the threshold of the bedroom. About 90% of husbands and 74% of wives cross that threshold with attitudes of eager anticipation; the remaining husbands and wives enter their marital chambers with attitudes of disgust, aversion, or indifference toward sexual relations. Of all married couples who stated that sex was about as important in marriage as they had anticipated, two-thirds rated their marriage as "very happy," whereas one-third rated their marriage as "average" or "less than average" in happiness. Even from these very few examples, it can be seen that marital coition is affected by manifold emotional and psychological attitudes. The impact on marriage of these attitudes and resulting behavior is observed constantly by marriage counselors.

Males. Only an exceedingly small number of married men do not participate, at least occasionally, in marital coitus; even among husbands in their late fifties, only 6% refrain from marital intercourse. These statements, of course, do not mean that marital sexual activity is confined to marital coitus; actually, marital intercourse provides only 85% of the total sexual outlet for married men, the remaining 15% being derived from masturbation, nocturnal emissions, petting, homosexual activity, extramarital coitus, and, in some rural areas, animal contact.

Many may be surprised to learn that about half the sexual outlets of the entire male population are socially disapproved, and, to a large extent, are illegal and punishable by law. Only 60% of the American male population are married at any one time, and between adolescence and old age, each 100 men average 231 orgasms a week; correcting for the increased incidence of coition and total sexual outlet in marriage, one is led to conclude that only 106 orgasms a week per 100 men are from marital coitus (45.9% of their total sexual outlet). If 5% of the total outlet is accounted for in nocturnal emissions, then approximately 50% of men's total sexual outlet is obtained through illegal or disapproved sources.

An interesting contrast in incidence of marital intercourse in relation to total outlet for men at the various educational levels is presented in Kinsey's investigations. In the lower educational groups, about 80% of the total outlet in the early years of marriage is provided by marital coitus, and the incidence for this group increases to 90% as the marriages continue. For the college-educated man, marital coitus provides 85% of the total outlet during the early part of marriage, but by the time he reaches the age of fifty-five, only 62% of his total sexual outlet is provided by marital coitus. The assumption is that these college-educated men have reevaluated the moral restraints placed on them during their early life and have found them to be less constrictive and threatening than they formerly were. These men then come to the conclusion that they should have the sexual experiences they missed earlier in their lives. However, it should be emphasized that half the remaining 38% of their total sexual activity aside from marital coitus is not with another woman (or man), but is in the solitary act of masturbation and through nocturnal emissions.

The frequency of marital coitus decreases with age, dropping from an average of 3.9 times per week during the teens to 2.9 at the age of thirty, 1.8 at the age of fifty, and 0.9 at the age of sixty. If a man reaches pubescence as early as the age of ten or eleven, and marries between the ages of sixteen and twenty, he averages five to seven orgasms a week; if he reaches pubescence at fifteen or later, and marries between sixteen and twenty, his average is slightly over three orgasms a week.

The sex drive is somewhat greater in men than in women, especially during the early years of marriage, although, curiously, each sex tends to overestimate the drive of the other. One serious problem arises from this misjudgment: if their sex needs differ sharply, a husband and wife may work out some sort of compromise in the frequency of their sexual activity that, unfortunately, does not meet the needs of either.

Petting in marriage is usually considered to be only an introduction to sexual intercourse, although every method of arousal known to man has been made a part of the erotic repertory of marriage. Educational achievement exerts considerable influence on attitudes towards precoital stimulation. About half the total population, especially those with less education, are uninterested in prolonging the sexual act; they want to proceed with coition as quickly as possible and to achieve orgasm in the shortest period of time. The man with only a low level of education may limit his precoital activity to a simple kiss without causing any upset to his wife; similar perfunctory behavior on the part of the college-educated husband, however, would be interpreted by his wife as rejection or a lack of interest. The average college-educated husband will spend from five to fifteen minutes—sometimes an hour or more—in precoital petting. Once coitus is under way, he will attempt, more often than a man of lower education, to delay orgasm (although three-fourths of the total male population reach orgasm within two minutes). About 90% of college-educated men prefer to have intercourse in the nude, but only one-half as many of the grade-school group have ever had intercourse without being clothed. Because college-educated men are capable of a higher level of abstraction than are men with only grade-school and high-school educations, they are also more excited by external erotic stimulation. Consequently, they prefer to have intercourse in a lighted room where they can observe the nude body of the partner and the act of coition itself.

Because marital coitus (again, excepting nocturnal emissions and orgasms) is the only sexual outlet totally sanctioned by all religious groups, one would expect the frequency of marital coition to be greater among the religiously devout than among the religiously inactive—or that, at the very least, there should be no differences in frequency between the two groups. The frequencies of marital intercourse, however, are lower among religiously active Protestants than among inactive Protestants. (Insufficient data on Catholic and Jewish groups prevent similar comparisons.) It is difficult to escape the conclusion that the severity of early religious training of devout Protestants carries over into marriage and continues to inhibit sexual expression, despite the couples' conscious acceptance of the "rightness" of marital coitus.

Marital coitus among older men occurs considerably more frequently than is commonly realized. About three-fourths (73%) of all men between the ages of sixty-five and sixty-nine experience satisfactory coitus, as do about 60% of the men between the ages of seventy and seventy-four, and 48% of the men between the ages of seventy-five and ninety-two. The fact is interesting that elderly physicians seem to have one of the highest rates of impotency, while elderly clergymen, as a group, have one of the lowest impotency ratings. Seven out of ten healthy married couples who are sixty years of age or older are sexually active, and the consistent clinical observation is that of both men and women, the ones with the strongest sex drive during youth retain the greatest sex drive and virility in old age. Furthermore, another means of retaining vigorous sexual capacity is a consistent pattern of sexual intercourse through the years of marriage. Once interest is allowed to wane, it is difficult to rekindle.

Studies of older men show that frequency of marital intercourse ranges from one to four times a month, with about 25% engaging in coitus four times a month. Even the 25% of older men whose sexual potency is unsatisfactory report that they engage in sexual intercourse three or four times a month. Over 60% of men seventy-five or older report having occasional morning erections, and 17% report that the condition recurs frequently. It has generally been found that, among older people, Negroes are more sexually active than whites, and persons from low socioeconomic levels are more sexually active than those from higher socioeconomic levels.

The sexual drive of older people generally follows their overall pattern of health and physical performance. Secretion of the male sex hormone androgen decreases from fifty-five units per twenty-four hours when a man is thirty years of age to about eight units during the same period at the age of sixty; the secretion remains fairly constant thereafter. From the age of forty, women begin to experience a sharp decrease in the secretion of estrogen, a decrease which continues gradually for the remainder of their lives. However, over 90% of the older men studied reported that they had no physical disability that interfered with sexual frequency. The factors that most often deter sexual activity in older men are such psychological agents as feelings of shame and guilt for having sexual needs and drives at their age, and the erroneous notion that older men are naturally unable to perform sexually.

Females. Practically all married women participate in sexual intercourse, although there is a gradual decline in frequency between the first two years of marriage and old age. Men, too, it will be remembered, experience marital coitus less frequently in later years of life, but the decline among women is somewhat steeper than among males. Kinsey showed that at the age of fifty, 97% of men and 93% of women are still having coitus; at the age of sixty, the percentages are 94% for men and 84% for women. Curiously, marital coition is the only form of sexual outlet among women that undergoes such a decline with advancing age.

For women who marry in their late teens, the average (median) frequency of marital coitus is nearly three (2.8) times a week in the early years of marriage, 2.2 a week at the age of thirty, 1.5 a week at the age of forty, once a week at the age of fifty, and once every twelve days (0.6) at the age of sixty. About 14% of all married women have marital intercourse seven or more times a week, although the percentage of wives involved in such frequency drops to 5% at the age of thirty, and to 3% by the age of forty. This decline in frequency is rather puzzling in light of Kinsey's findings that women reach their peak of sexual desire between the ages of thirty-one and forty. However, since the peak of men's sexual drive is reached between the late teens and the age of twenty-five, and thereafter shows a decline, it must be assumed that the aging of men rather than women's loss of sexual interest causes the decrease in marital coital frequency. During the first year of marriage, 75% of all women attain orgasm at least once during coitus; the percentage gradually increases to 90% after twenty years of marriage.

It should be remembered that the decline of frequency of marital coitus after the first two years of marriage does not mean that there is necessarily a decline in interest in other forms of sexual activity. The incidence of female masturbation and nocturnal dreams involving orgasm increases after marriage, and then remains fairly steady at its maximum level until wives become sixty years of age or even older. Between the ages of twenty-one and twenty-five, 89% of a married woman's total sexual outlet is derived from marital coition. After the age of twenty-five there is a gradual but consistent decline, so that by the time a woman reaches the age of seventy, only 72% of her total sexual outlet is provided by marital coitus.

There is little evidence that aging produces any decline in the sexual capacity of women until possibly quite late in life. Apparently women struggle (with some success) through the years of marriage to throw off the inhibitory shackles forged by the taboos of their early sex education, and once they reach their maximum sexual peak (between the ages of thirty-one and forty), they maintain this level. By this time, however, the husband's interest in sexual intercourse typically begins to slacken, with the unfortunate result of all-round frustration that frequently leads the wife to seek out other means of sexual gratification. From the late teens to the age of forty-five and after, the incidence of masturbation increases for all groups of women—from about 35% to 65% of single women, from 30% to 60% of the postmarital group, and from 25% to 45% of the married women.

There are few differences in frequency of marital coitus among women at different educational levels; however, for every age group there is an increase in coition to orgasm as the education level rises. For example, during the first year of marriage, 34% of the grade-school group, 28% of the high-school group, about 25% of the college-educated group, and only 22% of the graduate-school women fail to reach orgasm during marital coition. During the later years of marriage, the incidence of female orgasm in coition increases for all educational levels, although the incidence is consistently greater among the higher education groups. No changes in frequency of female coital experience in marriage according to decade of birth have been observed, but there are significant differences between the decade-of-birth groups in the incidence of response to orgasm in marital coitus—the women born during the 1919-1929 decade showing about a 25% increase in the incidence of orgasmic response over those women born before 1900.

It has been previously noted that the incidence of masturbation, premarital petting, and premarital coitus is significantly related to a woman's religious background—the more devout she is, the less likely she is to engage in such sexual activities. However, it has also been noted that once a woman has had these experiences, the frequency of her sexual activity continues, bearing little or no relationship to her religious background. This same pattern applies to marital coitus. A pattern of frequent coition is somewhat slower in developing among the more devout women, but once the frequency is established, there is no further relationship to the degree of religious involvement (in contrast to the findings concerning Protestant males).

There is a correlation, however, between the percentage of total sexual outlet provided by marital coitus and a woman's devotion to her religion, the more devout women experiencing from 4% to 12% more of their total outlet in marital coition than the women who are religiously inactive. Regarding religious affiliation, there are no differences in the incidence of sexual intercourse leading to orgasm, except that devout Catholic women are less likely to have orgasms during marital coitus than women of the other religious groups are. This tendency probably stems from fear of pregnancy because of the Catholic Church's prohibition of certain birth-control measures that does not bind women of other religions.

Precoital techniques of petting in marriage are similar to premarital ones; however, since marital coition is readily available, the length of time devoted to petting is usually not as protracted within marriage as before. Precoital marital petting is limited to less than three minutes in 11% of marriages, four to ten minutes in a third of them, and eleven to twenty minutes in another third. About 22% of couples—primarily in the groups with higher education—extend petting beyond twenty minutes (occasionally for as long as an hour or more). Decade of birth also affects marital petting techniques. Eighty percent of those women born before 1900 have manually manipulated and 29% have had oral contact with their husbands' genitalia; while among those women born between 1920 and 1929, 95% have manually manipulated and 57% have had oral contact with the male genitalia. About one-third of the married women born before 1900 remained clothed during coitus, while only 8% of those born during the 1920s keep clothes on during coition.

Kinsey and Terman have shown that almost 15% of all women regularly respond with multiple orgasms. Masters and Johnson conclude from their investigations that the percentage is somewhat higher. Masters and Johnson say further that "woman is naturally multiple-orgasmic in capacity."

Older women, like older men, are quite capable of sexual intercourse and other forms of sexual activity. About seven-eighths of all women aged fifty and 70% of those aged sixty continue to have intercourse with their husbands. Even of those women who no longer have husbands, 37% of the fifty-year-old group, 29% of the fifty-five-year-old group, and 12% of the sixty-year-old group continue to experience coitus. About 30% of the older married women supplement marital coitus with masturbation.

Many women past sixty avoid having an orgasm because of the painful uterine cramping they often experience afterwards. This pain can be relieved by their taking the proper combination of estrogen and progesterone to correct the imbalance in the sex-steroid level caused by the aging process. However, despite some obvious and predictable physical changes resulting from aging, there are apparently no physiological agents that should prevent a woman in her post-menopausal years from continuing satisfactory sexual expression with the frequency of her younger years.

Extramarital Sexual Activity

The phrase *extramarital sexual behavior* customarily means *adultery* in most people's thinking. However, many sexual outlets other than coition are technically implied in the total scope of extramarital behavior. In this discussion, unless otherwise indicated, extramarital sex relations will refer to extramarital coition only; that is, nonmarital sexual intercourse between a man and woman, at least one of whom is married at the time to someone else. Such behavior is condemned in practically all Western cultures because of the threat it poses to the family unit. Adultery, furthermore, is unequivocally condemned in Judaic-Christian moral theology. Nevertheless, at no time in the history of any culture has men's extramarital coition been consistently controlled or severely punished, whereas women have universally been subjected to a much more stringent code of sexual ethics. Furthermore, wives at every social level are more permissive of their husbands' extramarital affairs than husbands are of such behavior on the part of their wives. These differences in attitude are primarily a result of the fact that since the dawn of history, women have been regarded, more or less, as property of their husbands; if the woman were to engage in extramarital coitus, it would threaten the economic stability of the entire society, would reflect on the masculinity and social prestige of her husband, and, in the case of pregnancy, could raise the question of paternal responsibility.

For men, the frequency of extramarital coitus, as with other types of sexual activity, decreases with age. For women, in keeping with certain other forms of sexual activity, both the frequency of extramarital coitus and the percent of total outlet that it represents increase with age. Because of society's attitude toward extramarital affairs, the participants will usually go to rather extreme lengths to hide or deny their activity. As a result, only the most careful, detailed, and sophisticated investigations can uncover even an approximation of the actual incidence and frequency of extramarital coition—a state of affairs that is attested to by the experience of psychotherapists who find patients reluctant to admit to such behavior, despite an extended time in therapy and the confidential nature of the therapeutic relationship.

Although extramarital affairs incur moral, legal, and social condemnation, and often engender unique difficulties for one or both partners, the participants nonetheless frequently view their attachment as an opportunity for love, excitement, adventure, romance, renewed vigor, enhanced ego, and return to youth—all the dreams that marriage was supposed to fulfill, but did not, or no longer does. The partners, however, are frequently disappointed in their expectations. Although changing ethical values are producing a change of attitude toward both premarital and extramarital sexual activity, the censorious judgments of religious and social groups are still rigid and powerful enough to make adultery a relationship that is sometimes destructive to marriage —although it is questionable why couples would allow adultery, in most instances, to be so ruinous a force in their marriages.

Males. Almost three-fourths of all married men admit at least to an occasional desire to have an extramarital affair, and a conservative estimate is that about 50% of married men actually do experience extramarital coitus at some point during their marriage.

Men of the lowest educational group have more extramarital coitus during the early years of marriage (as well as more premarital coition) than men at other educational levels do. College men have less premarital coitus and less extramarital coitus during the early years of marriage than other educational groups do. As marriages continue, however, the involvement in extramarital intercourse decreases for the lower educated group from 45% during the late teens to 27% by age forty, and 19% by age fifty. In contrast, among the male teenage married group, only 15% to 20% have extramarital intercourse, but the incidence increases to 27% by the time this group reaches the age of fifty.

Frequency of contact of men of lower education drops from once (1.2) a week between the ages of sixteen to twenty, to once in two weeks (0.6) by the age of fifty-five; extramaritally involved college men average one contact in two or three weeks between the ages of sixteen to twenty, and the average increases to almost once a week by the age of fifty. Between the ages of sixteen and twenty, the men of lower education have over ten times (10.6) as much extramarital coitus as college men of the same age do; laborers and semiskilled workmen aged sixteen to twenty have almost seventeen (16.7) times more extramarital intercourse than do young men of the same age who later become members of the professions.

Men frequently become promiscuous in their nonmarital sexual behavior once they begin it, no matter whether it involves premarital or extramarital coition or homosexual contacts. Ultimately, married men derive between 5% and 10% of all their orgasms from extramarital coition, intercourse with prostitutes comprising from 8% to 15% of all their extramarital coitus. The most common cause for men's seeking coition with someone other than their wives is, no doubt, their desire for sexual variety, although dissatisfaction with their marital coition leads many men to extramarital intercourse.

Extramarital coitus causes more complications for the middle classes than it does for either the high or low social classes. Wives of low social status rather expect their husbands to form outside attachments, and they seem not to object to the affair so long as it is not conducted flagrantly under their noses. At the upper social levels, the persons involved in an extramarital affair exert sufficient and intelligent care so that no one becomes aware that it exists.

Females. Among white American married women, about one-fourth (26%) will have extramarital sexual intercourse by the age of forty. During the fourteen years from the age of twenty-six to the age of forty, the incidence of extramarital coition rises from 7% to 26%.

For most age groups, the incidence of response to orgasm in extramarital affairs is about the same as its occurrence in marital coition—from 78% to 100%, depending upon the group studied. For those having extramarital intercourse, the lowest frequency—once in ten weeks—is among married teen-age girls. From that point the frequency rises to one contact every two to three weeks by the age of forty. The notion is almost universal that men customarily prefer sexual intercourse with somewhat younger partners. Sexological investigations, however, have shown that men frequently prefer coition with middle-aged or older women. The reason is that since a woman's sex drive reaches its peak between the ages of thirty-five and forty, she therefore is ordinarily more responsive. Furthermore, she is more experienced sexually, and has a better knowledge of sexual techniques; she has also thrown off many of the taboos and inhibitions that plague most women during their earlier years, making her a freer and more responsive partner.

Education, decade of birth, and religious factors have a direct bearing on extramarital coitus among women. Nearly a third (31%) of the college-level women have extramarital intercourse by the age of forty, as compared with about 24% of those in the same age group who have only grade-school or high-school education. Of those women born before 1900, 22% have had extramarital coition by the age of forty, while of those born after 1900, 30% have had the experience. At every age level, the lowest incidence of extramarital intercourse is among the religiously devout.

For example, by the age of thirty, 7% of the active Protestant women have had extramarital intercourse, as compared with 28% of the inactive Protestant women.

About 41% of the women who have extramarital affairs limit their activity to a single partner; another 40% have two to five partners in their total extramarital experience; 16%, between five and twenty partners; and 3%, more than twenty. Up to the date their histories were taken, about 33% of those women involved had had extramarital coitus ten times or less. Forty-two percent limit their extramarital affairs to one year or less; about a fourth have their affairs over a two- to three-year period; and about a third continue their extramarital sexual experiences over a period of four years or longer.

The frequency of extramarital petting has risen in recent years, and all forms of petting are utilized. In fact, light petting under certain circumstances—for instance, at a cocktail party or dance—has become rather widely accepted in many groups. Almost 15% of married women reach orgasm when they engage in extramarital petting, including 2% who do not allow extramarital coitus but will pet.

Of those women who experience extramarital coitus, 68% also have had premarital intercourse (in contrast to 50% of the whole female population who experience premarital coition). Of those women who have not experienced extramarital coitus, 83% state that they have no expectations of doing so, while only 44% of those who have had extramarital intercourse state that they do not expect to renew their activity.

Allan Fromme

Toward a Better
Sexual Orientation

What is a sexually well-adjusted person? First of all, a man is glad to be a man and a woman is glad to be a woman. This is not to say that men do not have feminine components in their make-up or that women do not have masculine elements in theirs. What it does mean, however, is that the individual accepts the biological fact of his birth and develops a role in life consistent with it. There may be homosexuals who have been immensely productive in their fields of work, but it is doubtful if they are immensely well adjusted. Generally such individuals have greater than aver-age difficulty making an emotional go of things because they are out of step. At best, they achieve only marginal emotional adjust-ment, no matter how brave a front they may put up.

From: Allan Fromme, *Understanding the Sexual Response in Humans.* New York: Simon and Schuster Inc., 1966. Reprinted by permission of the author.

A sexually well-adjusted adult gets along with both men and women. He is aware of the differences, treats the two sexes differently, and enters into different relationships with each. Despite the variations history has presented to us from time to time, and even those which continue to exist in our society at present, sexual gratification is easiest and deepest when men and women find each other attractive. This is a basic requirement for the best kind of sex life.

A second requirement is to be glad that there is this major difference in the world. Boys and girls at eight and ten may find each other a nuisance, but eventually it becomes important that they learn to celebrate the fact that they have each other. In other words, another requirement for a good sex life is to like sex. Unfortunately many of us are brought up in such a way that we develop varying degrees of fear about sex. Fear of being caught, fear of pregnancy, fear of doing the wrong thing, fear of being turned down, fear of being inadequate—all these are more than enough to make anyone dislike sex. In other words, a certain amount of freedom is essential for the enjoyment of sex.

This notion of sexual freedom is not the same as promiscuity. As a matter of fact, promiscuity is often the result of other personal fears which may find an outlet in sexual expression. Although promiscuity, at first blush, sounds like a personal choice, it is more often a matter of compulsion. One young woman, for example, may be afraid of total rejection if she refuses a man sexually; another is so afraid of satisfying her parents' conventional standards that her promiscuity is only one of many expressions of defiance; a third is promiscuous because of a compelling need to prove how desirable she is. In none of these cases are we talking about real sexual freedom.

One of the most important areas of sexual freedom necessary for a fulfilling sex life has to do with freedom from notions of inadequacy about our bodies. Boys worry about their pimples, girls about their figures, and both have all too often been raised by parents who emphasize the *dangers* rather than the *pleasures* of the uses of the body. They were never allowed to get dirty, run, fall, tumble, hang from trees. And all too frequently they grow up hesitant about, rather than highly oriented to, the uses of their bodies. We learn to like our body not as a result of being extraordinarily well endowed, but as a result of the fun we derive from it. If we have used our body well, we enjoy it.

Sex involves a certain amount of exposure, exploration, intimacy—all of which can be enormously enjoyable if we think well of our bodies. We need not be narcissistic; we need not spend hours before a full-length mirror or in a weight-lifting gymnasium. Obviously such extremes can easily preclude the pleasures to be shared with others. What we do need for sexual pleasure is to be sybaritic enough or physically oriented enough toward pleasure in general to recognize sex as a particular part of this. Slithering into a warm tub or between the fresh coolness of clean sheets, filling one's lungs with the fragrance following a spring rain, the bite of the wind on a downhill ski slope, the touch of a woman's hand, the velvet smoothness of her skin—our enjoyment of all these things makes it easier for us to enjoy any one of them.

Now, of course, our ability to enjoy any of these, as well as any pleasures, is not a purely physical matter. Physical enjoyment or sexual enjoyment may be enhanced by healthy and sensitive physical endowment, but so can it be inhibited or enhanced by our emotional or psychological make-up. In fact, it is safe to say that the ability to enjoy life or any part of it is primarily a matter of personality. People who are secure and well adjusted find a large percentage of pleasure in life. People who are constantly fearful and anxious, pessimistic or given over to feelings of threat, rejection, not to mention chronic physical aches and pains, do not enjoy things so easily. Their opportunities for sexual pleasure are easily and often diluted or dissolved by fatigue, worry, or a general inability to recognize their opportunities when they occur. In other words, another most important cornerstone of a good sex life is a sound emotional life.

People who do not enjoy things easily generally will not enjoy sex easily, in particular. As a matter of fact, our sexual behavior is probably more easily disturbed than any other part of our behavior. It is really our true Achilles' heel. Because of the amount of conflict, contradiction, and confusion about sex in our world, we all have our share of difficulty in developing a sex life. Many men find it easier to make a good living than to create a good sex life for themselves. A certain amount of anxiety seems inevitably associated with part of our sexual growth. Many never get rid of this completely. It seems clear, however, that the better our overall personality adjustment, the better chance we stand to work out our sexual difficulties as well. Thus, a good sex life demands not only a healthy orientation to sex itself, but a healthy orientation to life. This is a very much bigger problem.

Children live in a world governed by the immediacy and imperativeness of their desires. Adults are not without their strong desires but part of their maturity leaves them with the ability to temper them, to postpone them. Adults can even take "no" for an answer, if that is necessary. Nor are they slaves of their sexual desires; such desires enrich their lives without tyrannizing them. A Don Juan or a nymphomaniac is more driven by sex than entertained by it. Desires do not fuel their lives; they take over. They do the driving. A grownup, in short, is not compulsive about sex. He enjoys it, but it does not dominate his life. There may be moments of passion and even recklessness but, in the main, sex is incorporated into the texture of the rest of his desires, needs, and even his respect for what is socially apropos.

The emotional and sexual growth found in grownups also involves fairly distinct expressions of sexuality unlike those we find in emotional minors. Sigmund Freud went to great pains to trace the earliest expressions of sex and claimed they began long before the child discovered the erogenous zones known as his genitalia. Oral and anal fixations predated genital expression in the Freudian scheme. Whether we accept this or not, there is little doubt that the earliest use of the genitalia is not in sexual intercourse. The child discovers how pleasant it is to rub himself or tickle himself, and herein we find the beginnings of masturbation. Although there is absolutely no scientific evidence whatever to believe that masturbation is harmful, we do expect some change in a person's behavior as he grows. As a matter of fact, it might even be added that masturbation is beneficial to a child, for it helps him to discover an important part of his body which later will be used in the service of love.

Although masturbation itself is not organically harmful, children invariably come to feel guilty about it. In fact, masturbation guilt is the most common form of guilt we find in people. After a while, the child does not even have to masturbate; merely wanting to masturbate will develop guilt feelings. Guilt is not only a deeply painful component of our psychological make-up but it has a way of spreading among our desires, discoloring them, and easily making them appear base. Masturbatory guilt can continue to plague an individual in highly subtle ways, and such a person is not always aware of it. It can even come to make him distrust his healthy sexual desires later on.

It is not at all uncommon, for example, to find women who object even to the most sacrosanct connubial sexual experiences. These reactions can vary from shyness and embarrassment to deeply disturbed feelings of loathing and shame. Needless to say, this is not a part of *emotional* maturity or *sexual* maturity. The grownup has put masturbation and its guilt behind him; nor is he shy, loathing, or guilty about his adult sexuality. He finds pleasure, love, and respectability in it. His enjoyment of sex leaves little room in his mind for worried questions about whether or not some of his tastes are perverse. A healthy man and a healthy woman ideally enjoy each other in any way they like, so long as it is not hurtful or a substitute for sexual intercourse. Such people are no more ashamed of their sexual appetites than they are of their appreciation for good food or drink. The loss of appetite, from a medical point of view, is associated with illness.

We need hardly be reminded that the opposite of illness is health, not immorality. There are many who are altogether too quick in making judgments of immorality. More often than not, they mistake bad taste for what they believe to be a breach in morality. But sex does not monopolize bad taste. There is bad taste in art, architecture, humor, clothes, and even in such simple matters as how we sometimes speak on the telephone. Perhaps if we were more sure of ourselves sexually, we would recognize bad taste as such and not confuse it with immorality. We already have a sufficiently difficult time developing our sexual maturity not to be additionally burdened by the hasty judgments of others. It is important for us to give sex every possible chance. It can be very good for us.

Sex is one of the few areas in life in which we can really let go of ourselves. As members of society, we are patterned and constrained by it. Although we have strong inner urges frequently pushing us beyond conventional dictates, we have few opportunities to express them. Philosophers, sociologists, political scientists, and now psychologists grapple with it. We are aware that freedom can degenerate into lawlessness and anarchy, just as restraint can easily become dull conventionality and even slavery. We try to develop some happy medium for ourselves; but it is difficult. Most of us feel some tension or restraint most of the time. Not that we are not capable of periods of intense concentration, but when we get lost in our business or in something at home, it rarely has the quality of a great giving of self.

This enormous freedom to express and give of oneself is frequently found in artists. This is why so many psychoanalysts say that despite the maladjustment so common among them, artists, nonetheless, enjoy the greatest opportunity for the best emotional adjustment. Sex can do the same for us as art. It can easily become a do-it-yourself art kit, eminently capable of elevating us to the status of artist. The necessary talents here are far more easily developed. And the satisfactions may even be greater. All we need for qualification is a healthy interest in sex, along with an adult ability to relate ourselves to others. Those who are friendless and fearsome have the greatest difficulties. We must learn to like ourselves enough to be able to expose ourselves to others sufficiently to enjoy them socially, or sexually, or both.

It should be clear that a sexual relationship is, after all, part of a bigger relationship between human beings. There are individuals who cannot get along with themselves, let alone with others. How can we expect our sexual relationships in the long run to be any better than our general human relationships are? This means that the way we sexualize is a reflection of the way we live. In order to understand sex better, it then behooves us to study the way we live. Although physiology is certainly an important science, we cannot expect to develop a truly sophisticated understanding of life exclusively on physiological terms. The human sexual response is no more physical than the human fear response. The latter too has marked physiological changes associated with it, but can we understand anxiety merely in such terms?

Man is a social animal. He is gregarious. His sexual relationships reflect and express only parts of his life with others. This is what we have to remember in order to understand his sexual difficulties. His most common sexual problems are not the inability to develop and maintain sufficient erection for intercourse and, secondly, premature ejaculation. His most common sexual problem is the inability to relate himself significantly enough to women to promote a gratifying sexual experience.

One of the interesting claims made in the Masters-Johnson report is that their sexual research program was in no way detrimental to those who participated in it. On the contrary, it insists that their participants' sexual effectiveness was either maintained or improved during the program. It also reports that people who had sexual problems were helped considerably in the course of their participation in the research program. Now, if sex is primarily to be enjoyed rather than merely studied, participation in it rather than study of it might be therapeutic. Like swimming or golf, one cannot learn to develop skill in sex merely from a book. Whatever information may have been imparted to those who had problems was perhaps not nearly so helpful as the actual participation made possible by the program. In short, opportunities to act on the relationships were provided. The added factor of social facilitation, that is, that others were participating too, frequently makes the difference between success and failure in trying to achieve a therapeutic goal.

Not all sexual difficulty lends itself so easily to symptomatic treatment. More frequently than not, symptoms reflect deeper disturbance. Erectile inadequacy, for example, may be one among several other symptoms of a deep-going sense of unworthiness. Being unable to perform sexually can be a man's irrational, unconscious way of asserting his basic lack of worthwhileness. Or, because of a long disturbed history with his mother, it may be his irrational unconscious way of getting even with all women. He stimulates and excites them, brings them to a point where they want him, and then cannot satisfy them. There are other types of deep, dark motivations involved in the inner conflicts of human beings. Sexual difficulty is generally looked upon as one among other expressions of these unconscious motives. Such cases all underscore the basic relationship between sex and personality.

Merely understanding sex offers little guarantee of sexual fulfillment. After all, doctors, nurses, and medical students know a great deal about human biology, but this does not necessarily make them great lovers. Before vaginal distention was measured, men even with large organs experienced and knew what has been referred to as being "lost in the vagina." College students for ages have countered their anxiety about phallic size by saying, "It's not the size but the English you put on it." It is not what we have, or even what we know, so much as how we use it which makes the difference between sexual frustration and sexual fulfillment.

How does one learn to use his body to maximum advantage? Some people want to respond and cannot. Others respond only if they want to, and still others respond whether they want to or not. The wonder and magic of sex seems to be unlocked *psychologically*, not physiologically. Our physiological capacity to respond becomes available to us as a result of the permission we give our bodies to respond. This need not necessarily be conscious. In fact, it is better for us that it be habitual. We enjoy a healthy sexual orientation by enjoying sex enough to be ready most of the time. This does not mean anybody, anywhere, anytime. A person can have healthy sexual appetites and remain moral and monogamous. What this does mean is that the person lives in a world he recognizes as masculine and feminine without shrinking from it. He is not at "the club" all the time. He enjoys the existence of sex.

This enjoyment of sex means both a liberal or accepting attitude toward it and the regular practice of what we believe. To say that some of my best friends have a rich sex life is not enough. A man is his own best friend when he bridges the gap between his own belief and his own behavior. If he fails to do this, he leaves himself with the sadness of Ecclesiastes who cried that "much knowledge increaseth sorrow."

The best practice of liberal attitudes toward sex is not to be found in our approval of others. There may be great largesse in this, but self-deprivation could render this almost hypocritical. There are things to be done every day in the week which involve varying amounts of direct and indirect sexual satisfaction. Keeping one's body alive and healthy is a good start. We can as easily learn to enjoy keeping our bodies well groomed and polished as so many of us do our automobiles. Our sense organs can open us to a world of brilliant color, subtle tastes, nostalgic aromas, not to mention art, music, and, most of all, delightful people. *These* are uses of the body for the pleasure. But we forget; we "lay waste our powers," as Wordsworth put it. True, people with deep-going sexual problems cannot be expected to do this without psychotherapy. *But most of us do not have such deep problems.* We have minor problems and bad habits, mostly of inattention to ourselves. Most of us could improve our life enormously, not by additions to it, but by using more fully what we already have.

Pleasure must become habitual for us to be happy. All habits require repetition. If sexual fulfillment is part of happiness, we must use our bodies sexually repeatedly. There are endless indirect expressions of sexuality which keep alive the habit of using the body for pleasure. There are endless direct expressions of sexuality short of intercourse for those who have reasons important to themselves for postponement. And finally, there are endless opportunities for direct expressions of sexuality involving complete and total gratification. All we have to do is to develop the habit of recognizing these opportunities.